KT-228-640

Sustainability Indicators
Measuring the Immeasurable?

Simon Bell and Stephen Morse

UNIVERSITY OF WOLVERHAMPTON
LEARNING RESOURCES

Acc No. 2214295

CLASS

CONTROL
1853834971

333.
714
Bel

DATE
18. JUL 2000

SITE
W

F
333
SAS

EARTHSCAN

Earthscan Publications Ltd, London

First published in the UK in 1999 by
Earthscan Publications Limited

Copyright © Simon Bell and Stephen Morse, 1999

All rights reserved

A catalogue record for this book is available from the British Library

ISBN: 1 85383 498 X paperback
      1 85383 497 1 hardback

Typesetting, figures and page design by PCS Mapping & DTP, Newcastle upon Tyne
Printed and bound by Biddles Ltd, Guildford and Kings Lynn
Cover design by Declan Buckley

For a full list of publications please contact:

Earthscan Publications Limited
120 Pentonville Road
London N1 9JN
Tel: +44 (0171) 278 0433
Fax: +44 (0171) 278 1142
Email: earthinfo@earthscan.co.uk
http://www.earthscan.co.uk

Earthscan is an editorially independent subsidiary of Kogan Page Limited and
publishes in association with WWF-UK and the International Institute for
Environment and Development.

This book is printed on elemental chlorine free paper from sustainabily managed
forests.

Contents

Part III Where Next? Humility and Honesty

List of Figures, Tables and Boxes

FIGURES

TABLES

BOXES

Acronyms and Abbreviations

AMOEBA	general method for ecosystem description and assessment (Dutch)
BAAC	Bank for Agriculture and Agricultural Cooperatives
BCCI	Belize Chamber of Commerce and Industry
BKK	Badan Kredit Kacamatan
BUD	Bank Rakyat Indonesia Unit Desa
CATWOE	customer, actor, tranformations, worldview, owner, environmental constraints
CBA	cost-benefit analysis
CBI	Confederation of British Industry
DDS	Diocesan Development Services
DfID	Department for International Development
DSD	degree of sustainable development
ECBA	economic cost-benefit analysis
FAO	Food and Agriculture Organization
FS	financial services
FSR	farming systems research
FSR/E	farming systems research and extension
GB	Grameen Bank
GIS	geographical informations systems
IITA	International Institute of Tropical Agriculture
ISD	indicators for sustainable development
IUCN	International Union for the Conservation of Nature
LF	logical framework or logframe
LISA	low input sustainable agriculture
LO	learning organization
M & E	Monitoring and Evaluation
MCA	multi-criteria analysis
MIS	Management Information Systems
MOV	Means of Verification
MSY	maximum sustainable yield
N	nitrogen
NEF	New Economics Foundation
NGO	non-governmental organization
ODA	Overseas Development Administration (now renamed DfID)
OVI	Objectively Verifiable Indication
P	phosphorous
PRA	participatory rural appraisal
PRAM	participatory and reflective analytical mapping
PSI	process SI
SCBA	social cost-benefit analysis
SDI	subsidy dependence index
SI	sustainability indicator
SSA	systemic sustainability analysis
SSI	state SI
SSM	soft systems approach or method

SWOT	strengths, weaknesses, opportunities and threats
TFP	total factor productivity
TUC	Trade Union Movement
UN	United Nations
UNEP	United Nations Environment Programme
USAID	United States Agency for International Development
WCED	World Commission on Environment and Development
WWF	World Wide Fund For Nature

Foreword

This book is the result or outcome of our personal journeys through a great deal of literature and opinion. Although both of us have spent several years working in development studies, Steve is a biologist with a background in the scientific tradition whereas Simon defines himself as a systems thinker with specific experience in the field of information systems development and computing. Both of us have come by separate routes to the current discussion relating to sustainability, and without being dramatic this book might be described as the fruit of a voyage of discovery.

For some time we have both been concerned, but from our different perspectives, with the literature on sustainability and the discussions which this literature has produced. On the one hand, we were worried by the numerous attempts to try and ascribe exact 'measures' to sustainability (for instance, sustainability = 42). On the other hand, it appeared that the politicians had created a storm by picking up on the word *sustainability* which was intended to be the marker and driving force for the development effort. Such an emphasis intensified the need for definition and measurement, and yet the very holistic and anthropocentric essence of sustainability continues to elude attempts at objective analysis and assessment.

We came to the conclusion separately that in trying to tie down and measure sustainability the civic, academic and developmental communities were engaging in a futile exercise of measuring the immeasurable. Although many have tried to quantify sustainability – with all the jargon and apparent rigour of the objective and reductionistic mindset of much of the academic community – when looked at more closely the approaches do not seem to work. Sustainability is not a thing to be simply measured, and an element of circularity appears inevitable. The approach to measurement is based on an individual's vision of sustainability, which in turn can be changed depending on the measurement mindset. Our concern grew in our analysis of theory and in our own practice as consultants and researchers; despite being told by some colleagues that to critically evaluate indicators was 'off the wall', we decided to both map our understanding of the sustainability indicator debate and to set out what we think might be a more holistic, realistic, participative and systemic approach to gauging sustainability.

At the outset we need to bring to the reader's attention problems with the use of the words system and systemic. In the first three chapters of this book, which review the work of academics and practitioners in developing sustainability indicators, the word system is frequently used; however, this is usually in a non-specific, everyday sense – the word could be replaced with 'related entities' or even 'things'! In Chapters 4 to 7 we use the words much more specifically and provide definitions of what they mean in precise terms

This book is both the outcome of a creative endeavour and the reflection of the current debate on sustainability indicators. We offer our thoughts on the discussion so far and suggest ways forward with humility. We both agree that there will be great need for fuller discussion before the issue is in any way resolved, and all we can hope to do is to contribute some personal insights.

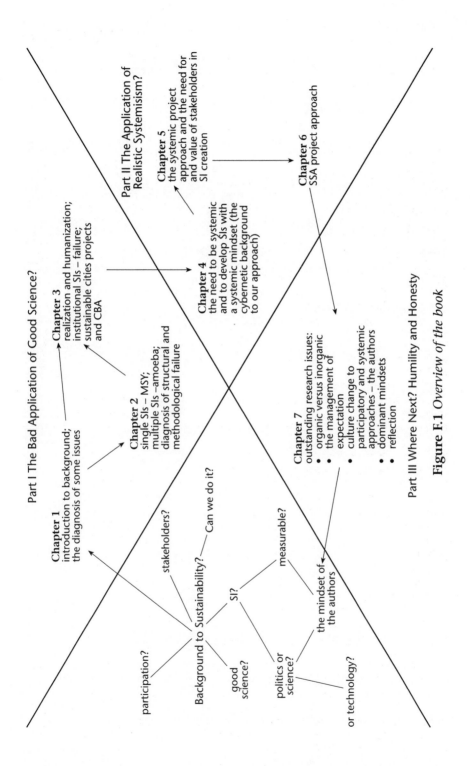

Part I The Bad Application of Good Science?

Chapter 1
introduction to background;
the diagnosis of some issues

Chapter 2
single SIs – MSY;
multiple SIs –amoeba;
diagnosis of structural and
methodological failure

Chapter 3
realization and humanization;
institutional SIs – failure;
sustainable cities projects
and CBA

Part II The Application of
Realistic Systemisism?

Chapter 5
the systemic project
approach and the need for
and value of stakeholders in
SI creation

Chapter 4
the need to be systemic
and to develop SIs with
a systemic mindset (the
cybernetic background
to our approach)

Chapter 6
SSA project approach

Chapter 7
outstanding research issues:
• organic versus inorganic
• the management of
  expectation
• culture change to
  participatory and systemic
  approaches – the authors
• dominant mindsets
• reflection

participation?

stakeholders?

Can we do it?

Background to Sustainability?

good
science?

SI?

politics or
science?

measurable?

the mindset of
the authors

or technology?

Part III Where Next? Humility and Honesty

Figure F.1 *Overview of the book*

The reader will find three distinct sections in the following pages.

- Part 1 deals with the review of the literature on the use of sustainability indicator (SI) in development. Chapter 1 provides background to the issue of SI development, Chapter 2 focuses on examples of single and multiple SIs and Chapter 3 looks at institutional SIs, sustainable cities and introduces the notion of using SIs in projects.
- Part 2 sets out an alternative, systemic manner for the development of SIs. In Chapter 4 the systemic approach is introduced. Chapter 5 describes the development of SI development tools within project contexts and Chapter 6 sets out the systemic approach to SI development – stressing the essential participative nature of understanding sustainability.
- In Part 3, Chapter 7 focuses on setting out a number of further questions arising from the discussion and provides an outline of future research interests.

We believe that the discussion which we present here comes together as one overall whole, bringing us back to some of the questions we started with. To assist the reader we have developed a route map of the conversation (see Figure F.1), and we provide step by step indicators on this as the conversation develops from chapter to chapter.

The authors encourage readers to engage in the discussion of SIs.

Simon Bell (s.g.bell@open.ac.uk)
Stephen Morse (s.morse@uea.ac.uk)
April 1998

Acknowledgements

Both authors would like to express their thanks to the members of Systems Discipline at the Open University and to the School of Development Studies at the University of East Anglia. Thanks go especially to Professor Ray Ison, Christine Blackmore and Bob Zimmer of the Open University and to Professor David Gibbon, previously of UEA and now of the University of Agriculture at Upsalla in Sweden. Thanks are also due to early helpers Bridgette Petite, Taran Sarwal, William Buhler and Graham Gass. The authors would like to express particular thanks to David Ellis and Liz Edwards of Norwich 21, at Norwich City Council, who provided rich detail relating to sustainable cities projects and also valuable comments on the text. It is impossible to thank all those who have provided contributions and insights to the formulation of this book, but we would like to express our gratitude to all our friends, colleagues and all the silent recipients of development projects worldwide who have for the last 20 years worked with the authors and helped them in their intellectual, moral and spiritual development.

Part I

The Bad Application of Good Science?

Chapter 1

Sustainability and Sustainability Indicators

INTRODUCTION AND OBJECTIVES

Few development interventions or research initiatives these days can success-fully attract funding unless the words 'sustainability' or 'sustainable' appear somewhere in the proposal to the funding agency. Indeed, if one listens to speeches by politicians or reads articles by economists, policy-makers or scientists the word sustainable appears with a remarkable regularity.

> *Sustainable development has become the watchword for international aid agencies, the jargon of development planners, the theme of conferences and learned papers, and the slogan of developmental and environmental activists.*
>
> Lele (1991)

Although some have questioned the motives behind this popularity (Bawden, 1997), there is no doubt that sustainable development is now a very dominant theme. Some even go so far as to say that 'everyone agrees that sustainability is a good thing' (Allen and Hoekstra, 1993), although to Fortune and Hughes (1997) 'it [sustainability] is an empty concept, lacking firm substance and containing embedded ideological positions that are, under the best interpretation, condescending and paternalistic'. The main catalyst for this popularity in recent years, particularly in terms of sustainable development, was the Rio de Janeiro Earth Summit held in 1992 (Haas et al, 1992). The Rio Summit agreed a set of action points for sustainable development, collectively referred to as Agenda 21 (agenda for the 21st century), and governments that signed up to these have committed themselves to action. In order to help put these points into practice, the summit established a mandate for the United Nations to establish a set of 'indicators of sustainable development' that will help monitor progress. In fact, the idea of using indicators as a means of gauging sustainability has become extremely popular, with many governments and agencies devoting substantial resources to indicator development and testing (see, for example, Kuik and Verbruggen, 1991; WWF and NEF, 1994; NEF, 1995; Reid, 1995). Even the idea of a sustainable city, an apparent contradiction in terms, has become so popular that prizes are now provided for those cities deemed to be the most sustainable, and indicators play a major role in this process. The central idea behind the use of such indicators is very simple, and essentially they are designed to answer the question: 'How might I know objectively whether things are getting better or getting worse?' Lawrence (1997).

Sustainable development is an example of a paradigm quite distinct from what some see as the contradictory term of sustainable growth (Daly, 1990).

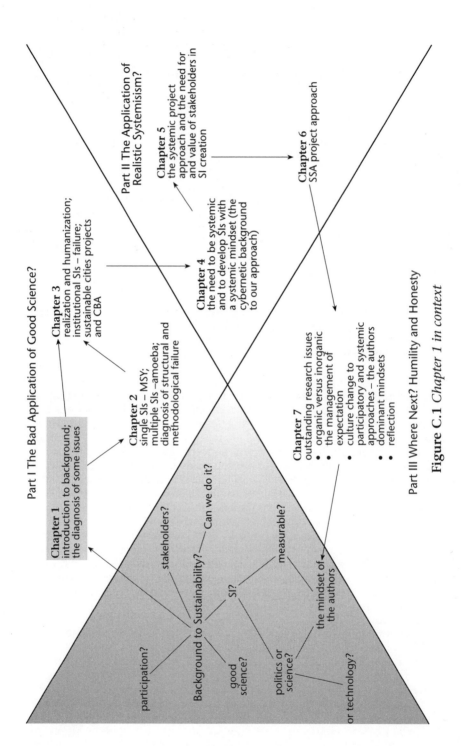

Figure C.1 *Chapter 1 in context*

Paradigms are important in that they are philosophical and theoretical frameworks within which we derive theories, laws and generalizations (Webster, 1995). In its broadest sense, the sustainable component of the sustainable development paradigm implies that whatever is done now does not harm future generations – a concept often paraphrased as 'don't cheat on your kids'. However, the precise meaning of sustainable, and what it embraces, varies depending upon who is using it and in what context, a critical point which we return to later. For example, can we sustain our environment within sustainable development yet 'cheat our kids' on other aspects, such as decline in economic performance or worsening social conditions? Sustainable development has indeed become a quintessential example of practical holism, but at the same time embodies an ultimate practicality since it is literally meaningless unless we can 'do' it; as such it is firmly rooted in the present.

This book is all about the 'doing' of sustainable development. In these pages the reader will frequently come across a liberal sprinkling of terms such as 'achieve', 'implement', 'practice', 'goal' and 'do' with regard to sustainable development. This reflects an important shift away from 'sustainable' as an appealing though rhetorical adjective. 'Sustainable' becomes both a descriptor of something and a target to achieve (Cox et al, 1997). Indeed, since it is the 'sustainable' part of sustainable development which particularly interests us, we have tended to refer to 'sustainability' in a generic sense, and our discussions of sustainability could be employed to anything which has sustainable as an adjective. Therefore, the same broad points we make apply to sustainable agriculture, sustainable cities and sustainable institutions – for this reason we have ranged freely between all these domains. The latter two, in particular, will form the focus for Chapter 3. This may appear to be rather cavalier, but 'sustainable' in each case refers to much the same, although the detail can be quite different. Taking sustainability in a broad sense allows us to compare and contrast facets of application across these domains, and to apply lessons from one arena to another.

In order to provide the reader with some background, we have begun this chapter with a discussion of a few of the current visions of sustainability, with a particular emphasis on sustainable development. There is, of course, an additional and substantial literature on the meaning of development but this will not be covered here. The aim will be to use these visions of sustainability to illustrate some of the difficulties inherent within its concept, and how some people have tried to address these.

As described above, many individuals have noted the need for measurement of sustainability, and this chapter will discuss a few approaches in this direction and the problems that people have faced. Again we cannot claim to be exhaustive, but the examples we have chosen illustrate the broad range of approaches with their associated advantages and disadvantages. In particular, the background to the use of indicators as a means of gauging sustainability will be discussed. Chapter 2 will deal with some specific examples of sustainability indicators in more depth. An important point to make is that the use of simple indicators as a means of following change in complex systems is not new. Biological indicators have been widely employed in environmental science for many years, and in this chapter we compare their use in this context to one of gauging sustainability. The final section of the chapter will draw together some of the main difficulties in using relatively simple indicators to gauge what is in fact, very complex. These problems will be pursued further in Chapters 2 and 3.

TWO ROOTS OF SUSTAINABILITY

In its original form, sustainability was closely associated with maintenance of environmental quality, although – as would be expected with a term that is so multifaceted – the origins of sustainability are complex. Excellent discussions can be found in Kidd (1992), Moffatt (1992), Munn (1992), Heinen (1994) and Mitcham (1995) and will not be repeated in depth here. Needless to say, concerns for the environment and views over humankind's place within the environment are ancient (Pepper, 1984). Kidd (1992) suggests that the contemporary view of sustainability in a broad sense has originated from six separate strains of thought (Figure 1.1). We do not intend to describe each of these, but two of them are particularly relevant for the purposes of this book as they will reappear in various guises in later chapters.

Ecological/Carrying Capacity Root

Of the six roots in Figure 1.1, a major contribution has come from the first – the ecological concept of carrying capacity and the idea of maximum sustainable yield (MSY) that partly flows from it. Carrying capacity is the notion that an ecological system (ecosystem) can only sustain a certain density (the carrying capacity) of individuals because each individual utilizes resources in that system. Too many individuals (overshooting the carrying capacity) results in overuse of resources and eventual collapse of the population. The MSY is a related concept in that it implies a sustainable utilization of a resource. If the MSY is exceeded, perhaps because of population increase or simply because of greed, then the system may collapse with potentially dire consequences for those dependent upon the resource.

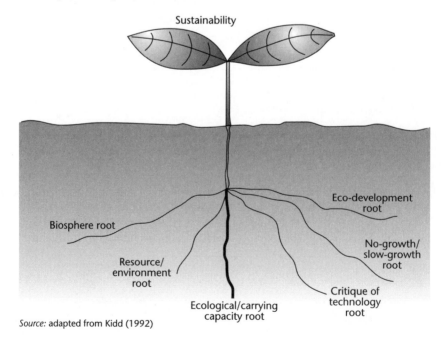

Source: adapted from Kidd (1992)

Figure 1.1 *The roots of the modern view of sustainability*

Carrying capacity has been and remains a central concept in ecology and can be found at the heart of the other five strains of thought in Figure 1.1. For example, the second root ('resource/environment') stems from a number of influential books written in the late 1940s and 1950s that question the ability of the earth to sustain a growing human population. In other words, these works argue that the earth is approaching its carrying capacity, and great dangers are ahead if we push too close to or exceed that limit. In the introducion to one of these books, written by William Vogt and published in 1949 entitled *Road to Survival*, the author suggests that:

> *Road to survival is, I believe, the first attempt – or one of the first – through carefully chosen examples, in large part drawn from wide first-hand experience, to show man as part of his total environment, what he is doing to that environment on a world scale, and what that environment is doing to him.*

> Vogt (1949)

The Critique of Technology Root

The critique of technology root of sustainability originated in the 1960s and 1970s as a counter to the perceived indiscriminate use and exportation of technologies that may pose dangers to the environment (Gilot and Kumar, 1995). A classic example is the well-known book by Schumacher entitled *Small is Beautiful: Economics as if People Mattered* (1973). There are a number of examples that come under the critique of technology, including nuclear power, but probably some of the best-known examples are in agriculture (Mitcham, 1995). Indeed, it can be argued that the problems arising from the indiscriminate use of pesticides, in particular, have had a major effect on the evolution of the sustainability concept. These dangers were highlighted in an immensely influential book, *Silent Spring*, written by Rachel Carson and published in 1962. The title invokes a spring without songbirds as they become decimated by the widespread use of pesticides. Indeed, it could be argued that agriculture has been at the heart of much of the sustainability debate, and this is not particularly surprising for two main reasons (Lele, 1991):

- Agricultural systems occupy large areas of land – far more land than any other industry with the possible exception of forestry. Therefore, what occurs within agriculture can often have major environmental effects.
- The end product of agriculture is often food, and we all eat! Agriculture is therefore one of the foundations of human society.

The result has been a move towards the promotion of sustainable agriculture (IITA, 1993; Otzen, 1993; Gibbon et al, 1995; Baldock et al, 1996), although terms such as agroecology, alternative agriculture, ecological food production (Begon, 1990), low input sustainable agriculture (LISA) and organic agriculture have also entered the frey and offer distinctive elements to their proponents (Beets, 1990; Neher, 1992; Zinck and Farshad, 1995). Alternative agriculture is taken to be a sort of antithesis to conventional agriculture without really being very clear as to what either term means (Frans, 1993). LISA is assumed to be sustainable agriculture with an accepted low-level of artificial inputs, although where one draws the line between this and high-input agriculture is again rather nebulous. Of all the terms, organic agriculture is the most definable:

Box 1.1 *Visions of sustainable agriculture*

- Those who appear to see no problem in equating sustainability with 'high-input', 'high-yield' conventional farming.

  ...profitability, consumer safety, resource protection, and viability of rural America.

  Kelling and Klemme (1989)

  What is sustainable agriculture after all? The only sustainable agriculture is profitable agriculture. Short and sweet.

  Ainsworth (1989)

  ...the concept of sustainable agriculture does not exclude the use of fossil fuels and chemicals: it only requires that the criteria of appropriateness and sustainability be applied to the whole system.

  Wilken (1991): quoted in Frans (1993)

  One of the key charges of the environmental activists is the claim that high-yield farming is 'unsustainable'. This has resonated with the public, probably because it implies a lurking, hidden threat. Actually ... high-yield farming is **more** *sustainable than organic farming... We also have strong evidence that high-yield farming can continue producing higher and higher yields on into the future.*

  Avery (1995)

- Those who do not appear to equate sustainability with high-input, high-yield conventional farming.

  'Sustainable' means the capability to continue producing food and fibre indefinitely and profitably without damaging the natural resources and environmental quality on which all of us depend.

  Schaller (1989)

  For a farm to be sustainable, it must produce adequate amounts of high-quality food, protect its resources and be both environmentally safe and profitable. Instead of depending on purchased materials such as fertilizers, a sustainable farm relies as much as possible on beneficial natural processes and renewable resources drawn from the farm itself.

  Papendick and Parr (1990)

  A sustainable agriculture is one that equitably balances concerns of environmental soundness, economic viability, and social justice among all sectors of society.

  Allen et al (1991)

  ...sustainable agri-food systems are systems 'that are economically viable, and meet society's need for safe and nutritious food, while conserving or enhancing ... natural resources and the quality of the environment.

  Science Council of Canada (1991): Cited in Lehman et al (1993)

  Sustainable agriculture refers to the use of agricultural land in such a way to ensure that over time no net quantitative or qualitative loss of natural resources occurs.

  Fresco and Kroonenberg (1992)

  Sustainable agriculture consists of agricultural processes, that is, processes involving biological activities of growth or reproduction intended to produce crops which do not undermine our future capacity to successfully practice agriculture.

  Lehman et al (1993)

  Only the most hard-bitten of intensive commercial farmers would now accept that conventional agriculture is sustainable.

  Gibbon et al (1995)

produce can be certified as organic depending upon the absence of defined substances (mostly pesticides and artificial fertilizers) during production. Indeed, for many the terms sustainable agriculture and organic agriculture have become synonymous precisely because the latter, by definition, minimizes if not eliminates the use of technologies that may pose dangers to the environment. However, do we minimize or eliminate such technologies, and if minimize is adequate, then by how much?

The answers, quite frankly, are very diverse and depend to a large extent upon who is defining sustainability in each individual context; the specific example of agriculture beautifully encapsulates this central paradox of sustainability. The comments in Box 1.1 provide a simple illustration of these diverse viewpoints. Further examples can be found in Dunlap et al (1992), Swift and Woomer (1993) and Hansen (1996). As can be seen from these, there are marked contrasts in how people envisage sustainable agriculture, and the views of Avery and Gibbon et al, both published in 1995, are very hard to reconcile.

THE MEANING OF SUSTAINABILITY

The confusion over the meaning of sustainable agriculture is also apparent when the meaning of sustainability in other arenas, for example in sustainable development, is considered. Although most would agree that sustainability implies 'not cheating on your kids', a clearer definition has proved to be elusive. This is a point that has been noted by many (Kidd, 1992, and Mitchell et al, 1995) and appears to be a source of much frustration. Almost every article, paper or book on sustainability bemoans the fact that the concept is broad and lacks a broad consensus; this is usually followed by the authors' own preferred definitions which in turn add to the lack of consensus! Some examples of this diversity can be found in Box 1.2, although it should be stressed that the examples in Box 1.2 are by no means indicative of the entire range of definitions that exist or indeed of the main elements that tend to be mentioned. To do this would be labouring the point and would make for rather staid and boring reading.

Given its ubiquitous use and popularity, the lack of a concrete definition of sustainable may appear to be very surprising. How can something so vague be so popular? The essence of the problem has been captured by Schaller (1993): 'As a destination, sustainability is like truth and justice – concepts not readily captured in concise definitions.' We all want truth and justice, but what these mean can also vary greatly from individual to individual and between societies. My justice may be your exploitation, and my truth may be your lies! Indeed, this failure to obtain a universal and concise definition of sustainability has lead some authors to take what may be thought of as a rather extreme position:

> *Many would argue that it is important to define what sustainability is, or might be, before any actions can be taken towards setting up more sustainable agricultural practices. We do not necessarily subscribe to the need to define sustainability in order to practise it, but the exercise of definitions is one useful way to examine several perspectives and to understand competing views.*
>
> Gibbon et al (1995)

This would seem to be an illogical stance. After all, how can we do something unless we know what we are trying to do? Surely we cannot farm or develop

---

Box 1.2 *Some definitions of sustainability*

• General definitions

...the capacity of system to maintain output at a level approximately equal to or greater than its historical average, with the approximation determined by the historical level of variability.

Lynam and Herdt (1989)

...maximizing the net benefits of economic development, subject to maintaining the services and quality of natural resources over time.

Pearce and Turner (1990)

The sustainability of natural ecosystems can be defined as the dynamic equilibrium between natural inputs and outputs, modified by external events such as climatic change and natural disasters.

Fresco and Kroonenberg (1992)

• Sustainable development

...development that meets the needs of current generations without compromising the ability of future generations to meet their needs and aspirations.

WCED (1987)

...development that improves the quality of human life while living within the carrying capacity of supporting ecosystems.

IUCN (1991)

---

sustainably unless we know what this implies? If we don't know what we are trying to get, how do we know if we have it? While one can sympathize with the view that a simple, concise definition may not be possible, surely some idea of where one is trying to go is an absolute necessity. Even a statement of intent that some factors should increase while others decrease, without specifying an ultimate goal, is still a definition.

This uncertainty over the meaning of sustainability has not reduced the popularity of the concept. On the contrary, it could perhaps be cynically argued that the resulting flexibility has allowed the concept to attain the heights that it has. If those involved in sustainable development can give their own individual 'spin' to the meaning of sustainability, then all definitions can remain fashionable and mainstream, and this may help strengthen its popularity. The uncertainty may, in fact, be self-reinforcing and sustainable in its own right. In a less cynical vein, this flexibility as to what sustainability means can also be a great strength in a very diverse world. People differ in the environmental, social and economic conditions within which they have to live, and having a single definition that one attempts to apply across this diversity could be both impractical and dangerous. As Kidd (1992) argues: 'there is not, and should not be, any single definition of sustainability that is more logical and productive than other definitions.'

Why is there so much diversity in viewpoint regarding the meaning of sustainability? After all, the oft-quoted World Commission on Environment

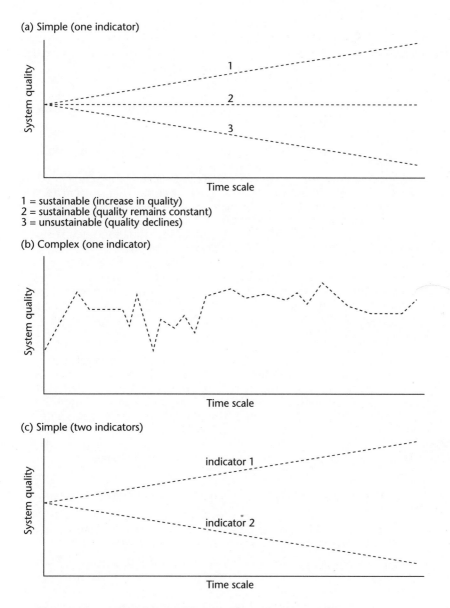

(a) Simple (one indicator)

1 = sustainable (increase in quality)
2 = sustainable (quality remains constant)
3 = unsustainable (quality declines)

(b) Complex (one indicator)

(c) Simple (two indicators)

Figure 1.2 *System quality and sustainability*

and Development (WCED) (1987) definition of sustainable development
appears to be a reasonable stance. Some of the fundamental reasons for this are
briefly illustrated in Figure 1.2a. In this figure sustainability is represented by a
change in a property referred to as 'system quality' – a very subjective term
open to all sorts of value judgements. Sustainable equates to a situation where
quality remains the same or increases. If quality declines then the system can
be regarded as unsustainable. This may at first sight appear to be clear, but there
are numerous problems that arise even in this simple graph. These can be listed
as follows (Lele, 1991; Costanza and Patten, 1995; Zinck and Farshad, 1995):

1   *What exactly is the system we are ascribing some notion of quality to?* Who is in
    this system and who isn't? This may equate in a rather crude sense to the
    spatial dimension of the system being evaluated, and one can ask where the
    system 'boundary' resides? Indeed, is there really a boundary at all?
2   *What do we take as a time scale across which quality is being gauged?* For
    example, in Figure 1.2b system quality fluctuates with time, but taken
    across the whole length of the time axis it remains more or less the same
    (= sustainable). If one only looked at small segments of the time axis
    rather than the whole length the picture could be quite different. Some
    segments show marked unsustainability as quality declines rapidly while
    other segments show a rapid increase.
3   *What is meant by system quality and how is it determined?* This problem is
    probably the most intractable. Quite frankly, given the same system and
    time scale it is possible for two people to arrive at very different views
    depending on what they see as important components of quality (Figure
    1.2c). To one person the quality may be increasing while to someone else
    it is decreasing. This point can be illustrated from another angle – the costs
    of achieving sustainability, or what some call the 'profitability versus
    environment debate' (Schley and Laur, 1996). In the literature there is
    frequent reference to two types of sustainability (Box 1.3) depending upon
    the costs incurred in attaining them (Common and Perrings, 1992;
    Rennings and Wiggering, 1997): strong sustainability and weak sustain-
    ability.

There are fundamental differences between strong and weak sustainability, and
they can be regarded as mutually exclusive rather than as two ends of a
spectrum (Common and Perrings, 1992). As an illustration of this, Tisdell
(1988) raises the following set of questions with regard to various definitions of
sustainable development broadly based around the notion of 'not cheating on
your kids':

> *Do they imply that no development is desirable which temporarily
> raises the income of existing generations?*
>
> *To what extent should the potential of future generations to meet their
> needs be maintained?*
>
> *Is it, for example, ever acceptable to engage in current developments
> that reduce the potential of future generations to meet their needs?*
>
> *What trade-offs, if any, are acceptable between present generations and
> future ones?*

In other words, how much 'cheating of our kids' can we get away with! Quite
simply, if one believes that sustainability should be strong then anything less is
simply not acceptable, and the above questions cannot even be considered.
    The three questions regarding spatial and time scales and meaning of
'quality' have to be resolved before sustainability can be achieved because they
provide the context within which the process takes place. In any one circum-
stance the answer may not appeal to all, but individuals need to have a clear
vision as to what is being attempted. In the following sections we will examine
these questions in greater depth and illustrate how some people have
attempted to provide answers. We will begin with a discussion of spatial and
time dimensions, and we will progress to that most intractable of questions –
what comprises system quality?

Box 1.3 *Two different visions of sustainability*

• Strong sustainability
In strong sustainability there is little if any consideration of the financial or other costs of attaining sustainability. It equates to what some call ecological sustainability and the focus is primarily on the environment. In this case system quality is taken in terms of the physical measures of things (eg population, soil erosion, biodiversity).

• Weak sustainability
The second type of sustainability is referred to as weak sustainability. Costs of attainment (financial or otherwise) are important and typically based on a cost-benefit analysis (CBA) which inevitably involves trade-offs between environment and social and economic benefits (Young, 1997). Weak sustainability equates to a sort of economic sustainability where the emphasis is upon allocation of resources and levels of consumption, and financial value is a key element of system quality.

SPACE AND TIME IN SUSTAINABILITY

As mentioned above, there are two questions that need to be answered before achieving sustainability (Fresco and Kroonenberg, 1992; Spencer and Swift, 1992):

• Over what space is sustainability to be achieved?
• Over what time is sustainability to be achieved?

The answers to these may at first appear rather obvious. The spatial scale may correspond with a farm, village, town or city, region, country and so on until the whole planet is considered. However, the difficulty is that these scales are all interlinked (Niu et al, 1993). The smaller the scale, the harder it is to know where to draw the line. In other words, where does the system boundary reside? If the aim is to change the agriculture in an area from what is considered to be unsustainable to sustainable, then are the units for consideration fields, farms or a collection of farms? If the latter, where does the 'collection' stop? Political boundaries (such as local government, state or county) may not be of much theoretical use. Even within clear spatial units such as villages, towns or cities there are difficulties. Urban areas are not self-contained entities but have links with other urban areas and the rural environment, which may extend for many miles around the centre. Sustainability in the urban area may be heavily influenced or even dependent upon what happens outside of that area. Do we include these? Sustainability in urban centres will be returned to in more depth in Chapter 3. Even if a boundary can be defined, what lies outside it can be of great importance.

From a theoretical perspective the spatial scale is clearly very important when one attempts to put sustainability into practice or when one judges the level of sustainability of an existing system. However, even if individuals can clearly define the boundary there are problems in implementing sustainability. To begin with, there are simple logistical considerations brought about by limited budgets. The larger the scale and the more unsustainable the system, the bigger this problem is likely to be. What does one do? Redraw the spatial scale to take account of the budget? Limit one's objectives and perhaps even abandon the goal of full sustainability, implementing instead a sort of partial sustainability? Even worse may be the fact that development funding, and hence project boundaries, may well have to work within political borders rather than with more reasonably formulated system boundaries. Clearly what comprises the spatial scale for sustainability is of major importance and is by no means simple.

There are numerous examples in the literature illustrating how the spatial scale has been defined. In some cases the boundary of the system was a defined 'settlement' (Izac and Swift, 1994; Jansen et al, 1995). Indeed, the clearest examples of defined spatial scales are those based on human habitations. 'Sustainable cities' is now a common phrase, and there are even awards for the most sustainable city in a number of countries and regions. One of the pioneers is the Sustainable Seattle programme in the US.

The time scale over which sustainability occurs is a further dimension. The definitions in Box 1.2 imply an intergenerational scale (also referred to as 'futurity') to sustainability, but over how many generations? Does one consider ten, 100 or 1000 years? Different systems may well require different time scales (Ehui and Spencer, 1993). Another complication is that different components of sustainability in the same system may best be measured in different time frames. For example, agricultural sustainability has a number of elements including build-up of pests and levels of land degradation. In this case Harrington (1992a and 1992b) suggests that pest problems are best looked at over scales of five to 20 years, while land degradation requires scales of 20 to 100 years. Indeed, Harrington (1992a and 1992b) also suggests that some factors are best looked at over 1000 years, although achieving this would certainly be a challenge unless one limits oneself to historical trends.

A very practical consideration flows from this discussion of relevant time scales. In Boxes 1.1 and 1.2 the reader encounters words such as current, future, improve, maintain, equilibrium, conserve, and enhance. All of these words have one thing in common – they are relative. This relativity lies at the heart of sustainability, and the latter is only meaningful if it is based on a trend over time and if we apply a value judgement as to what that trend should equate to. The non-attainment of 'sustainable' becomes de facto 'unsustainable'. Clearly a starting point, or reference condition, is required in order for the trend to be gauged, but the choice of the starting point can influence the results.

Figure 1.3 presents a rather simplistic explanation of the problem. As in Figure 1.2, this figure presents the change in system quality over time, but the time axis has been divided into four blocks (each representing ten years perhaps). The vertical lines labelled A, B, C and D are arbitrary starting points for the gauging of system quality. Over all four time periods quality fluctuates, but a general trend would be more or less horizontal as indeed it was in Figure 1b (no increase or decline). However, if divided into smaller time horizons that may perhaps equate more to human planning horizons (eg ten years) then the interpretation of the trend in each block of time may be quite different. The last segment (number four) suggests a very unsustainable system while segment three suggests the opposite. To make things even more complex, it is apparent that the situation could be quite different with smaller (eg five years) or larger (eg 20 years) scales. Although fixing a scale at X years (no matter how arbitrary) provides some clarification, it does not in itself yield all the answers. Clearly we need to know where the length of the time scale is to start. Even if the time scale is kept constant at X years, one could 'prove' almost anything one wishes by careful selection of the starting point in Figure 1.3.

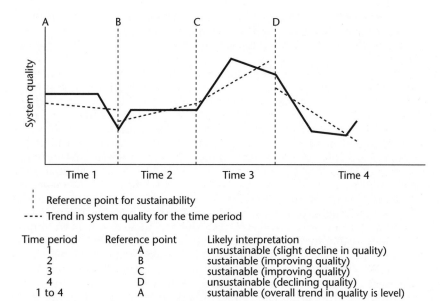

Figure 1.3 *Importance of the reference point for gauging sustainability*

SYSTEM QUALITY

Spatial and time scales are key components of achieving sustainability; as has already been stressed, they are problematic in the sense that careful selection of scale or reference point can be used to prove almost anything. However, as difficult as these may be, they pale when put alongside another consideration in sustainabilty – the meaning of system quality and, in particular, the meaning of quality of life as an element of system quality. This element is a key component of many definitions of sustainability (especially sustainable development) and reflects a major evolution in the 'sustainable' concept. Earlier views of system quality and sustainability focused on the natural resource base and environment, with emphasis on physical entities such as the level of water and air pollution, soil erosion, soil acidity or alkalinity, crop yield, biodiversity, and so on. Gauging these over particular spatial and time scales may be difficult and interpreting the results is open to some debate; however, at least one is dealing with measurable factors, and system quality may be expressed in a manner which is a composite of these (see Miller and Wali, 1995, for a review of soils and sustainability). Later considerations of sustainability began to question whether human quality of life should be included as a component within system quality and hence sustainability, particularly since we are usually concerned with the sustainability of systems within which humans not only have a stake but which they actively manage (Jeffrey, 1996). Sustainability, like development, is all about people, and there may be little point achieving a sustainable system that reduces the quality of life of the people in that system. This issue is returned to in Chapter 6.

Although a logical extension of the sustainability concept, this complicates the issue further. Just what does quality of life comprise? It has been defined by Cutter (1985) as:

> *...an individual's happiness or satisfaction with life and environment including needs and desires and other tangible and intangible factors which determine overall well being.*

There are a number of terms used more or less synonymously with quality of life such as well being in Cutter's quotation. However, others see these as being quite distinctive. For example, a related term –level of living – has been defined by Knox (1974) as 'the level of satisfaction of the needs of the population assessed by the flow of goods and services enjoyed in a unit time.'

Although the approach of including quality of life within sustainability has been broadly accepted, there is not so much unanimity about what it is and how it should be included (see Livermann et al, 1988 and Mitchell et al, 1995 for just two discussions of this topic). Pollution and erosion may be measured, but how can quality of life and well being be assessed? There are numerous examples of gauging well being through employment, income, crime, travel, migration and house prices. However, just which of these or others are important will presumably vary dramatically from individual to individual and over time. Calibration and interpretation would also appear to be problematic. Are they all to be treated equally or is crime to be rated higher than travel? What about leisure activities and culture? Although the inclusion of quality of life considerations within sustainabilty may be desirable, the practice appears to raise many difficult questions.

SUSTAINABILITY IN PRACTICE

While the previous sections have discussed some of the questions central to sustainability, we are faced with a conundrum. Although sustainability may have much in common with truth and justice – what it comprises is heavily influenced by value judgements and ethics – like these two it has to be put into practice by imperfect human beings. Given that sustainable development, like agriculture, cities and institutions, is a practical goal to be reached by intervention of some sort, one clearly needs to be aware of whether the system is still unsustainable or whether the goal of sustainability has been reached. Obviously this will depend upon one's particular vision of sustainability (Mitchell et al, 1995), and answers to questions regarding relevant spatial and time scales; however, even so, once the goal has been clearly identified one needs to know whether the target has been reached.

> *Sustainability must be made operational in each specific context (eg forestry, agriculture), at scales relevant for its achievement, and appropriate methods must be designed for its long-term measurement.*
>
> Heinen (1994)

An illustration of the approach taken in this direction is provided by the results of a meeting held in November, 1996, at Bellagio, Italy. The meeting was funded by the Rockefeller Foundation, and the aim was to set some principles for monitoring progress towards sustainable development. The results of the meeting are referred to as the Bellagio Principles for sustainable development (Hodge and Hardi, 1997) and are summarized in Box 1.4.

Some of these address broad issues already discussed:

• the need for a clear definition (principle 1);
• the focus on holism in sustainability (principle 2);
• the importance of time and spatial scales (principle 4).

These are elements closely associated with the goal of sustainable development – finding them listed amongst the first principles in Box 1.4 is no surprise. Clearly, they need to be addressed before any progress on sustainability can be made.

Box 1.4 *A summary of the ten Bellagio Principles for gauging progress towards sustainable development*

(1) What is meant by sustainable development should be clearly defined.
(2) Sustainability should be viewed in a holistic sense, including economic, social and ecological components.
(3) Notions of equity should be included in any perspective of sustainable development. This includes access to resources as well as human rights and other 'non-market' activities that contribute to human and social well being.
(4) Time horizon should span 'both human and ecosystem time scales', and the spatial scale should include 'not only local but also long-distance impacts on people and ecosystems'.
(5) Progress towards sustainable development should be based on the measurement of 'a limited number' of indicators based on 'standardized measurement'.
(6) Methods and data employed for assessment of progress should be open and accessible to all.
(7) Progress should be effectively communicated to all.
(8) Broad participation is required.
(9) Allowance should be made for repeated measurement in order to determine trends and incorporate the results of experience.
(10) Institutional capacity in order to monitor progress towards sustainable development needs to be assured.

Source: adapted from Hodge and Hardi (1997)

As for the gauging of sustainable development, principle 5 emphasizes the use of a limited number of indicators, and this is followed by principles 6, 7, 8 and 9 which broadly lay out how the indicators should be developed and employed. It should be noted that in recommending the use of indicators for this purpose the Bellagio meeting was simply echoing similar calls made by others. For example, in Chapter 40 ('Information for decision-making') of the Agenda 21 document flowing out of the Rio conference in 1992 there is a call for the development of indicators for sustainable development (ISDs). Indeed, there is a strong literature stretching back a number of years prior to 1992 calling for the use of indicators as a means of gauging sustainability (sustainability indicators: SIs), and indicators have been widely employed in a diverse range of circumstances for perhaps thousands of years. For example, farmers have long employed simple indicators of soil fertility, such as soil colour and presence of certain plant species, and other important considerations in agriculture (including the weather). Biologists have also been developing and applying indicators to ecological systems for many years. Ecosystems can comprise thousands if not millions of different components, some of which will be living (animals, plants, micro-organisms, etc) while others will be inert (soil and water). Indeed, people (with all their attendant socioeconomic and cultural dimensions) can also be components of the system. Clearly, with thousands, if not millions, of components and interactions in such a system one cannot measure everything; instead, biologists focus on key components and interactions that represent the system as a whole.

Given the extensive experience of farmers, biologists and others, an extension of the indicator approach into sustainability is certainly not surprising and one could even say is inevitable. In the following two sections we will explore some aspects of the use of indicators to gauge complex systems. We will begin by exploring the use of indicators by biologists to monitor the effects of pollution, and then progress to the use of indicators to gauge sustainability.

INDICATORS OF ECOSYSTEM HEALTH

The widespread introduction of human-made chemicals and other pollutants into the environment has resulted in a host of literature on the use of biological indicators as a means of gauging environmental impacts or, as some put it, the health of the ecosystem (Hellawell, 1986; Callicott and Mumford, 1997). It has been suggested that there are two broad approaches to these 'environmental indicators' (see Figure 1.4), with the top-down approach particularly popular. Within the top-down category the two most common approaches are:

* to look for certain 'indicator' species that are sensitive to changes in the environment;
* to measure the biological diversity (biodiversity).

However, in practice these two will often go together – the indicator species will be the first to be lost when a stressed system shows a reduction in biodiversity.

Use of Indicator Species

There are numerous studies that illustrate how species composition reflects ecosystem health, and one could select an example from almost any system or country worldwide. One particular example dating to the late 1960s and early 1970s is provided by Learner et al (1971). This example has the advantage of referring to a system with a clear spatial (and to some extent, administrational and political) boundary – a river and its catchment – covering an area of 108 square kilometres. Furthermore, since a number of the key texts in the sustainability paradigm were published in the early 1970s (Goldsmith et al, 1972; Meadows et al, 1972), an example that predates them may be pertinent.

The study is based on a survey of fish and macro-invertebrates (insects, worms etc) of the Cynon River, a tributary of the River Taff that flows through Cardiff, the capital of Wales. The study intended to determine how the distribution of species was influenced by effluents from sewers and various industries, including coal washery plants and coal tips that enter the river. Figure 1.5 is a diagrammatic representation of the river and its associated streams, along with an indication of where effluent enters the river and sampling stations (C1, C2,

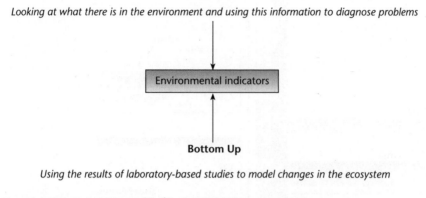

Top Down

Looking at what there is in the environment and using this information to diagnose problems

Environmental indicators

Bottom Up

Using the results of laboratory-based studies to model changes in the ecosystem

Two of the most common methods in the top-down approach are to:

- Measure the biological diversity (biodiversity): when communities are put under stress (eg pollution), they generally become simpler as some species die and the relatively small number of tolerant species come to dominate the system.

Therefore, more biodiversity = better ecosystem health

- Use the presence of certain indicator species: some species are very sensitive to a change in the environment (temperature, acidity, pollutants etc).

Therefore, presence/number of individuals of these species = better ecosystem health

Source: Cairns et al, 1993

Figure 1.4 *The two broad approaches to the use of environmental indicators*

C3, etc) where the fauna was checked. Distributions of six fish species (such as brown trout, bullhead and eel) are illustrated in Figure 1.5: there were clear effects on fish distribution, especially below the point where the Rivers Groes and Aman join with the Cynon. This corresponds with a major, but intermittent, discharge of industrial effluent. It is also noticeable that of all six species, minnows were found closer to the point of discharge, although this probably reflected their higher mobility and ability to recolonise rapidly after pollution incidents, rather than an innate ability to withstand the toxicants. The results of the pollution could even be found some distance downstream of the point where the Cynon meets the Taff. Again, minnows in the Taff appeared to be the least affected.

Measuring Biodiversity

Another way to gauge the state of the environment is to measure biodiversity. Ecologists have been measuring biodiversity for a long time, and various methods and indices exist (Southwood, 1978). These tend to be of a rather technical nature; one example is the Shannon–Wiener index (H) illustrated in

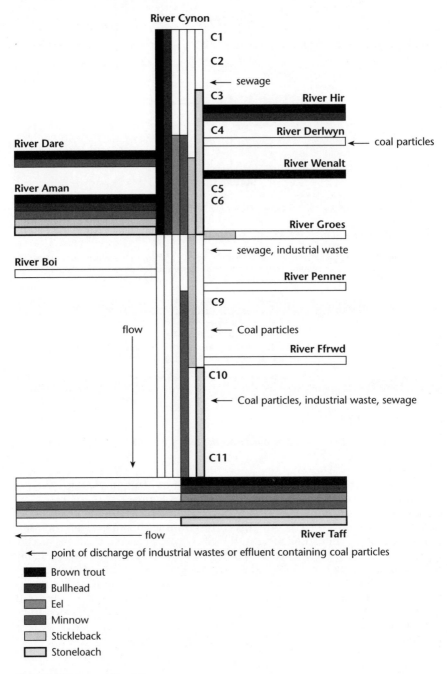

Figure 1.5 *Fish distribution in the Cynon River system in South Wales, UK*

Box 1.5 *The Shannon–Wiener index (H) of biodiversity*

$$H = - \Sigma \, (p_i) \, (\log_2 p_i)$$

Σ	=	sum of
S	=	the number of species
p_i	=	the proportion of total sample belonging to the $_i$th species
p_i	=	n_i / N
		where n_i is the number of individuals in species $_i$ and N is the total sample size.
$\log_2 =$		logarithm to the base 2

The negative sign converts the results of the calculation from negative to positive. It is required because the logarithm to the base 2 of values less than 1 are always negative ($\log_2$ of 1 = 0).

The higher the value of H, then the greater the biodiversity of the sample.

EXAMPLES: In both cases there are two species (S = 2), and the sample size is 100 (N = 100).

(a) 50 individuals of each species

$$\begin{aligned} H &= - (0.5 \times \log_2 (0.5) + 0.5 \times \log_2 (0.5)) \\ &= - (0.5 \times -1) + (0.5 \times -1) \\ &= - (-0.5 + -0.5) \\ &= 1 \end{aligned}$$

(b) 99 individuals of species 1 and 1 individual of species 2

$$\begin{aligned} H &= - (0.99 \times \log_2 (0.99) + 0.01 \times \log_2 (0.01)) \\ &= - (0.99 \times -0.0145) + (0.01 \times -6.6439) \\ &= - (-0.0144 + -0.0664) \\ &= 0.08 \end{aligned}$$

THEREFORE, H is higher in (a) than (b), suggesting that there is more biodiversity.

Box 1.5. The higher the value of H, the greater the biodiversity of the sample. In effect, the index is a composite of the number of species in the sample (S) and the number of individuals of each species in the sample (represented in p_i). Example calculations of H are also shown in Box 1.5. The application of the Shannon–Wiener index can be illustrated by using the Learner et al (1971) example already described. Figure 1.6 presents the values of H for nine of the sampling stations (C1 to C6 and C9 to C11) on the River Cynon (location shown in Figure 1.5). The index has been calculated for species of macro-invertebrates (insects, worms, etc), and fish and other animals have not been included. As can be seen from Figure 1.6, the value of H declines between stations 4 and 5, but gradually increases from stations 5 to 11. The point between station 4 and 5 corresponded with a discharge of coal particles into the river, and interestingly did not correspond with the location of the discharge that had a major effect on fish distribution as outlined above (this discharge lies between stations 6 and 9). It is also interesting to note that the biodiversity increases between stations 2 and 3, probably as a result of sewerage entering the river and providing a source of enrichment.

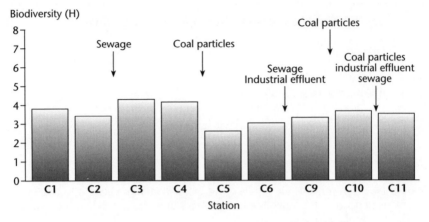

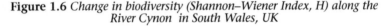

Note: arrows indicate points of discharge of sewage, coal particles and industrial effluent.
Source: adapted from Learner et al, 1971

Figure 1.6 *Change in biodiversity (Shannon–Wiener Index, H) along the River Cynon in South Wales, UK*

The advantage of such an index is that it simplifies complexity into a single value that readily allows comparison. However, although this biodiversity index is useful for biologists it does have a number of limitations.

- Strictly speaking it can only be applied when the total number of species in the ecosystem is known, although in practice this may not be the case. For example, although Learner et al (1971) included a total of 126 macro-invertebrate species in their survey, and sampling was very thorough, there is no guarantee that *all* of the species were sampled.
- The index has no qualitative element since the same value of H can be found in the same system that has undergone a dramatic shift in species composition. For example, stations C1 and C10 in the Learner et al (1971) example both had an H value of around 3.7, yet the species composition at those two stations was quite different. In other words, it simply measures biodiversity without allowing for differences in the species that comprise that diversity.
- As can be seen from the equation and calculations, it is a rather technical expression that may not resonate very well with those not conversant with biology.

The first limitation is essentially technical in nature. The second represents an inevitable loss of information as we create a simple index out of complex data. The third is not a consideration for biologists but would be important if the index was employed as a means of informing policy-makers or the public about environmental quality. Although the fundamental ideas of indicator species and biodiversity do resonate with lay people (Hawkins et al, 1994), the means of presentation is critical. Very technical expressions such as H that speak volumes to biologists may simply not be the best format to use in situations where a much wider audience is being addressed.

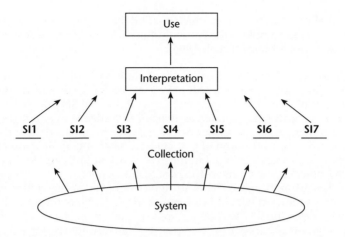

Note: SIs 1 to 7 collect pieces of information (indicated by arrows) about the large, complex system.

Figure 1.7 *The concept behind sustainability indicators (SIs)*

SUSTAINABILITY INDICATORS

Given that indicators have been widely employed by biologists for many years to gauge ecosystem health, it is not surprising that indicators have been seen by many as the core element in operationalizing sustainability (Jansen et al, 1995; Syers et al, 1995; Zinck and Farshad, 1995; Rennings and Wiggering, 1997). However, unlike the sort of system described in the Learner et al (1971) example, sustainability incorporates many more dimensions, including quality of life. While the presence of just a few indicator species and the calculation of biodiversity were all useful in tackling the specific problem of pollution in the River Cynon, the frontiers of sustainability are much grander and a number of indicators are almost certainly required (Harrington, 1992a and 1992b; Cairns et al, 1993; Mitchell et al, 1995). The theory is indicated in Figure 1.7. The values of the seven SIs shown here are gauged; one then has to interpret the results and make use of the interpretation. The problem, of course, is how many and which indicators to use? Clearly one cannot use every SI that may potentially be available, and an element of simplification, while at the same time maximizing unique and relevant information, is essential (Cairns et al, 1993).

SIs are often grouped in various ways depending upon what dimension or element of sustainability they are trying to gauge. The simplest division is into two groups:

1   *State SIs.* These are SIs that describe the state of a variable. For example, in the case of environmental quality one may determine soil physical and chemical properties (Swift and Woomer, 1993; Jansen et al, 1995; Miller and Wali, 1995; Penfold et al, 1995), or the concentration of a pollutant in water. Other more social examples may be the human population density, income equality, female and male wage ratio, life expectancy at birth and maternal mortality rate.

2   *Control (also referred to as pressure, process or driving force) SIs.* These are SIs that gauge a process that in turn will influence a state SI. For example, a

control SI may be the rate at which a pollutant is passed into the environment. A good example is the amount of pesticide used in an area (eg. the 'Biocide Index' of Jansen et al, 1995).

State and control SIs can be related. An obvious example is that the rate of pesticide application in an area will have a major influence on the measured concentration of pesticides in drinking water. A suite of SIs may need to have both state and control SIs included as changes in a state SI may not necessarily provide information on the causes of change (Harrington, 1992a and 1992b). The link between concentration of pesticides in water and application in a river catchment may be clear enough, but life expectancy at birth and income equality will be influenced by many factors, not just one.

This basic distinction between state and control SIs is also employed by the United Nations for their ISDs, flowing out of the 1992 Rio conference; however, the UN includes a third type called 'response' indicators. These are employed to gauge required progress in the response of governments, for example, to achieve adequate values of state and control indicators. It is also interesting to note that the term driving force instead of control was preferred by the UN when developing its list of ISDs in order to fully incorporate the notion that impact of a factor on sustainable development can be positive or negative.

A further feature of the UN indicators is that they have based their selection of SIs on the chapters of the conference document, so that the latter essentially becomes the frame. The chapters themselves can be broadly divided into four categories:

* social aspects of sustainable development;
* economic aspects of sustainable development;
* environmental aspects of sustainable development – further subdivided into water, land, atmosphere and waste;
* institutional aspects of sustainable development

A set of SIs is then determined for points arising in each of the chapters. A summary of the results is presented in Table 1.1. For example, in Chapter 17 of Agenda 21, entitled 'Protection of the Oceans, all Kinds of Seas and Coastal Areas', we have three driving force (= control) SIs and two state SIs. The driving force SIs cover population growth in coastal areas and levels of pollution. One of the state SIs follows the first rule given by Rennings and Wiggering (1997), namely that resource use should not exceed regeneration. This is the much studied and discussed concept of maximum sustainable yield (MSY) mentioned earlier in this chapter. We will return to the MSY in Chapter 2. The second state SI, the algae index, is an index of algal (includes phytoplankton) biodiversity and abundance. It comprises information on the type and quantity of algae present in a volume of water. As of August 1997 the UN has not suggested any response SIs for this chapter. The UN set of SIs is still in the development phase, with extensive field testing in a number of countries due to be completed by the end of the century. The plan is to make a set of SIs available to planners by the end of the century

Nevertheless, although there is much agreement that SIs are the way forward, there is disagreement over what SIs to use and even about the broad nature and characteristics of the SIs. However, the decision over what SIs to adopt is vital to the final outcome. Included here are just four more examples to provide the reader with a taste of the diversity.

Table 1.1 *The United Nations working list of sustainable development indicators*

Category	Main chapter heading	Chapter numbers
Social	combating poverty	3
	demographic dynamics and sustainability	5
	promoting education, public awareness and training	36
	protecting and promoting human health	6
	promoting sustainable human settlement development	7
	Driving force: 11 State: 21 Response: 7	
Economic	changing consumption patterns	4
	financial resources and mechanisms	33
	Driving force: 9 State: 11 Response: 3	
Environmental	promoting sustainable agriculture and rural development	14
	combating deforestation	11
	conservation of biological diversity	15
	protection of the atmosphere	9
	environmentally sound management of biotechnology	16
	Driving force: 22 State: 18 Response: 15	
Institutional	science for sustainable development	35
	information for decision making	40
	strengthening the role of major groups	23–32
	Driving force: 0 State: 3 Response: 12	
Totals	Driving force: 42 State: 53 Response: 37	

Total Number of SIs: 132

Note: the UN prefers to use the term driving force instead of control, pressure or process SIs.
Source: based on the chapters of the Agenda 21 document (Rio de Janeiro, June, 1992)

Example: *Protection of the Oceans, all Kinds of Seas and Coastal Areas (Chapter 17)*

Driving Force	State	Response
Population growth in coastal areas	Maximum sustained yield for fisheries	None
Discharges of oil into coastal waters	Algae index	
Releases of nitrogen and phosphorous to coastal waters		

Sustainability indicators: example 1

Another indicator framework developed as a response to the Agenda 21 document of the Rio Summit is provided by Harger and Meyer (1996). The framework was created by a UN interagency working group for south and south-east Asia; as would be expected there is much overlap with the UN SI list. Agriculture, fisheries, population and education all feature, but there are some interesting additions. Military considerations, for example, are listed as a category and one can but speculate over what SIs could be included here and how they are to be measured and presented, given the enormous sensitivity of such a topic.

Harger and Meyer (1996) suggest that SIs should have the following characteristics:

- Simplicity;
- Scope: the SIs should cover the diversity of issues mentioned above (environmental, social and economic) and overlap as little as possible;
- Quantification: the SIs should be measurable;
- Assessment: the SIs should allow trends with time to be determined;
- Sensitivity: the SIs should be sensitive to change;
- Timeliness: the SIs should allow timely identification of the trends.

There is much here in common with the selection of suitable bioindicators by biologists to measure pollution or some other environmental change. The quantum jump from bioindicators to SIs is clearly in the scope – the need for a range of SIs that cover the breadth of the sustainability vision.

Sustainability indicators: example 2

Niu et al (1993) have developed a framework for sustainable development that builds on the basic definition of sustainable development given in the WCED report (1987). They suggest employing a spatial systems approach, with each spatial system comprising five sub-systems:

- richness of resources;
- strength of the economy;
- stability of society;
- tolerability of the environment;
- soundness of decision.

SIs are then selected to gauge each of these.

Sustainabilty indicators: example 3

Rennings and Wiggering (1997) suggest that SIs should be chosen to reflect three management rules which they feel characterize a sustainable use of natural resources:

- Harvest rates of renewable resources should not exceed regeneration rates.
- Waste emissions should not exceed the relevant assimilative capacities of ecosystems.
- Nonrenewable resources should be exploited in a quasi-sustainable manner by limiting their rate of depletion to the rate of creating renewable substitutes.

Sustainability indicators: example 4

Izac and Swift (1994) have developed a matrix of SIs for small-scale agriculture in sub-Saharan Africa (see Table 1.2). The two scales of the matrix relate to spatial scale (cropping system, farm and village) and three categories of 'products' from the system (main products, by-products and amenities). As can be seen from the

Table 1.2 *Some sustainability indicators for sub-Saharan African agroecosystems*

	Cropping system	*Scales* Farm	Village
Products	ratio of annual yield for all products to potential and/or farmer's target yield	profit of farm production	economic efficiency
		ratio of profit to farmer's target income	social welfare
By-products	soil pH, acidity and exchangeable aluminium content	ratio of aggrading to degrading land area	
	soil loss and compaction	nutritional status of household	nutritional status of community
	ratio of soil microbial biomass to total soil organic matter		stream turbidity, nutrient concentration and acidity
	abundance of key pest and weed species		human diseases and disease vectors biodiversity and complexity
Amenities		drinking water quality	drinking water availability
		source and availability of fuel	

Source: adapted from Izac and Swift (1994)

table, production forms a major element of their vision of sustainability, and they cope with the spatial scale problem by adopting the village as the largest scale for gauging sustainability; the time scale is set at ten years.

It is interesting to note that in all of the above examples, those who have set the framework are for the most part either politicians, policy-makers, social or natural scientists. Logically, one may feel that those best placed to define sustainability and to set relevant SIs would be the beneficiaries (also referred to as the stakeholders) of the programme. For example, Mitchell et al (1995) state the following as the first principle in the development of SIs:

> *Stakeholders [should] reach a consensus on the principles and defini-tions of sustainable development that are used and the objectives of the sustainability indicators programme.*

However, this has rarely been put into practice, and for the most part the SIs, or at least the methodology for developing SIs, have been set by outsiders, with perhaps a nod in the direction of those the SIs are ultimately meant to serve. Indeed, is sustainability really an important consideration for all stakeholders, and if it isn't, should an outsider impose it? The following comment by Tisdell (1996) related to agricultural sustainability is very sobering: 'In fact, sustain-ability is unlikely to be an overriding consideration of a farmer from an economic viewpoint.'

Given that participation has been central to much development since the late 1970s, particularly in terms of guiding research priorities, and the fact that a huge and highly accessible literature has grown around the subject (see Chambers et al, 1989; Chambers, 1991 and 1997; Scoones and Thompson, 1994), it is interesting how the 'sustainable' part of sustainable development has retained such a top-down and Western emphasis. The issue of participation in sustainability, and particularly in the development of an SI framework, is, we believe, of paramount importance and will be returned to in greater depth in Chapters 5 and 6.

CALCULATION, PRESENTATION AND INTERPRETATION OF SUSTAINABILITY INDICATORS

Once a set of SIs has been agreed upon, they have to be measured. The fewer the SIs to be considered, the easier this may be, although the tendency may be to include a large number of SIs in order to cover the breadth of sustainability.

Obtaining the value of an SI may be a relatively easy task if good quality data is already available, or if the means of getting such data is already well established. Indeed, the availability of relevant data may not be a problem at all, and all the difficulties will revolve around choice, interpretation and use of SIs.

> *In the developed world, we often have far more data than we can ever use. In most cases, what is lacking is not data but an understanding of what is important and the resolve to act.*
>
> Lawrence (1997)

If new data has to be collected, then the precise methodology for determining an SI will, of course, depend upon what it is. For example, in the Izac and Swift (1994) set of SIs, the soil nutrient status, organic matter content, water holding capacity, and the abundance of an animal or plant species can be determined by employing standard analytical and ecological sampling techniques (see, for example, Penfold et al, 1995). Clearly, there is the problem of variation, given that in the same field there can be marked differences in, for instance, nutrient status within very short distances depending on slope, previous cultivation and the presence of trees or termite nests; however, given the resources these problems are resolvable. In the same list, issues surrounding social welfare and economic efficiency can be found using standard social science surveying techniques. It should be noted, however, that although many of these tools are well established, they are not without limitations.

Although a single SI may be relatively easy to interpret provided one has a clear reference point, the interpretation of a suite of SIs may be problematic. What does one conclude if some are within the reference limits and some are not? Does one take an all or nothing point of view (the 'binary' view of sustainability – either a system is sustainable or not), or can one conceive of gradations of sustainability (van Pelt et al, 1995)?

At one extreme, some have attempted to encapsulate SIs 'using an appropriate weighing scheme' into a single measure of sustainability. An ambitious example is the calculation of the degree of sustainable development (DSD) suggested by Niu et al (1993). Another, perhaps more focused, example is the use of an economic approach for measuring sustainability in tropical farming systems (Lynam and Herdt, 1989; Monteith, 1990; Ehui and Spencer, 1993;

Box 1.6 *The theory behind the calculation of the total factor productivity (TFP) indicator of sustainability in tropical farming systems*

Lynam and Herdt (1989) define the TFP as:

$$TFP = \frac{\text{value of outputs from farming system}}{\text{value of inputs into framing system}}$$

Lynam and Herdt suggest that changes in TFP over time equates to a measure of sustainability (ie change in productive capacity of the system). In its simplest form:

INCREASE IN TFP = SUSTAINABILITY
DECREASE IN TFP = UNSUSTAINABILITY (decline in resource base)

Tisdell (1996) suggests a slight modification of this idea to focus instead on profitability (P) of the system:

$$P = \frac{\text{value of output} - \text{value of input}}{\text{value of input}}$$

This is fundamentally an economic approach based on the productivity of the farming system, and works as long as inputs (including the natural resource base) and outputs can be given a monetary value. Other environmental and social effects that many consider central to sustainability are not included.

Tisdell, 1996; Cox et al, 1997). This is the total factor productivity index (TFP), and the ideas behind it are illustrated in Box 1.6.

The notion of a numeric value for sustainability, as in the DSD and TFP, is attractive for the very reason that the Shannon–Wiener biodiversity index, and others like it, is attractive. Simplifying system complexity into single values that allow easy comparison has a definite appeal, but don't we run into the very same qualitative problem as we did with H as a measure of biodiversity? The answer is clearly yes, and in order to avoid this other individuals have attempted to keep the richness of sustainability intact by using various tabular or diagrammatic formats. An example of the latter is the AMOEBA (Gilbert, 1996) which will be described in Chapter 2. In some cases the SIs are superimposed on maps of the area to illustrate how they vary over space (Jansen et al, 1995). This may become more common with the increasing use and power of geographical information systems (GIS) on microcomputers.

If SIs are taken over a period of time, they can be used to determine a trend – do they stay the same, increase or decrease, and if so by what rate? In a sense, the absolute values of the SI may not matter (just as well if it is based on 'guesstimates'!); instead, the emphasis is on how they change with time. The problem is what happens if the trends for different SIs go in opposite directions (see Figure 1.2c) – some stay the same while others go up and down. Furthermore, what if the same SI shows a complex pattern of increases and decreases with time as in Figures 1.2b and 1.3? In addition, although the trends can be useful to illustrate sustainability, they need to be combined with estimates of what is acceptable. After all, sustainability can be achieved at a very low level of system quality, but is the low level acceptable? Single values of SIs with units require some sort of baseline for interpretation. A value of X units is meaningless unless we have an idea of what range equates to sustainability or, in other words, what represents the target or reference condition (Gilbert, 1996). This is not easy! Jansen et al (1995) were able to establish limits to nutrient balances that reflect sustainability; however, for the biocide index mentioned earlier: 'No clear-cut relation exists between the calculated index of biocide use and the sustainability of the system, making calculation of a limit to the biocide index impossible.' Instead, a limit to the biocide index equating to sustainability could only be set 'subjectively'.

SUSTAINABILITY INDICATORS: A REALISTIC AND REASONABLE APPROACH TO MEASURING SUSTAINABILITY?

As one may construe from all of the foregoing, the selection and measurement of SIs is hardly a fine art and is subject to many pressures, agendas and biases. Governments often wish to portray themselves in the best possible light, and it is certainly not hard to imagine that 'reference' conditions may be set with a political agenda in mind. Indeed, given all of the above, the reader could be forgiven for thinking that the development and application of SIs as a way of gauging system sustainability may be unrealistic. There are a number of critics of SIs, and the following two chapters will illustrate some of the major planks upon which these criticisms are based. It should first be noted that the problems discussed so far in this chapter, including defining sustainability, and the setting of spatial and time scales, are well known to the proponents of SIs; as has already been illustrated, workers in the field attempt to provide various solutions.

One of the major criticisms regarding SIs is that they attempt to encapsulate complex and diverse processes in a relatively few simple measures. This is not a new problem. The world is a complex place, and people have had to make sense of it for a long time! The obvious approach is to deal with the world in manageable bits. Scientists deal with a complex system by breaking it down into components and studying how these work in isolation and then together; this is the reductionist approach. Reductionism has received much criticism by authors such as Capra (1982; 1996) and MacRae et al (1989) on the reasonable basis that some systems are so complex, with millions of interactions, that we are unable to look at every one. However, do we need to? Biologists have been dealing with complex ecosystems for many years, and they have long used indicators as a tool for gauging ecosystem health. Their experience suggests that:

> *The number of possible interactions among species is astronomical. If ecosystems science is strictly a study of species interactions it is hopelessly complex. But just as we need not consider all cell-to-cell interactions whenever we discuss a single organism, so we need not consider all possible species-to-species interactions whenever we discuss ecosystems.*

> Slobodkin (1994)

Allied to reductionism is a common perception that scientists, policy-makers and others are obsessed with quantification (MacRae et al, 1989). The distillation of information on biodiversity into a single value such as the

Shannon–Wiener index is but one example of quantification. Interestingly, some argue that belief in quantification is itself generated and reinforced by paradigms; this in turn requires proof of the wider application of a paradigm. In other words, the evolution of sustainability as a paradigm inevitably leads to a need to quantify sustainability; hence sustainability indicators were developed as a means of keeping the paradigm alive. Quantification, however, does have limitations, and clearly it is not possible to measure all human experience (MacRae et al, 1989). Indeed, for all their attempt at holism (see, for example, the second Bellagio principle) and a desire to incorporate the richness of humankind's complex interrelationships with nature, SIs are still a classic reductionist set of tools based on quantification. Indeed, we find it very ironical that those who scorn attempts to give value to sustainability, or to produce tables of SIs such as those proposed by the UN, still employ a language that has quantification at its heart. This has clear relevance, and indeed we feel it is central to the whole sustainability debate. Can we really use simple SIs to gauge such a complex issue as sustainability? Although aware of these pitfalls, many of course do just that. As Harrington (1992a) points out: 'it is never possible to deal with any problem (not just sustainability problems) in all its real-world complexity. Scientists "have to simplify to survive."' But how much simplification is acceptable? Clearly there is a trade-off between necessary simplification and at the same time having SIs that are meaningful. However, this is not a problem unique to sustainability or indeed to ecology. As Slobodkin (1994) states:

> *Any simplification limits our capacity to draw conclusions, but this is by no means unique to ecology. Essentially, all science is the study of either very small bits of reality or simplified surrogates for complex whole systems. How we simplify can be critical. Careless simplification leads to misleading simplistic conclusions.*

Harrington (1992a and 1992b) rejects the notion that quantifying sustainability is not possible precisely because it has been successfully achieved with complex biological systems. After all, what about the species indicators and biodiversity measures described earlier in this chapter? Farming systems research has also provided a wealth of experience in dealing with complex systems. Indeed, here is the nub! If the development and application of SIs was purely an academic exercise with no real immediate and practical relevance, then one may be willing to accept initial problems of oversimplification as an essential and necessary part of a lengthy learning curve. It should be remembered that ecologists and agriculturalists can make predictions about system behaviour based on their knowledge of the system's components and their interactions. If the results do not match reality, it is back to the drawing board for refinement. Ecology is a science, and like all science any predictions (hypotheses or models) are compared to the hard reality of what actually happens. If the predictions fail, then a good scientist will acknowledge the fact and build this new knowledge into future predictions. The result is an evolving body of knowledge accumulated over many years by a rich process of hypothesis formulation and testing.

While it is true that ecologists are part of a wider society, and are not isolated from socioeconomic, cultural and political pressures that set priorities for research and how results are used, the science itself should be immune to these pressures. Similarly, farming systems research (FSR, also sometimes referred to as farming systems research and extension – FSR/E – or more generically: on-farm research) combines a systems framework of analysis with research in which the farmers and their families play a central role in the process (Flora, 1992; McNamara and Morse, 1996). The language is certainly similar to that of sustainability – holism, systems perspective, incorporation of social perspectives and methodologies are all central to FSR. However, the setting of hypotheses, and testing, acceptance or rejection are also a part of the FSR process, albeit under different guises and by different means than in ecological science.

Does the development and use of SIs parallel the scientific approach of ecology, or even FSR? Frankly, it does not since the sustainability–SI combination involves a degree of circularity. Sustainability itself is a human vision that by definition is laced with human values (political and ethical) and SIs are not necessarily developed through a long process of hypothesis setting and testing, intended to arrive at a deeper understanding of sustainability. Granted, an element of refinement can be built in; but one does not develop a host of SIs, then test them to see whether they adequately describe sustainability. Rather, the starting point is a description of sustainability, with all of its human subjectivity, followed by an identification of SIs to gauge attainment of that description. Indeed, if we are planning to make major policy and economic changes to a system in order to get the SIs moving in the right direction, we do not want the SIs to be continually changing while all of this is happening. Not only can confusion result, but one is left open to the charge of changing SIs to suit. The reader should not take this to mean that SI selection is somehow inferior to more rigorous approaches in science. It is not inferior, but different.

An additional and very important factor is the role of those involved in setting agendas and the provision of funding for development initiatives. Money is inevitably a scarce commodity, and phrases such as value for money, cost effectiveness, project appraisal and evaluation are commonly employed by funding agencies. Given this background, donor agencies have become concerned about the sustainability of organizations charged with development in the field as well as the sustainability of the outcomes of development. These two visions of sustainability are quite different and not necessarily complimentary. An excessive emphasis on the sustainability of the method may inevitably result in less emphasis on the sustainability of the final outcome.

In the next two chapters we will examine some of these two concerns in greater depth. In order to do this we will describe SIs at a number of levels. To begin with, we will illustrate the limitations of the reductionist, mechanistic and quantitative approach to sustainability by looking at some of the ecological ideas behind one SI recommended by the UN: the maximum sustainable yield in fishery management. This will be followed by a description of an attempt to forge different SIs together into one overall picture of sustainability – the AMOEBA approach. As both MSY and AMOEBA are essentially located in natural resource management, we will examine how holism in sustainability (combining environmental, social and economic concerns) is attempted by focusing on the use of SIs in sustainable city programmes. Finally, we will discuss some of the points that arise out of the need for agencies to appraise field projects on the basis of sustainability. The example chosen is the expanding area of financial service provision in developing countries.

It should be stressed that sustainability and SIs cover a huge amount of ground, and the examples in Chapters 2 and 3 certainly do not imply that these are the only ones, or indeed are necessarily the best. Our aim, instead, is to choose areas that link to debates in later chapters and hence are illustrative of general principles rather than specifics.

Chapter 2
Sustainability Indicators in Practice

INTRODUCTION AND OBJECTIVES

Chapter 1 set out some of the background issues in the debate surrounding the development and use of sustainability indicators. In Chapters 2 and 3 we will take this further and provide some examples of SIs in practice. The theme throughout the two chapters will be to examine SIs at different levels.

- individual SIs and the combination of SIs
- SIs with a narrow focus and those with a broad focus

In this chapter we will examine a single SI in some detail, and move on to how SIs can be combined to provide a picture of sustainability. In both cases there will be a narrow focus on the technical issues of natural resource and environmental management. Chapter 3 will continue to look at collections of SIs, but this time we will discuss how socioeconomic factors can be included alongside environmental concerns.

We begin here with a detailed examination of one SI, suggested by the UN following the Rio Earth Summit. The example we have selected is maximum sustainable yield (MSY), and is suggested by the UN as a state SI for the 'protection of the oceans, all kinds of seas and coastal areas' (Chapter 17 of the Rio document). This is followed by a discussion of how SIs can be pooled to form an overall picture of sustainability. The example we have chosen is AMOEBA, which has been developed to pictorially represent SI values relative to a baseline. Although by no means the most common approach, AMOEBA does have advantages since its originators have given substantial thought to interpretation; this immediately raises the issue of how one is to deal with a collection of SIs, some of which may be pointing in quite different directions.

MSY and AMOEBA were also developed with a marine environment in mind, although they do have quite a different emphasis. MSY is concerned with the management of single fish species, while AMOEBA was developed with a much broader emphasis on environmental management. MSY also has a long history dating back to the last century, although its more modern form

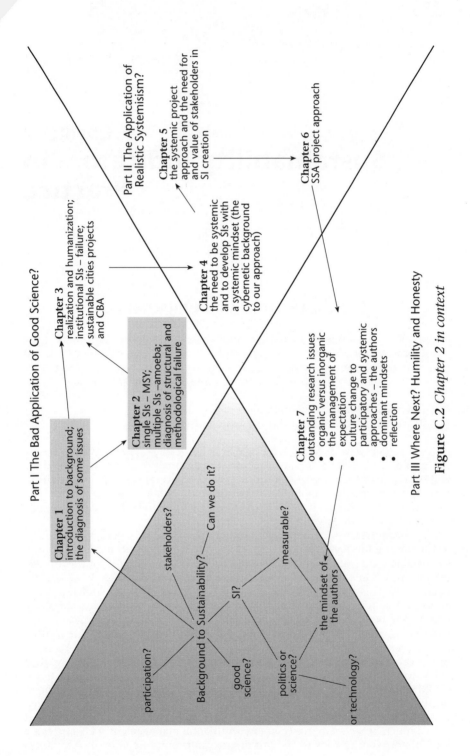

Part I The Bad Application of Good Science?

Part II The Application of Realistic Systemisism?

Part III Where Next? Humility and Honesty

Chapter 1
introduction to background; the diagnosis of some issues

Chapter 2
single SIs – MSY; multiple SIs –amoeba; diagnosis of structural and methodological failure

Chapter 3
realization and humanization; institutional SIs – failure; sustainable cities projects and CBA

Chapter 4
the need to be systemic and to develop SIs with a systemic mindset (the cybernetic background to our approach)

Chapter 5
the systemic project approach and the need for and value of stakeholders in SI creation

Chapter 6
SSA project approach

Chapter 7
outstanding research issues
• organic versus inorganic
• the management of expectation
• culture change to participatory and systemic approaches – the authors dominant mindsets
• reflection

Background to Sustainability?

participation?

stakeholders? — Can we do it?

SI?

good science?

politics or science?

measurable?

the mindset of the authors

or technology?

Figure C.2 *Chapter 2 in context*

originated in the 1930s. It now makes a regular appearance in many contemporary discussions of sustainability (see, for example, Daly, 1990, and Munn, 1992) In contrast, AMOEBA is a much more recent device for gauging sustainability and its inventors have taken on board the need to combine a broad set of indicators into a visual device suitable for use by planners. For our purposes, MSY provides other advantages because:

- It is based on some fundamental ecological concepts of population growth that incorporate the notion of carrying capacity, often taken as a key element in the history of the sustainability concept. Indeed, MSY encapsulates in microcosm the very essence of sustainability – continuous but not detrimental exploitation of a resource.
- The MSY encapsulates many of the arguments summarized in Chapter 1 with regard to the reductionist, mechanistic and quantitative nature of modern science. It represents one of the first attempts to sustainably manage a resource based on knowledge derived from ecological science.

MSY represents a useful example of an SI to illustrate some of the issues outlined in Chapter 1; however, in order to fully appreciate the origin of the concept and the problems with its use, one needs to have some background knowledge of the ecological principles that lie behind it. Therefore, we have included some of this theory in the chapter. It is not necessary for the reader to fully comprehend the mathematics but to appreciate the relative simplicity of the equations being used.

THE MAXIMUM SUSTAINABLE YIELD

Carrying capacity basically represents the maximum number of individuals of a species that an ecosystem can sustain. It follows, therefore, that if the carrying capacity is exceeded, the population will be limited through lack of resources. Following on from this in part is the concept of MSY, the number or biomass of individuals that can be removed from an ecosystem without driving the population down. Since these ecological concepts have had a major influence on the broad thinking that lays behind sustainability, it is worth spending some time looking at these concepts and their limitations in practice.

MSY is one of the key state SIs put forward by the UN in Chapter 17 ('Protection of the Oceans, all Kinds of Seas and Coastal Areas') of the Rio Summit document. It is described by the UN as 'an expression of the state of fishery resource exploitation to its sustainable size'. It is worth noting that there has been a large influence of ecosystem concepts and ecological theory in fishery management, and this influence goes back many years. Indeed, it may not be an exaggeration to say that fishery management was the first concerted attempt by humankind to effectively manage a resource based on fundamental ecological ideas, derived via classic Western science. This is reflected in research and published work on fish population dynamics and age structure that dates back to the last century. After World War II, MSY took root as a fishery management concept, and some have even called the decade after 1945 the 'golden age for the concept of maximum sustained yield' (Larkin, 1977). MSY appeared to offer a panacea for fishery management that can be summarized in the following dogma:

> *Any species each year produces a harvestable surplus,*
> *and if you take that much,*
> *and no more,*
> *you can go on getting it forever and ever.*
> *(Amen)*
>
> Larkin (1977)

MSY's influence in fishery management worldwide has been immense (Larkin, 1977), and although it has had numerous critics, it has been remarkably resilient even to the point of its inclusion as an SI by the UN (Hoenig et al, 1994). Given this, one is entitled to ask why fishery management has received such a strong influence from ecology? It is interesting to note, for example, that this influence has been far less marked in the case of wild game management or indeed in the management of rangeland. There are a number of possible reasons (Wagner, 1969), one of which is that fisheries tend to have a clearly defined spatial boundary (Cushing, 1981). The spatial boundary is distinct if one considers a lake; however, even in oceans, fisheries often have defined boundaries where fish concentrate (Cushing, 1981). These boundaries include:

- isotherms (patterns of temperature change in the water);
- physical boundaries (ridges, troughs);
- areas of upwelling or divergence (water rises from lower depths to the surface); these often bring nutrients to the surface and phytoplankton production can be intense.

As discussed in Chapter 1, defining a spatial boundary for sustainability is often problematic, but in fishery management the problem is made simpler.

The central question regarding population management is quite simply: how many animals can be taken without destroying the stock? There are a number of ways of approaching this, and one is to consider the basic elements of population growth. Scientists have been producing mathematical models of animal populations for a very long time (Jensen, 1973; Dempster, 1975; Watson and Ollason, 1982). The earliest (and simplest) examples were all based on the fundamental idea that at time (t) one individual in the population becomes two, and the overall effect is an acceleration of population growth with time. Therefore, at its simplest, population growth represents the difference between births and deaths in a population. The larger this difference is, the greater the rate of population growth. It is also reasoned that populations will continue to increase provided there is plenty of food or other vital resource and there are no natural enemies or disease (Figure 2.1a). An outline of the equations behind this curve are shown in Box 2.1. In reality, of course, populations do not increase to infinity, since limitations of space and food usually become apparent. A population tends to increase up to a certain point until basic limitations start to operate and the growth rate slows down. Eventually the growth rate becomes zero (the population is static). The equations given in Box 2.1 will not reflect this process since they will always describe a population increasing to infinity. Nevertheless, a slight alteration in the equations can take these limitations into account, and the result is shown in Figure 2.1b. The equation behind Figure 2.1b is shown in Box 2.2.

The key point we would like the reader to take from Boxes 2.1 and 2.2 is not necessarily the mathematical detail; instead we would like to emphasize the relative simplicity of the equations. Each only has a few components, and some of these (r and K) are assumed to be constant. Quite clearly we are emulat-

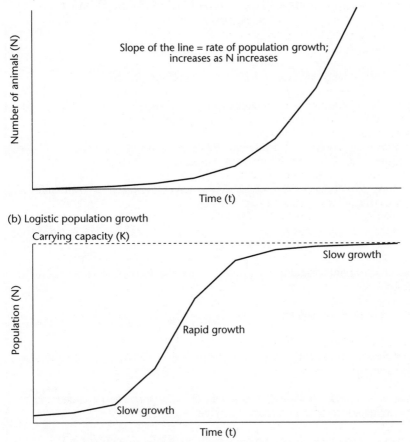

(a) Exponential (=organic) population growth

Number of animals (N)

Slope of the line = rate of population growth; increases as N increases

Time (t)

(b) Logistic population growth

Carrying capacity (K)

Population (N)

Slow growth

Rapid growth

Slow growth

Time (t)

Note: numbers of animals (N) plotted at each time (t)

Figure 2.1 *Examples of population growth curves*

ing nature in a very simplistic manner. For example, is it realistic to assume that carrying capacity (K) is a constant? After all, real environments fluctuate greatly from year to year and hence the value of K may also fluctuate. One should also point out that in practice animals do not instantaneously disappear when the population approaches K! There is always a time lag for this influence, and populations can exceed the carrying capacity for short periods. Secondly, real populations are made up of two groups: sexually mature individuals (individuals who can contribute to population growth) and those individuals who cannot add to population increase because they are too old or not yet sexually mature. The value of r will be a constant only if the proportion of sexually mature individuals is constant. In other words, r is a constant only if the population has a stable age distribution (Figure 2.2). In practice, age distributions may not be stable over time. Therefore as Slobodkin (1994) points out: 'Due to the simplistic nature of their initial assumptions, these [logistic] equation systems, regardless of particular modifications, do not mimic any actual population.'

Box 2.1 *The mathematical equations behind the population curve in Figure 2.1(a)*

It can be shown that :

population growth rate = constant X population size (N)

Constant = an indicator of the multiplication rate of each individual in the population. By convention, the constant is given the symbol 'r'.
Population growth rate = change in number of individuals (N) over a time period (t). This can be expressed as dN/dt, where 'd' means 'a very small change in' (we consider very small changes for technical reasons).

Therefore, the above expression in English can be written in mathematical language (a differential equation) as:

$$\frac{dN}{dt} = rN$$

Also, the differential equation can be rearranged= to make it more useful in practice:

$$\frac{dN}{dt} = rN \rightarrow N_t = N_0 e^{rt}$$

    Differential   *Integral*
      form   *form*

where 'e' is another constant (2.71828, etc), N_t is the population at time t and N_0 is the population at time zero (starting population).

Therefore, higher values of 'r' $\rightarrow$ more rapid growth rates of a population.

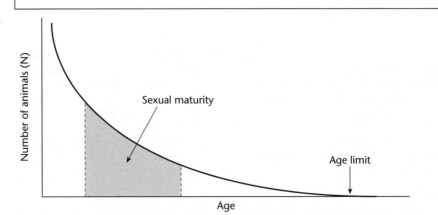

Note: A stable age distribution occurs when the proportion of adults at sexual maturity remains constant (curve moves evenly up and down but does not change shape). Intrinsic growth rate (r) is a constant only if the population has a stable age distribution. In this example there is a high mortality rate amongst the younger age groups.

Figure 2.2 *Example of an age distribution*

Box 2.2 The mathematical equation behind the population curve in Figure 2.1(b)

$$\frac{dN}{dt} = r \left(\frac{K - N}{K} \right) N$$

Differential Form

K = another constant commonly referred to as carrying capacity.
Other symbols as in Box 2.1.

Therefore, population growth rate changes depending on how close the population is to K.
As N approaches K, the (K–N)/K part of the equation becomes closer to zero and hence the growth rate becomes static.

However, although it has its limitations, even the simple equation in Box 2.2 provides the basis for some resource management models that are referred to as the surplus yield models (or more precisely, biomass dynamics models). These models introduce a further component, namely harvesting, into the equation of Box 2.2, as shown in Figure 2.3. If immigration and emigration into a defined population are constant, then the numbers that can be removed by harvesting will depend on the balance between births and deaths (on the population growth rate). Clearly, the maximum gap between births and deaths will be the maximum number of animals that can be removed without reducing the size of the population. This is referred to as the maximum sustainable yield (MSY) and is illustrated in Figure 2.4. The concept of MSY has been widely applied in fishery management, and problems that have been associated with this widespread use will be discussed later.

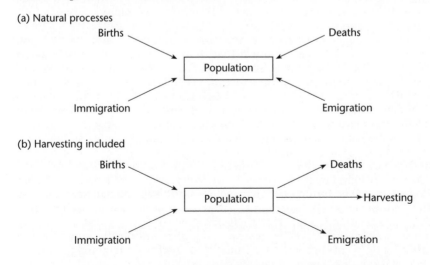

(a) Natural processes

Births   Deaths

Population

Immigration   Emigration

(b) Harvesting included

Births   Deaths

Population ————→ Harvesting

Immigration   Emigration

Figure 2.3 *Main elements contributing to population change*

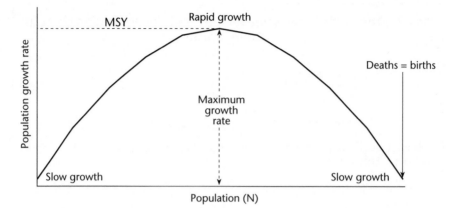

Note: Population growth rate from the logistic curve is plotted against population (N)

Figure 2.4 *The concept of maximum sustainable yield in harvesting a population*

It should be noted that the basic ecological ideas behind MSY are not particularly complex or, indeed, new. The mathematics within which the basic ideas in Boxes 2.1 and 2.2 are expressed (calculus) was 'invented ' by Leibniz (1646 to 1716). The logistic curve was proposed by Verhulst in 1844, while the application of the logistic curve to animal populations was proposed by many biologists from the 1930s onwards (for example, Gause, 1934). However, the application of the MSY concept is much more recent. Given the age of the elements that make up MSY, why did it take so long to apply the concept? Part of the problem is that in order to use the MSY equation we have to create a curve such as that in Figure 2.4 by finding either the values of r and K or the population growth rate for a number of populations. In practice, it can be difficult to do this as it requires very detailed knowledge of the animal population. Fortunately, the yield obtained from a fishery is demonstrably related to the 'fishing effort' (weight per boat per day); MSY (and also optimum fishing effort) can then be found from this relationship (Schaefer, 1954, 1957). With a lot of mathematical juggling, starting with the basic logistic equation in Box 2.2 (and some assumptions), it can be shown that there is a theoretical link between yield from a fishery and the fishing effort. The relationship is illustrated in Figure 2.5, and the mathematical equation behind the curve is shown in Box 2.3. Again, the main point to note is the relative simplicity of the equation; yield is determined by just three factors, two of which (U and b) are assumed to be constants over the period in which the curve is fitted.

The beauty of the Schaefer approach is that it is simple: only data on yields and fishing effort are required (Polacheck et al, 1993). There is a relative abundance of such data for many fisheries and the individual values of 'b' and 'U' are usually found by fitting curves to these data. There are a number of ways of doing this, but unfortunately these methods can give different values for the optimal fishing effort (Polacheck et al, 1993). In addition, the determination of MSY by this method requires that there are some data points beyond the MSY in order to fit a curve. In other words, and perhaps ironically, some level of overfishing (ie points beyond the optimal fishing effort) is required in order to obtain the MSY with a degree of confidence.

Given the foregoing, it is not difficult to see why MSY achieved the prominence it has. The equations are very simple and are firmly rooted in good

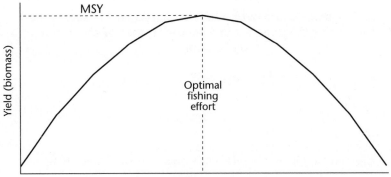

Figure 2.5 *The Schaefer model employed to determine MSY based on the fishery yield for a particular fishing effort*

Box 2.3 *An equation relating fishing effort to yield from a fishery.*

The general equation for the curve in Figure 2.5

$$Y_e = U f - b f^2$$

where Y_e = the fishery yield for a particular effort
f = the fishing effort (usually expressed in terms of trawler fleet tonnage)
b = a constant which comprises a number of factors, such as the efficiency of the fishing gear and the intrinsic growth rate of fish biomass (fish catches are normally expressed in biomass not numbers)
U = maximum fish catch/unit fishing effort

Both b and U are assumed to be constants.

Example equation fitted to data from the Peruvian anchovy fishery (Figure 2.7).

$$Y_e = 0.722 f - 0.0121 f^2$$

---

mechanistic science. Given a reasonable set of effort and yield data – and many fisheries have such data – simple statistical techniques can be employed to fit curves (Hoenig et al, 1994; Prager, 1994). Indeed, one doesn't have to be a scientist to do this. Techniques have even been developed to estimate MSY in the absence of effort and yield time series data (Garcia et al, 1989). If MSY can deliver sustainable utilization of a resource, then all is well; but can it deliver?

PROBLEMS WITH THE APPLICATION OF MAXIMUM SUSTAINABLE YIELD

Although surplus yield models (such as the Schaefer model) are useful, they do have a number of problems. These are largely centred around the assumptions made for the logistic curve (the Schaefer model and others like it have been

---

Box 2.4 *A population growth equation based on the assumption that the size of the population is linked to that of the previous generation*

The simplest example is as follows (May, 1989):

$$N_{t+1} = N_t \, \lambda$$

N_{t+1} = population in generation t+1
N_t = population in generation t
λ = multiplication rate (number of offspring/individual between time t to t+1)

For example, assuming a one-year time period this equation means :

population this = population last **X** number of offspring
   year (t+1)   year (t)   per individual

Allowing for carrying capacity (K) limitations as in the logistic equation:

$$N_{t+1} = N_t \left(\frac{K - N_t}{K} \right) \lambda$$

---

derived from the logistic growth curve). The logistic equation may provide some interesting insights, but there is a danger in using them as the basis of management models. An inkling of some of the problems encountered can be illustrated by deriving another surplus yield model from a different starting point. Instead of relating population size to time, what happens if it is related to the size of the population in the previous generation? After all, this is a far more logical stance to take. The result of such a derivation is shown in Box 2.4. However, such a basic and logical assumption can generate very complex population curves since they incorporate the notion of feedback. The size of the multiplication rate is a major factor in producing such chaotic behaviour (see Figure 2.6). Although higher values of the multiplication rate generate complex population curves, these capture the essence of what we observe in practice (May, 1989; Fielding, 1991). Wild populations fluctuate widely (an effect caused by an array of environmental and biotic factors) and do not increase smoothly to a maximum before levelling off (Dempster, 1975). Therefore, by taking another simple starting point the foundations of the MSY appear to be insecure.

Quite clearly, MSY is a very simple concept, and the sort of equations evident in Boxes 2.1 to 2.3 do not fully take account of the complex nature of the ecosystem MSY is meant to manage. As Pitcher and Hart (1982) point out:

> *In its classical form, MSY excludes the effects of competition, symbiotic or commensal relationships with other species, tropic relationships, or changes in carrying capacity due to pollution or other human influences.*

Indeed, there are numerous echoes of this concern, and for the sake of brevity we only give two more spanning a 17-year period, beginning with Mohn's 1980 study of bias and error in estimating MSY:

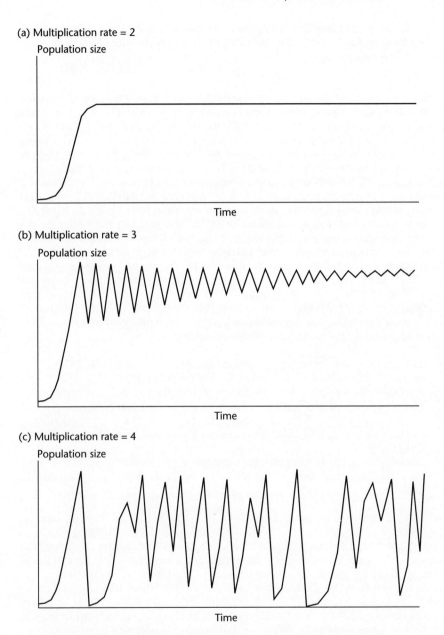

Figure 2.6 *Population growth curves based on the equation in Box 2.4*

As experimental verification of MSY is unlikely for a commercial stock and the yield is affected by many factors, sustainable yield estimation will be slow in changing from an art to a science.

Mohn (1980)

...the supposed catch-effort relationship underlying the concept of MSY is apparently illusory. The level at which these stocks are 'sustainable'

> *is not known and is unlikely to be known for many years, if ever,*
> *because of the lack of basic information on the landings and biology of*
> *fish species.*
>
> Aikman (1997)

A classic example of the problems that could occur from a narrow application of MSY to fishery management is that provided by the collapse of the Peruvian anchovy fishery in 1972 (Boerema and Gulland, 1973; Idyll, 1973; Pitcher and Hart, 1982; Laws, 1997). This fishery exists largely as a result of deep water being brought to the surface of the sea by the prevailing wind, moving the surface water north-westerly. The deep water brings nutrients to the surface, encouraging the growth of phytoplankton, which in turn provides a source of energy for the whole ecosystem. It has been estimated (Idyll, 1973) that this was the world's largest fishery, accounting at one time for 22 per cent of all fish caught throughout the world. Even in 1971, just prior to the collapse, the fishery still accounted for 15 per cent of the world catch of fish (Pitcher and Hart, 1982). However, after the collapse, the fishery switched from one dominated by anchovy to one dominated by the South American sardine (*Sardinops sagax*); only in the late 1980s and early 1990s has there been any suggestion that the ecosystem may revert back to its pre-1972 conditions (Patterson et al, 1992). Just what caused this switch has been the subject of much research and debate, and an excellent history is provided by Laws (1997). There appears to have been three main causalities:

- The anchovy was heavily exploited during the 1960s and early 1970s, although this exploitation was within the predicted MSY.
- Anchovy and sardine appear to have a relationship in that a collapse in the population of one leads to a boom in the population of the other (Walsh et al, 1980). One link is that both may feed on the same organisms, but anchovy and sardine larvae are normally separated in space (Sameoto, 1982).
- Conditions in the Peru upwelling were subject to regular disruption by a climatic fluctuation that occurs in the Pacific every two to ten years (the El Niño event).

Since the establishment of the anchovy industry in the mid 1950s, catches have soared, although this has been at the expense of the sea bird population that also survived on the fish. Sea-birds were not just of aesthetic interest, but were also the basis of a thriving guano industry. Estimations of total catch and fishing effort have been made (Boerema and Gulland, 1973), and a Schaefer model can be fitted to these data using standard statistical techniques that are readily available with many computer packages. Indeed, as Pitcher and Hart (1982) point out: 'MSY is seductively easy to calculate; in fact, no biologists need to be employed in the fishery and managers do not even have to get their hands and feet wet in examining actual fish.' An example for catches and effort in the 1960s (1960 to 1969) is shown in Figure 2.7. The fit of the curve is highly significant statistically (see Box 2.3), engendering a high level of confidence in the result. It is interesting to note that as the sea birds were significant catchers of fish up until the mid 1960s, the yield and fishing effort were based on a combination of human and bird activity. The total catch removed by the birds was estimated, and the total human fishing effort that would give this catch was calculated. The resulting curve suggests that MSY was approximately ten million tonnes and occurs at a fishing effort of about 30 million tonne trips.

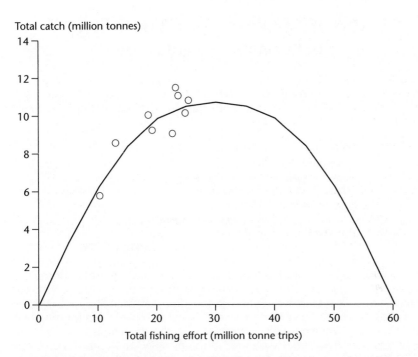

Figure 2.7 *Schaefer model fitted to data from the Peruvian anchovy fishery*

As can be seen from Figure 2.7, the actual catches in the 1960s were generally at or below MSY, suggesting that the fishery was being exploited to the maximum and that the exploitation was sustainable. However, as mentioned above, the equations upon which all of this is based assume a stable age distribution in the population. If this is not the case due to an excessive removal of fish at reproductive age, or because of environmental fluctuations, then recruitment can decline rapidly. Such a decline occurred with anchovy in the early 1970s following a period of heavy fishing effort between 1967 and 1970. Ironically, the fall in recruitment was noted, but heavy fishing continued over the three-year period. Secondly, the El Niño event in 1972 started to bring warmer water into the fishery. This warmer water had a negative effect on the anchovy population in the fishery, possibly because it encouraged increased numbers of horse mackerel, which is a major predator of anchovy (Laws, 1997); nevertheless, heavy fishing was allowed to continue. It was almost as if the use of the Schaefer model generated a 'misplaced confidence' that the MSY was around ten million tonnes. The result was a collapse in the anchovy population and an upsurge in the sardine population. When it was clear that the fishery had collapsed, the industry was nationalized by the military government and effectively reduced to half its size. The number of boats was cut from 1500 to 800, the number of fishmeal plants reduced from 100 to 50, and the number of people employed was reduced from 25,000 to 12,000 (Laws, 1997). Since the changes in the early 1970s, the fishery has been subject to other El Niño events, and the industry has passed through a number of changes. However, it can hardly be said to represent the epitome of sustainable resource utilization.

MAXIMUM SUSTAINABLE YIELD AS A SUSTAINABILITY INDICATOR

As will have been gleaned from the previous pages, the MSY concept – in practice – has had its problems. Indeed, MSY has even received some light-hearted derision as the following, often quoted by fishery scientists, poem illustrates:

> *Here lies the concept. MSY.*
> *It advocated yields too high,*
> *And didn't spell out how to slice the pie,*
> *We bury it with the best of wishes,*
> *Especially on behalf of fishes.*
> *We don't yet know what will take its place,*
> *But we hope it's as good for the human race.*
>
> Larkin (1977)

MSY as a management tool has gradually been replaced by other approaches (Pitcher and Hart, 1982), although the term has been remarkably resilient. The UN, for example, while including MSY as one of its key state SIs, acknowledges that 'fishing at the MSY level is now seen to be excessive, and determining MSY where it is not yet known involves overfishing, which is obviously undesirable.' Yet no fewer than five SIs based on MSY (plus one based on biomass rather than on MSY) have been proposed by the UN to address issues in Chapter 17 ('Protection of the Oceans, all Kinds of Seas and Coastal Areas') of the Rio document:

1   ratio of MSY abundance and actual average abundance;
2   the deviation in stock of marine species from the MSY level;
3   ratio of current fishing effort to the effort at MSY;
4   ratio of current fishing mortality to that at MSY;
5   ratio of current population biomass (or spawning biomass) to that at MSY;
6   current biomass to that under 'virgin' conditions (before fishing began).

The last SI is an alternative indicator where MSY is unknown. Ratios of MSY to abundance, fishing effort and mortality are considered to be more precise than absolute estimates (Prager et al, 1996). It is suggested that the Schaefer method should be employed to find the MSY; once the SIs have been calculated it will be possible to check whether the resource is being exploited in a sustainable fashion. Problems with the MSY concept are acknowledged in the UN documents and are essentially those already highlighted above. Indeed, 'For many countries, suitable data to calculate these indicators are scarce. In addition, major deficiencies are characteristic of many available data sets.'

Given these problems, and the dangers with MSY as highlighted above, one may perhaps be forgiven for registering some surprise at the emphasis placed on MSY as an SI. After all, the Peruvian anchovy example was founded on an apparently good estimation of MSY, and SIs based on MSY under those prevailing conditions would have suggested 'sustainability' – while it was clear that the system as a whole was far from being sustainable. If that wasn't enough, the UN admits that 'For many global fish stocks, MSY levels have not yet been determined.' While it may be argued that these SIs are better than nothing, and our knowledge of how to find, test and implement an MSY has improved, one still can't help but feel some anxiety about the expectation surrounding the use of MSY as an SI. Surely we have a classic example of reductionism applied to a complex ecosystem, with a strong emphasis on 'simplify to survive'; yet the potential dangers for the sustainable management of a resource are very apparent.

The supreme irony of all of this is that many scientists involved in natural resource management have pointed out, over many years, the simplified nature of MSY and the problems that may arise from its unquestioned use. Two of the most respected workers in this field have stated:

> ...like some other simplified concepts, maximum sustainable yield has become institutionalized in a more absolute and precise role than intended by the biologists who were responsible for its original formulation. It is being expected to perform functions for which it was never intended, serving, for example, as the sole conceptual basis for or goal of management in some cases. Once a concept has been adopted and institutionalized, it is difficult to change it. In this case, because of its institutionalization, the concept of maximum sustainable yield is now an obstacle to the acceptance of concepts that derive from present ecological knowledge, and that would provide a more adequate basis for management.
>
> Holt and Talbot (1978)

Given all this, why has MSY enjoyed such longevity, including its presence in an exclusive list of SIs put forward by the UN at the turn of the 20th century? For example, although the European Union no longer aims to fish at MSY, it still uses it as a sort of benchmark in the $F_{0.1}$ objective (which corresponds to fishing slightly below MSY) – although 'arbitrary biological reference points' were also included for some stocks (Corten, 1996). Its relative simplicity as a concept, and the fact that equations such as that in Box 2.3 can be easily fitted to existing data, have no doubt been of enormous importance in this regard. It also provides a single figure answer as to what sustainability is – S really can equal 42! Single figure crystallizations of complex data appear to have an instant appeal for some.

SIS IN MARINE ECOSYSTEMS – THE AMOEBA APPROACH

In the previous section we looked in detail at one SI based on the MSY concept in fishery management. The main point was to provide the reader with some knowledge of the indicator, and to illustrate how SIs by definition imply a level of simplification, which can be dangerous when dealing with a very complex ecosystem. In this section we will move to the next level in the use of SIs and consider how a number of different sets of data may be combined to derive a composite SI for a system.

As mentioned in Chapter 1, indicator species and biodiversity have commonly been employed as a gauge of ecosystem quality. However, the limitations of technical measures of biodiversity such as the Shannon–Wiener index have led others to propose alternative approaches to measuring diversity as an element within an SI. An example is the AMOEBA approach (Ten Brink et al, 1991; Ten Brink, 1991), an acronym which in Dutch stands for 'general method for ecosystem description and assessment'. AMOEBA has one major advantage in that it is a highly visual approach to encapsulating sustainability , and this is largely a result of the fact that it has been created with non-specialists in mind. In Chapter 1 we pointed out that one of the limitations of the Shannon–Wiener biodiversity index, and others like it, is that they have been developed by scientists for scientists. The same is essentially true of MSY, and although MSY equations are relatively simple, a basic understanding of what is in them is still required. The AMOEBA approach attempts to reduce this limitation.

The AMOEBA approach arose out of the third national policy document on water management which focused on the management of the North Sea and Dutch inland waters. As well as stressing the need for a visual representation of sustainability, Ten Brink et al (1991) took a broad view of sustainability and concluded that there were three categories of 'valuable characteristics, whose sustainability is desirable':

- yield;
- biodiversity;
- self-regulation.

The first two have already been discussed. The third characteristic, self-regulation, relates in essence to the stability or resilience of the system – how stable the system is in the face of interference by humans or natural 'shocks'. Ten Brink et al point out that 'self-regulating ecosystems have low management costs'. In other words, if the system is robust, then continual, and expensive, management from humans is not required to maintain it.

The second key element in their approach is to assume that they can define sustainability in terms of how far the current ecosystem departs from an identified 'reference' ecosystem. The reference represents the natural state of the ecosystem with as little human interference as possible. The assumption is that this natural state is a sustainable system. The further a system departs from this, the less sustainable it is assumed to be. However, how can one identify the reference system? One possibility is to refer to the same system some time in the past before human interference began to have a major impact, although a key question is whether there is data available on the ecosystem for the chosen time. This is especially the case if one has to go back a long time to find a suitable reference system. For example, Ten Brink et al suggest the year 1930 for the North Sea, as this represents 'a pragmatic compromise between, on the one hand, the available knowledge and, on the other hand, a relatively low level of human interference.'

An alternative approach is to employ a reference system separated in space from the one studied, but which has not received any interference. Selecting a reference system that is separated in space is easier in the sense that one can see what is there and also identify whether there has been human interference. The main problem is quite simple: is such a 'twin' system available? For a relatively large ecosystem such as the North Sea this may be impossible. Secondly, even if a likely ecosystem can be found, how sure can we be that it represents a true twin for the system interfered with by humans?

The third key element in the Ten Brink et al methodology is what to measure in order to gauge the three 'key characteristics'. In other words, what are the specific SIs? One could, presumably, include SIs for each of the three characteristics, or indeed any other characteristics that one wishes to apply to sustainability, including the more nebulous quality of life. In practice, Ten Brink et al describe the use of a population index for 60 selected target species that include managed fish species and others that are assumed to be indicators of pollution or ecosystem disruption. As mentioned in Chapter 1, the use of certain species to indicate pollution or disruption is not new in ecology; but even so, what are the criteria for selecting these species? After all, there are literally thousands or even millions that could be included, and as pointed out by Slobodkin (1994): 'the strength of the interaction between a particular species and the ecosystem in which it occurs varies enormously among species'. In the face of such an obvious and major problem, Ten Brink et al suggest the following list of criteria for selecting these species.

- Quantitative data on abundance must be available for the species.
- The species must be susceptible to human interference.
- The species must be accessible for easy and accurate measurement.
- The species should have some 'indicative value for the condition of the system'.
- The species should ideally have some 'political and social appeal'.

The first four criteria are logical from a standard ecological perspective, but the fifth is a novel departure from the more usual technical approaches in the ecological literature. Ten Brink et al state that 'we believe it to be more effective and more appropriate to select species which society and the authorities know and understand.' Therefore, although the species indicator and biodiversity example in Chapter 1 focused on macro-invertebrates (Learner et al, 1971), and these may be acceptable under Ten Brink's first four points, it is very doubtful whether they would fulfil the last point. Clearly, the kind of organisms that would satisfy point 5 are birds, fish and other large vertebrates, particularly mammals.

The final element in the methodology is presentation. One could, of course, use the sort of biodiversity indices and graphs already described in Chapter 1. It is interesting to note that this was rejected by Ten Brink et al because 'water authorities and policy makers require a clear and simple presentation' rather than scientific models 'which nobody can understand'. Their suggestion was to use a visual presentation of diversity rather than calculated indices, and an example is provided in Figure 2.8. The circle represents the 'reference' condition (numbers/extent of that species in 1930), and the arms are the 1988 numbers/extent of the species as a proportion of the reference numbers/extent. The diagram is referred to as an AMOEBA because of the resemblance to the unicellular animal of the same name; as can be seen, the number of some species (for example, common seal, harbour porpoise, bottlenose dolphin, herring and lobster) have declined dramatically from the 1930 reference condition, while others, notably algae and some sea birds, have increased dramatically.

One can extend the basic AMOEBA approach further and compare different AMOEBAE. These may be AMOEBAE calculated for different years; however, each is still related back to the reference year. For example, if data was available, one could calculate AMOEBA for 1940, 1950, 1960 and 1970 as well as for 1988 in order to chart how the system's sustainability has changed with time. One could also calculate predicted AMOEBA based on various policy interventions. In order to make multiple comparisons of AMOEBA, Ten Brink et al have suggested the use of what they call an 'ecological Dow Jones index'. For each AMOEBA the sum of the gaps between the reference point and each of the arms is calculated. The assumption is that the smaller this value, the closer the system is to sustainability.

The AMOEBA approach based on the numbers of key indicator species

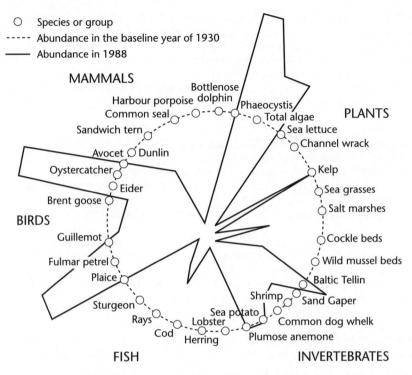

○   Species or group

----   Abundance in the baseline year of 1930

——   Abundance in 1988

MAMMALS

Bottlenose
Harbour porpoise dolphin
Common seal
Sandwich tern
Avocet ○ Dunlin
Oystercatcher
Eider
Brent goose

BIRDS

Guillemot
Fulmar petrel
Plaice
Sturgeon
Rays
Cod
Herring

FISH

Phaeocystis
Total algae   PLANTS
Sea lettuce
Channel wrack
Kelp
Sea grasses
Salt marshes
Cockle beds
Wild mussel beds
Baltic Tellin
Shrimp Sand Gaper
Sea potato
Lobster   Common dog whelk
Plumose anemone

INVERTEBRATES

Note: Abundance of selected species and groups (eg total algae, salt marsh) is shown relative to a baseline year. The example given here is based on that presented by Ten Brink et al (1991) with 1930 as the baseline year and the counts are from 1988.

Figure 2.8 *Example of an AMOEBA approach to presenting sustainability indicators*

addresses a number of the issues outlined in Chapter 1. Sustainability is defined as changes in the number of those species from a clear reference position. The time scale is also handled by defining the reference condition as a sample year. In the above example, the time scale is between 1930 and 1988 – a period of 58 years. The spatial scale is also defined clearly since one has to draw geographical lines in order to estimate the number/extent of the indicator species.

The approach has many advantages, and its appeal as a means of gauging sustainability is not difficult to understand. It also has a very practical feel, primarily because it was designed to be used as a decision-making tool in environmental management. However, it has been criticised (Rennings and Wiggering, 1997). To begin with one should note that because the AMOEBA is fundamentally based on numbers (population sizes) it does not in itself provide any information on the mechanisms involved in the changes – these have to be inferred from elsewhere (Slobodkin, 1994). In other words, the AMOEBA is essentially a set of 'state' SIs without 'driving force' SIs. Another problem is linked, ironically, to the underlying emphasis of combining different indicators within one diagram. Although there is an attempt at taking a holistic view of sustainability, the approach is based on simple addition (all indicators are combined into one diagram). However, is this realistic when dealing with a diverse set of stakeholders? Is it not likely that some groups are likely to weight some SIs more than others? For example, are fishermen more likely to emphasize the importance of cod and herring numbers than brent geese? It is also

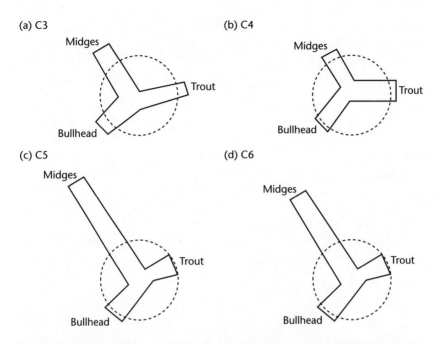

Figure 2.9 *Biomass of trout and bullhead and numbers of midges at four sampling stations on the River Cynon relative to station C1 (the reference condition)*

likely that members of the public will place more emphasis on mammals such as dolphins than kelp or sea potato, a point we will follow up in Chapter 6.

The third problem with the AMOEBA approach is centred on the choice of a reference condition, and this can be illustrated by using the familiar Learner et al (1971) example referred to in Chapter 1. The reader will recall that the researchers looked at the fauna (fish and macro-invertebrates) of a river in South Wales subject to pollution from a number of sources along its length. The population of various fish species and macro-invertebrates changed in response to a number of factors, but pollution was a major factor. Of the sampling stations (C1, C2, C3, etc) along the river, two of them (C1 and C2) occurred before the first input of pollution (a sewage inlet exists between C2 and C3). Therefore, it seems reasonable to use C1 or C2 as the reference condition and to compare incidence of species at other stations to one of these.

Following the logic of AMOEBA, and only including a few indicators to illustrate the point, it would make sense to focus on density (biomass/surface area of river) of trout and bullhead along with a number of individuals in the midge family of insects. Trout and bullhead were both found at stations C1 and C2, and biomass is a better indicator of relative abundance than numbers. These two species also have the advantage of being apparent (that is, they have some 'political and social value'). Midges were identified by the authors as being the most abundant insects in the Cynon system, and indeed comprised almost half the total number of macro-invertebrates sampled at each station. Therefore, although midges do not have any positive particular social value (the opposite if anything!), they do at least conform to the other criteria listed by Ten Brink et al. Figures 2.9 and 2.10 are AMOEBAE constructed with C1 and C2 as the reference conditions. There are some similarities between the

(a) C3 (b) C4

(c) C5 (d) C6

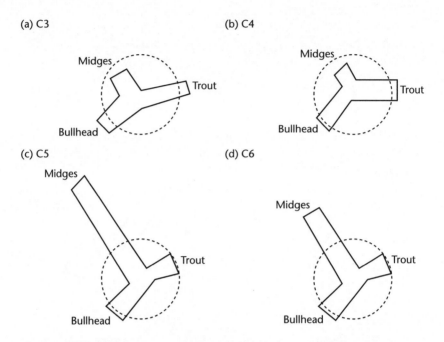

Figure 2.10 *Biomass of trout and bullhead and numbers of midges at four sampling stations on the River Cynon relative to station C2 (the reference condition)*

AMOEBAE, but there are also some differences. It should be remembered that in addition to the fact that both C1 and C2 are located upstream of the first pollution discharge point, the stations were only about two kilometres apart and had similar biodiversity indices. However, even a minor alteration in reference condition has resulted in significant changes in the AMOEBAE.

The choice of a reference becomes even more problematic if one calculates the Ecological Dow Jones index as suggested by Ten Brink et al. This can be found by summing the percentage change in the three indicators from the reference condition (ie C1 or C2) as shown in Box 2.5. The percentage change in these indicators relative to C1 is 100 times that relative to C2. Clearly the two different reference conditions have had a major impact on percentage change.

If one takes a time dimension instead of the spatial dimension given here, the fundamental problem remains. Although Ten Brink et al provide a logical rationale for the year 1930 as their reference condition, how would the results have looked if the reference year was 1920? Are we not faced with a C1:C2 dilemma in time as opposed to space, and could this potentially result in quite different conclusions regarding sustainability of the system?

The final point to make here is that given that AMOEBA has been developed as a practical tool rather than as an academic exercise, one could ask the reasonable (although hypothetical) question: would it have helped with the case of the Peruvian anchovy collapse? Here we are dealing with a defined ecosystem that was well researched and which was under clear management (at least from 1965 onwards) receiving regular technical reports on the state of the fishery. Managers had the power to suspend fishing for any period of time if they saw fit, or to change catch limits. Surely this should provide the ideal scenario under which SIs could be applied to allow a continued sustainable use

Box 2.5. *The calculation of ecological Dow Jones indices for three indicators (trout and bullhead biomass and midge numbers) from the River Cynon in South Wales*

Example calculation

| | | Indicators | |
Stations	Trout biomass	Bullhead biomass	Midge numbers
Reference stations C1	0.06	2.45	686
C2	3.13	4.82	5369
C3	7.36	11.8	2992

(a) Comparing C3 with C1

Total percentage change:
Trout = (7.3/0.06) x 100   = 12,167%
Bullhead = (9.35/2.45) x 100   = 382%
Midges = (2306/686) x 100   = 336%

Total = 12,885%

(b) Comparing C3 with C2

Total percentage change:
Trout = (4.23/3.13) x 100   = 135%
Bullhead = (6.98/4.82) x 100   = 145%
Midges = (2377/5369) x 100   = 44%

Total = 324%

Source: adapted from Learner et al (1971)

of the resource. There were certainly signs in the ecosystem that something was wrong prior to the collapse in 1972. Recruitment was known to have declined in 1971, and there was 'increasing evidence of unusual oceanographic conditions' (Boerema and Gulland, 1973) in 1972 about the same time as the collapse. The El Niño phenomenon developed rapidly in 1972 with no prior warning, although in 1971 there was an unusual occurrence of a tropical crab (*Euphilax*) along the coast, which presumably was linked to an increase in sea temperature. It should be noted that although El Niño is a regular occurence, it is unpredictable, and even now it is not known whether the perterbations in the ocean–atmosphere system originate in the atmosphere or the ocean. Presumably the SIs that would have helped to detect the collapse would include numbers of tropical species associated with warmer water (horse mackerel, yellowfin tuna, dolphinfish, manta ray and the hammerhead shark), as well as numbers of the anchovy itself and sardine.

Nevertheless, all of these were changing rapidly in just one to two years, and except for the clear decline in anchovy recruitment, it is highly debatable whether these SIs would have given adequate warning of a full-scale collapse. Indeed, the influence of a factor whose origin lies outside of the ecosystem represents a classic example of the problem of defining ecosystem boundaries. Even if an El Niño was known to be on the way, could the fishery managers have done anything about it? The answer quite simply would be no. On the other hand, the fishery was known to be under stress because of the observed poor anchovy recruitment, and it is likely that the eventual collapse was brought about by a combination of the two factors and maintained by the dominance of the sardine. The key indicator of recruitment was not given enough weight by the fishery managers, and catches remained high until El Niño arrived in full. Would an earlier suspension or reduction in fishing, in order to improve recruitment, have helped prevent the impact of El Niño? In previous years (such as 1965) there had also been a devastating El Niño, but in that case the stock had been able to recover. Overfishing in the late 1960s and early 1970s had greatly reduced this robustness, but what level of fishing could be sustainable when faced with an event like El Niño which has an unpredictable occurence and also varies in force?

The use of a suite of SIs based on species abundance as in the AMOEBA approach outlined by Ten Brink et al may not have prevented the collapse of the Peruvian anchovy fishery. The ecosystem itself is subject to massive disruption from an event that lies outside its boundaries and which is uncontrollable and unpredictable. Instead, the best one can do is build in an element of 'white noise' into the management models in order to aim for the best sustainable yield over a period of time. However, the key information for management of the resource would still be centred around the population biology of the fish stock rather than the sort of index that the AMOEBA represents. Where the AMOEBA approach could potentially play a role is as a measure of long-term ecosystem health rather than as a predictor of drastic short-term events; however, even here care would need to be taken in the interpretation of the results. Wild fluctuations in abundance of key species are likely to follow El Niño events and may last for some years (for instance, seabird abundance after 1965). Comparing species abundance prior to and just after an El Niño event may not be of much benefit, but longer term abundance may allow a measure of more subtle and yet still harmful environmental effects. Similarly, what does one choose as the reference condition? A year preceding a severe El Niño event is likely to be quite different from a year just after. The seabird population plummeted after the El Niño of 1965 not because of human activity but because of natural causes. Quite clearly, one needs to be aware of the processes involved in changes in species abundance and not just the fact that those changes have occurred.

SOME CONCLUSIONS

This chapter has examined two levels of SI – an individual SI (MSY) and an attempt at collecting individual indicators together as a single diagram (AMOEBA). Based on our discussion we can conclude that the main problem with such SIs is that they attempt to encapsulate a very complex system in a few simple measures. As has been illustrated, MSY makes many simplifying assumptions that may not exist in reality, and unquestioning adherence to MSY as a resource management tool can result in catastrophe. MSY itself is based on good scientific principles, but the scientific knowledge is simply incomplete. This is certainly not a criticism of those who have developed the ideas behind logistic population growth, yield/fishing effort relationships or even MSY. The criticism is aimed, instead, at those who extrapolate these ideas to complex systems without taking on board their inherent simplicity. Sustainable management is certainly a goal worth pursuing, and like Corten (1996) we too lament the fact that EU 'biologists have lost their initial enthusiasm for optimal management, and have stopped recommending specific management actions'; but we have to be realistic about what we can achieve with the knowledge that we have or are likely to get in the near future. The problem with lists of SIs such as those produced by the UN is that the holistic nature of sustainability encompasses a huge breadth of knowledge – economics, social science and natural resources.

MSY is but one SI out of 132 in Table 1.1, but can similar pictures be painted for the others as we have done here for MSY? Have we been unfairly selective in our choice of the MSY? Each of the UN indicators produces its own difficulties, some of which have been identified by the UN itself. Moreover, if each is examined in the same depth as we have done for MSY, would other problems also emerge? By definition each indicator is a simplification, and the dangers of taking them at face value without an appreciation of this simplification are just as real as they are for MSY. Lack of space prevents us from developing this argument for each of the SIs, and the reader is encouraged to pursue this line of thought as we have done for any of the SIs. However, to extend our horizons a little more we will consider the other SIs listed by the UN for Chapter 17 ('Protection of the Oceans, all Kinds of Seas and Coastal Areas'). As can be seen in Table 1.1, there are four other indicators (three driving force and one state) that relate to Chapter 17. Two of these (population growth in coastal areas and discharges of oil into coastal waters) are still under development at the time of writing and little information is available. The third driving force indicator – releases of nitrogen (N) and phosphorus (P) to coastal waters – has been described by the UN, and they list the following limitations for this indicator:

- Effects of N and P release depend on assimilative capacity of the water body (ie how the water can cope with the N and P).
- The indicator does not include cumulative impact (it only looks at N and P release in a year).
- The indicator does not differentiate between sources of N and P unless more detailed information is collected. It can be difficult to differentiate between human generated and natural sources of N and P.
- Very little data is available for the calculation of the indicator.

These appear to be formidable, but it has to be said not insurmountable limitations. However, the very fact that limitations have been identified by the UN personnel concerned does not remove the potential dangers arising from simplification, and decisions being made on incomplete information.

The second state indicator put forward by the UN alongside MSY for Chapter 17 is the algae index. This is described as the amount of algae, also called phytoplankton, measured in terms of biomass per litre of water. It is suggested that the algae is subdivided into species, and therefore the indicator combines a consideration of biodiversity with biomass. This indicator is particularly interesting since some of the early concerns with environmental damage that motivated meetings such as the United Nations Conference on the Human Environment, held in Stockholm in 1972, focused in part on concerns arising from the potential widespread poisoning of phytoplankton by pesticides (Munn, 1992). As a result, some scientists predicted a sharp drop in atmospheric oxygen concentration by the end of the century.

Box 2.6 *Two simple factors that complicate the use of the algae index as an SI*

The algae index is calculated on the basis of algal biomass per litre of water, with subdivision into species. The two complications described in this box are, firstly, how biomass can alter measurements of biodiversity based on numbers, and, secondly, how a standing crop measurement of biomass may not necessarily provide a clue on productivity.

(1) Biomass and biodiversity
As in Box 2.5, two species ($S = 2$) and a sample size of 100 ($N = 100$). Consider 50 individuals of each species but individuals of species A weigh twice as much as individuals of species B. Let weight of an individual of species A = one unit, and the weight of an individual of species B = two units (total sample weight = 150 units).
- biodiversity based on numbers (calculation in Box 2.5)
  $H = 1$
- biodiversity based on biomass
  proportion of species A = 50/150 = 0.33
  proportion of species B = 100/150 = 0.77
  $H = -(0.33 \times \log_2(0.33) + 0.77 \times \log_2(0.77))$
  $= -(0.33 \times -1.6) + (0.77 \times -0.38)$
  $= -(-0.528 + -0.2926)$
  $= 0.82$
  Therefore, in this case the Shannon–Wiener index based on biomass suggests that biodiversity is less than the calculation based on numbers. If the individual biomass of species A and B were more or less the same, then the disparity would not be so pronounced.

(2) Standing crop biomass as a measure of productivity
In an ecosystem where energy accumulates unused in an end-product, then standing crop can be an index of productivity:

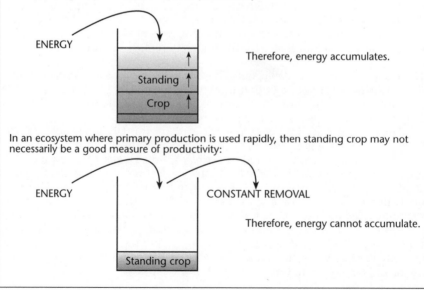

ENERGY

Therefore, energy accumulates.

Standing
Crop

In an ecosystem where primary production is used rapidly, then standing crop may not necessarily be a good measure of productivity:

ENERGY   CONSTANT REMOVAL

Therefore, energy cannot accumulate.

Standing crop

At first glance, the algae index would appear to be straightforward in the sense that it can be regarded as an extension of the Shannon–Wiener biodiversity index described in Chapter 1, with proportion of numbers (p_i) replaced by proportion of total biomass for each species. Clearly, biodiversity calculated on the basis of numbers and biomass can give quite different results (Box 2.6); however, provided the mass of each individual is more or less equivalent, then such an approach is perfectly reasonable. Biomass is also a far better indicator of productivity than numbers (Wagner, 1969), although again one should be careful: a 'standing crop' measurement can be a misleading measure of productivity (Box 2.6). However, given the data, such calculations are straightforward, and indeed some examples of the calculation of the Shannon–Wiener index have already been provided in Box 1.5, along with a discussion of some broad difficulties with the use of such indices. Nevertheless, the extension of this approach to algae in oceans introduces some methodological complications. Most of the ocean's algal biomass is in the form of phytoplankton, and these may be single cells (eg diatoms) or groups of cells rather than the large organisms counted by Learner et al (1971) in the River Cynon example used for Box 1.5. This is not to say that estimations of biomass are not possible with such small organisms. Given specialized equipment and expertise, estimations can be made, for example, by measuring chlorophyll fluorescence as a means of separating algae from other organisms (the zooplankton) present in samples.

There are well-established techniques for doing this and for relating chlorophyll to biomass. Dividing the biomass amongst individual species, and allowing for substantial spatial and temporal variability (patchiness) in both diversity and biomass, are certainly more difficult aspects of the methodology required by the algae index, especially when these will have to take place on a routine basis rather than just once. After all, the river described by Learner et al is minuscule in volume, let alone biodiversity, when compared to the oceans, and Learner and his colleagues only worked with the relatively easy to count fish and macro-invertebrates. Interpretation of the algae index in the context of sustainable development provides yet more concern. How will human-induced change be separated from natural change, and how much time and data will allow us to make such a distinction in any one situation? In other words, do we really know enough about such complex ecosystems and are we going to commit realistic resources to making a reasonable judgement as part of a programme of sustainable development? Again, we are not criticizing those involved in such vital and challenging research; instead, it is the potential misuse of the data as part of a short-term drive towards someone's vision of sustainability that provides concern.

The second dimension of SIs examined in this chapter is an attempt to combine indicators into a single diagrammatic representation of sustainability. The AMOEBA approach of Ten Brink et al is fundamentally a visual representation of indicator species abundance, but the species appearing in the AMOEBA represent but a small proportion of those existing in the ecosystem; abundance can change dramatically due to natural events that may in themselves be poorly understood. With a system that can undergo rapid switching, the use of species abundance as a measure of sustainability can lead to erroneous conclusions if the time scale over which sustainability is being measured is too small. AMOEBA has other problems as highlighted in this chapter, but the underlying concept has to be praised. For all its faults, the approach represents a genuine attempt to pool indicators together in a visual manner aimed at non-scientists. Unlike some other approaches that try to generate a single value for sustainability (like the Shannon–Wiener index does for biodiversity), AMOEBA is an attempt to keep the richness intact and to let the reader judge. It is a pity that Ten Brink et al spoil it by collapsing AMOEBA into single indices (their Ecological Dow Jones index) and again trying to prove that S = 42.

Both MSY and AMOEBA share a feature of all indicators in attempting to reduce complexity, and like all indicators a price has to be paid. Indicators can be very useful, as illustrated in Chapter 1 with pollution in the River Cynon, but they work best when dealing with limited, well-defined situations and when the methodology and interpretation can undergo rigorous testing (with rejection of the indicator possible if it is found to be a poor representation). The concept of sustainability takes us away from limited, well-defined situations; allied with an emphasis on immediate implementation, this does not allow rigorous testing of indicators. Development of SIs usually takes place in tandem with a wish to implement sustainability now! River pollution can be defined chemically and then matched with species abundance and biodiversity. Workers may differ in what pollutants they consider to be important, and how they are to measured; however, whatever the case each individual has to clearly define their viewpoint and their results are open to repetition and scrutiny – as a result, all views are open to rejection. It can also be acknowledged that the value of such changes in fauna and flora relative to the industrial output may well be subject to value judgements. It has to be said that the two SI examples given here (MSY and AMOEBA) are at least somewhat tangible. After all, we will ultimately know if the MSY indicator is successful by monitoring fish stocks and checking to see if these show signs of collapse. At least MSY is a very well-defined and clear (albeit simplistic) indicator that is open to scrutiny. However, do we limit our concerns purely in terms of a volume of water (and the life it contains) where fishing is done, or do we see a fishery in the context of an industry (the business of fishing)? If the latter, then the very point of sustainability is that it encompasses a broad range of considerations – the fishermen, their families, the micro- and macro-economy, politics and so on are all important considerations of a fishing industry. Ironically, given this wider perspective, it is possible for a fishing industry to become unsustainable despite the fact that fish stocks remain constant. Costs may increase or alternative sources of revenue may emerge that tempt fishermen away from the resource. Either way, the fish stock remains but the industry collapses. It is these wider concerns about sustainability and SI development that form the basis of the next chapter.

Chapter 3

Indicator's, Cities, Institutions and Projects

INTRODUCTION AND OBJECTIVES

In Chapter 2 we examined SIs at two levels. Firstly, a detailed description of one SI, maximum sustainable yield (MSY), was provided. It was shown that although MSY is put forward by the UN as an SI, it is problematic for a number of reasons. The second level examined how a collection of SIs could be combined together to develop an overall picture of system sustainability – the AMOEBA approach. Both the examples in Chapter 2 focused primarily on the management of natural resources, specifically fish and the ocean environment. MSY has its origin in fishing and can be regarded as having a basis in bio-economic calculus; therefore it is essentially designed to maximize production output. AMOEBA, in its original form, is a pictorial representation of indicator species abundance, although the choice of species is subjective. However, do we take sustainability of a fishery, or any other resource, to be measured just in terms of production? What about the people whose livelihood depends upon that resource; do we not also consider their well being? As can be imagined, the collapse of the anchovy fishery off the coast of Peru was devastating for the industry. However, if one implements changes in catch quotas that can vary, perhaps dramatically, from year to year, what will be the effect on the industry and the people that work within it? As Laws (1997) points out, 'maximizing the long-term fish catch does not necessarily maximize the social benefits or economic rewards of the fishery'. The SIs required here are beyond the scope of the relatively simple MSY and species abundance SIs described by Ten Brink et al in the AMOEBA approach, and much more complexity is introduced. As we have seen, even with the biologically based and defined MSY and AMOEBA, there are dangers of oversimplification, and these problems certainly do not disappear when socioeconomic factors are introduced – quite the opposite.

In order to explore how socioeconomic factors have been dealt with when considering sustainable development, we have chosen to focus on human communities, institutions charged with delivering development and development projects. In a sense, these provide extreme examples since they are all entirely human constructs which revolve immediately around human wants

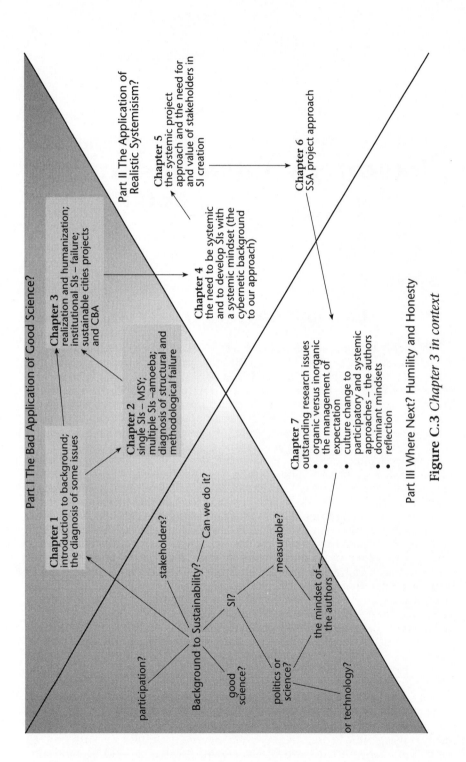

Figure C.3 Chapter 3 in context

and desires. We have also selected these examples because of their very defined spatial, and often temporal, dimension. Urban centres have defined boundaries based on a responsibility for administration often allied with politics. Therefore, there are city, town and village councils elected by the population of the centre and responsible for an area which can be very clearly delineated. Furthermore, since urban centres are, by definition, collections of people in a defined space, sustainability concerns move far beyond environmental considerations; economics, culture, crime and entertainment all become very important.

The defined space and time dimensions also apply to development institutions and, indeed, to development projects. The sustainability of an institution charged with facilitating development can be quite distinct from the sustainability of a development process; nevertheless, it is still very amenable to the use of SIs. Indeed, as we point out in this chapter, we believe that institutional sustainability provides an example of how the use of SIs can be very dangerous in a development context. Development projects, typically implemented by an institution of some sort, in many ways provide the clearest context for the use of SIs and will form the basis of our discussions for the remainder of this book. Much development takes place via projects intended to achieve a specific set of goals in a defined space and time scale. Given that funding for development is always limiting, using projects as a vehicle allows an easy monitoring of costs and benefits.

This chapter, therefore, has a number of aims:

- to broadly examine how socioeconomic factors can be included in SIs;
- to discuss the use of SIs in one of the most common development contexts – the project;
- to look at the use of SIs to gauge institutional sustainability, and the dangers inherent within this.

SUSTAINABLE COMMUNITIES

There are a number of examples of initiatives by urban administrators to make their centre more sustainable. Sustainable Seattle, in the United States, is one well-known example, but there are many others (Zachary, 1995). There is a Sustainable City award in Europe, and the UN has selected a number of cities worldwide to promote the sustainable city concept. However, what is meant by sustainable in the context of urban areas is interesting in terms of the breadth of dimensions considered. To begin with, the juxtaposition of the words sustainable and city may appear to be a gross contradiction – can any urban centre be regarded as sustainable when it clearly depends on goods and services created from outside? However, sustainability in this context has quite a distinctive meaning. For example, at a seminar held in California in 1991, the following definition was adopted:

> *Sustainability may be defined as a dynamic balance among three mutually interdependent elements: (1) protection and enhancement of natural ecosystems and resources; (2) economic productivity; and (3) provision of social infrastructure such as jobs, housing, education, medical care and cultural opportunities.*
>
> Dominski et al (1992)

Table 3.1 *Top ten key components of sustainable development suggested by 100 households in a Scottish village, UK*

Component	% saying 'very important'
Health	70
Security	69
Standard of living	59
Education	57
Environment	56
Culture, recreation and leisure	50
Housing	49
Transport/access to goods and services	36
Tranquillity	29
Community spirit	22

Source: adapted from a table in MacGillivray (1996) which summarizes data presented by the New Economics Foundation (1996)

There are two points worth noting about this definition. Firstly, although there is some resemblance to definitions of sustainable development given in Chapter 1, it is relatively precise. Secondly, there is a clear emphasis on economic and social factors. Indeed, given this definition, what is the difference between a sustainable city and good planning? Provision of jobs, housing and education is a very clear mandate, but does it require the paradigm of sustainability as an umbrella? Politicians have been promising these for decades – long before sustainability became such a dominant paradigm. What is noticeable is that the inclusion of these dimensions, although central to many definitions of sustainability, introduces much more complexity into the choice and interpretation of SIs. A taste of the diversity is provided in Table 3.1. This table summarizes the results of surveys conducted in a small village in Scotland where people were asked to rank what factors they considered to be important for a sustainable community (MacGillivray, 1996). Not only was environment included, but also other components such as education, housing and transport. While these may be seen as relatively straightforward components to gauge (number of school places, new homes, length of roads, etc), what does one do about components such as community spirit and tranquillity?

Another example of SIs developed for an urban centre is provided in Table 3.2. This is a list of SIs adopted by Norwich City Council in the UK, although very similar examples can be found for many other sustainable city programmes. They are divided into three groups: environmental protection, economic development and social development – very much in line with the above definition. The SIs were largely developed in 1997, but this will continue into 1998 and indeed will be reviewed on a regular basis. They have been chosen by a Norwich 21 Steering Group that represents a manifestation of a central element of the UN Agenda 21 – the need for local involvement and planning (so-called Local Agenda 21). The steering group consists of various prominent people in Norwich, and unlike AMOEBA, the Norwich SIs do not derive from scientists or technocrats, but represent what can best be termed the views of lay people; the results will be made widely available to the people of Norwich.

It is interesting to note that although the Norwich 21 plan has had its origins in the UN Agenda 21, the SIs employed by Norwich have not been broken down into driving force, state and response SIs, although there are some

Table 3.2 *The Norwich 21 set of SIs*

SI	Notes	Target	UN Chapter
Environmental protection			
1 Clean air	number of days of good air quality	increase	9
2 Less domestic waste	tonnes of waste produced per household; total domestic waste recycled	decrease increase	21
3 Saving water	cubic metres of water consumed by all users in a year	decrease	18
4 Saving energy	energy (gas and electricity) consumed by domestic and industrial users per year	decrease	4
5 Clean river water	quality of water in the two main rivers in Norwich (dissolved oxygen, BOD, ammonia)	increase	18
6 More wildlife	the number of swans living and breeding on the two main rivers in Norwich	increase	15
7 Protecting open spaces	area of green field sites developed within the Norwich area	increase	
8 Clean streets	amount of litter on the streets	decrease	
9 Less traffic	number of trips each year by:		7
	• cars	decrease	
	• public transport	increase	
	• cycle	increase	
	• foot	increase	
10 Safer streets	length of streets which are fully pedestrianized and traffic calmed	increase	
Economic development			
11 Less unemployment	the unemployment rate	decrease	3
12 More skilled people	percentage of the population achieving national training and education targets	increase	12
13 More jobs	net increase in number of jobs	increase	3
14 The regional capital for business	number of medium to large firms with regional or national headquarters in Norwich	increase	
15 More money from tourism	number of overnight stays by visitors in hotels	increase	
Social development			
16 Less poverty	percentage of the population living at or below the poverty line	decrease	3
17 Reduced housing problems	the number of:		7
	• homeless people	decrease	
	• people in need of specialist accommodation	decrease	
	• people in overcrowded accommodation	decrease	
18 Improved local services	number of people who live within walking distance of a centre of local services	increase	
19 More people involved in local democracy	percentage of eligible people voting in local elections	increase	
20 More sports facilities	number of sports facilities as measured against English Sports Council targets	increase	
21 A safer city	the level of reported crime (domestic violence and burglary, non-domestic violence)	decrease	
22 More arts and culture	number of seats/venues (cinema, theatre etc.)	increase	
23 Maintaining our heritage	number of listed buildings; number of collections/museums open to the public	maintain increase	

Source: the Policy Unit, Norwich City Council, City Hall, Norwich

clear associations between the UN indicators and those of Norwich 21 as indicted in Table 3.2. Although there are a number of parallels with the UN SIs, especially in the environmental sphere, it is interesting that there are few associations with the UN indicators in the social sphere. Local services, democracy, sports facilities, arts, culture and heritage have no parallels with the UN list, though of course the UN indicators are not meant to be definitive and each country and local group is encouraged to develop its own set of SIs. There are also echoes of some of the principles behind the AMOEBA. A good example is the focus on swan numbers as an indicator of wildlife (biodiversity). Clearly, swans are much more visible and recognizable by inhabitants of the city, and in addition have a strong sentimental value that other animals (such as the midges used for the AMOEBAE in Chapter 2) do not possess. Indeed, the choice of swans as an SI in Norwich mirrors the emphasis on numbers of salmon in local rivers by the people of Seattle, US (MacGillivray, 1996).

Clearly, the problems already highlighted in Chapter 2 regarding SI selection and interpretation of a collection of SIs applies to those of the Norwich 21 initiative, but with a vengeance! Each of the SIs listed in Table 3.2 are open to much the same sort of problems of oversimplification as with MSY. While acknowledging that in a country such as the UK much of this data is readily available, some information is politically sensitive and the manner in which it is calculated has been changed over the years. Unemployment rate is a classic example: the methodology by which this is calculated has been altered 30 times since 1979 (MacGillivray, 1996), and we will leave the reader to judge how much of this change was politically driven. One should also note that like MSY, each of the SIs will be influenced by many factors, some of which lie well outside the administrative boundary of Norwich. Just as with MSY, examining any one of these without appreciating the underlying nature of the forces that drive it may be dangerous.

However, what are the Norwich SIs intended to achieve? It is interesting to note that SIs for urban communities have a very clear application that may, in part, be a reflection of the more precise vision as to what sustainability means. Zachary (1995) suggests that there are four functions of these SIs:

1   enabling a community to identify what it values and allowing it to prioritize those values;
2   allowing the community to hold individuals and groups accountable for achieving goals identified by the community;
3   encouraging democracy;
4   allowing people to measure what is important and to make decisions based on those results.

The Norwich Agenda 21 SIs have a very similar set of functions. The city makes it clear that they are intended as a 'snapshot, and not as a complete picture', and are intended to measure the health of the city. However, the broad approach is one of enablement in much the same mode as described by Zachery (1995). The Norwich SIs will be presented to the public each year, and the public is encouraged to both judge progress and at an even more local level (blocks, streets) to develop their own set of SIs. Therefore, the SIs are an attempt to increase the appreciation of the many issues that are behind each SI, and the words of Gary Lawrence (1997), one of the people behind Sustainable Seattle, resonate very strongly here: 'For indicators to lead to change, there needs to be emotional content: people need to care in their hearts as well as in their minds.'

Indeed, it is the participative nature of sustainable city programmes that largely distinguishes them from many other initiatives to put sustainability into practice. If one looks at almost all of the other examples of SI development, including those of the UN, the flavour is very much one of top down, with a nod in the direction of those who are expected to benefit from the programmes. The Norwich initiative, and others like it throughout the world, start and end with the people; participation is a bedrock of the whole process. One could conceive of a further set of SIs alongside those in Table 3.2 that gauge participation (number of local initiatives, attendance at meetings, feedback, etc). It should be noted that quantification is just as much a part of this as it is with MSY, and it would be misleading to regard the Norwich approach as different in this regard. Granted that the Norwich SIs are directional (the concern is whether they move up or down), but the heart of that direction is still based on numbers.

In the next section we will contrast this emphasis on participation in the development and application of SIs with a very different approach – one where the institution delivers the development (often referred to as institutional sustainability). While this may seem to be a quite different issue, there are many similarities, and the application of SIs in this context has been markedly different from their use as part of sustainable community initiatives. Indeed, in some respects SIs as a gauge of institutional sustainability provide the other extreme to examples such as the Norwich initiative, and the results have been very sobering.

INSTITUTIONAL SUSTAINABILITY

Development is often planned, initiated, implemented and evaluated by an institution. This can take the form of a government agency or ministry, an international agency (such as the United Nations, World Bank, International Monetary Fund), an aid agency (for instance, the Department for International Development, DfID, in the UK) or a non-governmental institution such as the Catholic Church. At first glance, institutional sustainability has some parallels with the sustainable cities concept. An institution, even a very diverse one, is like an urban area in that it is a very definable entity. It may consist of a group of people and physical structures. The boundary within which sustainability operates is therefore very clear. Secondly, what is meant by sustainability in this context is evident and is typically encapsulated in factors such as financial self-reliance or some other measurable activity (Gustafson, 1994). Therefore, although this is a different perspective from that of sustainability in a city, both share a clarity of purpose. There are two remaining advantages to viewing sustainability in an institutional context:

- The time scale over which sustainability is deemed to operate is also more defined (the emphasis is on shorter scales).
- The institution, although complex, may not approach the complexity of an ecosystem or a city.

Institutional sustainability has become a major consideration of the general process of sustainable development. For example, the OECD (1989) maintains that 'sustained and self-reliant development depends on the strength and quality of a country's institutions', and van Pelt et al (1990) point out that 'in general terms, sustainability refers to the long-term availability of the means required for the long-term achievement of goals'. Van Pelt et al (1990) also make the important statement that:

> *The OECD (1989), focusing on development aid, considers develop-*
> *ment sustainable when the recipient country is willing and able to*
> *provide sufficient means and resources (financial, managerial, ecologi-*
> *cal, and so on) for an aid activity after the donor has withdrawn his*
> *assistance.*

However, it should be noted that sustainability in this context has two quite distinct, interrelated and perhaps even competing meanings. The institution itself may be sustainable in the eyes of the donor, but what it is doing may not be sustainable in the longer term. Sustainability of the 'means to an end' is therefore quite distinct from sustainability of the 'end', and the information one needs to collect to determine the two will also be different. For instance, one could consider institutional sustainability as part of a sustainable city programme by focusing on the institutions promoting sustainability in the city (such as the city council and its departments). However, in all of the literature pertaining to sustainable cities (Norwich, Seattle, etc) there is little if any reference to the sustainability of the institutions facilitating the vision – perhaps because of the political sensitivity behind the idea since it could be interpreted as sustaining administrators and even politicians in office! If institutional sustainability in a sustainable city context meant freeing the inhabitants from the necessary taxes to fund the programme, then the story would be different; but will this be popular with those charged with implementation?

In a development context, however, is not institutional sustainability a good idea? It certainly has resonated well with funding agencies for obvious reasons. Of course, one must be careful not to be too naive. After all, many institutions producing 'valued outputs' have been closed for a host of reasons, not least of which is naked politics. Nevertheless, given all of the above, institutional sustainability is an achievable target desired by some powerful groups, and progress to that target can be measured. Nevertheless, although theoretically attainable, the practice may not be so easy (Gustafson, 1994). For example, Brinkerhoff and Goldsmith (1992) report two studies by major donors, one by the World Bank and the other by the United States Agency for International Development (USAID), on the sustainability of projects that they have funded. Of 550 projects evaluated by the World Bank, nearly 50 per cent had 'sustainability difficulties'. Only 52 per cent had successfully achieved sustainability. Similarly, of 212 projects evaluated by USAID, only 11 per cent were thought to be sustainable.

One area of development activity where the increasing emphasis on institutional sustainability has been particularly noticeable is in the provision of financial services (FS) for the urban and rural poor (Adams and von Pischke, 1992; Levitsky, 1989; Otero and Rhyne, 1994; Hulme and Mosley, 1996a and 1996b; McNamara and Morse, 1998). The idea is very simple – problems of underdevelopment are assumed to be linked to a lack of money and if funds can be provided then people living in developing countries can invest in small-scale enterprises, including agriculture, thereby breaking the so-called poverty trap. For example, in agriculture access to machinery, land, labour and agricultural inputs may be limited because of the inability of farmers to purchase or hire them. The argument is that if these farmers had access to FS, they could afford these inputs and improve their production. This 'free enterprise' vision of tackling development has proved to be extremely popular with a number of development agencies, and some have poured vast resources into FS schemes. Indeed, a high-profile summit on FS held in Washington in early 1997 (the Microcredit Summit) put forward the target of expanding access of the world's poor to FS to 100 million by the year 2005 (Slavin, 1996).

Because there are many borrowers collecting relatively small sums the processing costs of such FS schemes for development tend to be high. Furthermore, in order to reduce costs for the beneficiaries, interest rates for credit often have to be set much lower than commercial rates (Adams, 1984; Jackelen and Rhyne, 1991). Partly as a result of these and other factors, the formal FS sector (banks) tend not to be interested in the provision of FS for resource-poor individuals and groups (Bouman, 1984; Thomas, 1992; Soyibo, 1996), and the tendency instead has been for non-governmental organizations (NGOs) and others, including government institutions, to step in and provide such a service. However, given the costs of FS provision some subsidization is often required either from the government or from an outside donor, and this may need to take the form of regular grants. However, in recent years there has been a move towards encouraging the field partner providing the FS to achieve sustainability and thereby remove the need for a constant injection of funds (Jackelen and Rhyne, 1991; Yaron, 1992; Bennett and Cuevas, 1996; Dichter, 1996). The emphasis is firmly upon the sustainability of the field partner rather than on the sustainability of what is being financed (the outcome); this equates very simply to financial self-sufficiency.

As sustainability in this context can be given a very narrow and defined meaning, it is no surprise that SIs have been developed in order to measure progress of the field partner towards achieving the goal of self-sufficiency. Two examples are presented in Box 3.1. Although the second equation (for the subsidy dependence index, SDI) may appear to be complex, it is, in fact, relatively easy to calculate since the values of the parameters can often be gleaned from the institution's accounts. Some practical examples calculated by Yaron (1992) and McNamara and Morse (1998) are given in Table 3.3. Indeed, like MSY and all SIs, the relative simplicity of the SDI may be problematic. It is primarily expressed in terms of the increase required in on-lending interest rates for the institution to become sustainable, and does not take into account other possible options. For example, rather than increase the interest rate, the institution may try to reduce the amount of outstanding loans by applying more 'aggressive and efficient loan collection' (Yaron, 1992).

Indeed, there are a host of other indicators that one could use to judge progress towards institutional sustainability or simply the performance in general of an organization providing FS. The number of loans issued, the number of savings accounts held, the amounts saved, and loan repayments rates are all easily quantifiable. In contrast, other development activities such as provision of primary health care or an agricultural extension service are not so easily and readily quantifiable; as a result Tendler (1989) has stressed that some 'organizations tend to look at commitment, honesty and hard work as proxies for performance. Mediocraty gets tolerated more, simply because the results of what these organizations do are more difficult to see.'

Even with just the two SI examples given in Box 3.1, it is clear that their use is a much easier and less daunting prospect than discussed in a wider context in Chapters 1 and 2, or even with the sustainable cities in this chapter. Given this, and a major emphasis on institutional sustainability from donors, it is interesting to note that FS institutions generally have a bad record of attaining sustainability (Yaron, 1992). Indeed, this drive towards sustainability based on such narrow criteria can be problematic in a practical sense (Dichter, 1996). To begin with, in order to attain sustainability, the field partner is pushed to take on the characteristics of more formal financial institutions (Jackelen and Rhyne, 1991; Schmidt and Zeitinger, 1996). In particular, interest

---

Box 3.1 *Two indicators that can be employed to gauge the self-sufficiency of development institutions in providing financial services to resource-poor groups*

(1) the percentage of total costs covered by income (Johnson and Rogaly, 1997); for any particular period of time:

$$SI = \frac{\text{total earned from FS programme}}{\text{total FS programme costs}} \times 100$$

The higher the SI, the more self-sufficient the institution.

(2) calculate the change required in interest rates charged by the lender in order to remove the need for a subsidy; this is termed the subsidy dependence index (SDI; Yaron, 1992):

$$SDI = \frac{\text{subsidy received}}{\text{outstanding loans} \times \text{interest rate}}$$

The denominator in the equation is, in effect, the income due from loans that have not been paid. More precisely:

$$SDI = \frac{A(m-c) + [E * m] - P] + K}{LP * n}$$

The numerator in the above equation is the annual subsidy received by the institution:
A = concessional borrowed funds outstanding (annual average)
m = interest rate that the institution would be assumed to pay for borrowed funds if access to borrowed concessional funds were eliminated
c = average annual concessional rate of interest actually paid by the institution on its average annual concessional borrowed funds
that are outstanding (A)
E = average annual equity (capital)
P = reported annual profit (adjusted, when necessary, for loan loss provisions, inflation, etc)
K = the sum of all other types of annual subsidies received by the institution (such as partial or complete coverage of operational costs by the state)

The denominator is the income generated by loans:

LP = average annual outstanding loan portfolio of the institution
n = average on-lending interest rate of the institution; this can be estimated by dividing the interest earned by the total value of loans issued.

The higher the SDI, the more the interest rate needs to be increased in order to make the FS institution self-sufficient. In other words:

SDI = 0   The institution has achieved sustainability (ie requires no annual subsidy from an outside donor).

SDI = +ve   The institution has not achieved sustainability and requires an annual subsidy from an outside donor. The higher the SDI, the greater the annual subsidy required.

SDI = –ve   The institution has not only achieved sustainability but also makes a profit. The 'higher' the negative value, the greater the profit.

Table 3.3 *Values of the subsidy dependence index (SDI) for some rural finance institutions*

Institution	Country	Year	SDI (%)
Badan Kredit Kacamatan (BKK)	Indonesia	1987	24
		1989	20
Bank Rakyat Indonesia Unit Desa (BUD)	Indonesia	1987	3
		1989	−8
Bank for Agriculture and Agricultural	Thailand	1986	28
Cooperatives (BAAC)		1988	23
Grameen Bank (GB)	Bangledesh	1987	180
		1989	130
Diocesan Development Services (DDS)	Nigeria	1982	89
		1987	20
		1996	11

Note: the SDI can be thought of as an indicator for institutional sustainability
Source: adapted from data provided in Yaron (1992) and McNamara and Morse (1998)

rates have to be commercial, operational costs have to be covered and loan defaulting has to be minimized. The latter requires a screening programme akin to those implemented by commercial organizations; however, the danger is that only those best able to repay will benefit from the service, while those who are the poorest may be rejected (Slavin, 1996). Furthermore, in order to minimize costs and target effort into screening and repayments, there may be pressure for the partner to concentrate solely on the provision of FS and to disregard other types of development activity or support services (Mutua, 1994). This approach is referred to as minimalist FS delivery, or sometimes more specifically as minimalist credit (Berenbach and Guzman, 1994; Dichter, 1996), while the opposite viewpoint is often referred to as the non-minimalist or integrated approach.

It is possible, of course, that even in integrated programmes the FS element can be made sustainable while the other activities are financed from grants (Holt, 1994). Indeed, some funding agencies (notably USAID) have required the supported institutions to split into two parts: a component that supplies the FS and which should become sustainable, and a second component supplying technical services and training that continues to be subsidized (Hulme and Mosley, 1996a).

There are well-recognized dangers in placing an excessive focus on FS and institutional sustainability. As pointed out by both Dichter (1996) and Slavin (1996), development is a complex process that may involve a number of differ-ent yet closely interrelated activities, and the idea that FS can solve these is simplistic, to say the least. The problem may be that since institutional sustain-ability is such a clear and easily measured concept, particularly in terms of FS provision, then it may encourage this narrowing of scope. Given that sustain-ability has taken on such a holistic and all-embracing meaning in recent times, this is ironic. After all, the weakness of the concept of institutional sustainabil-ity is also its strength. By focusing on institutional sustainability one can develop clear and precise definitions and indicators. However, since the people in the institution know the importance of these indicators and how they are calculated, and given that they clearly wish the institution to be sustainable for their own benefit, is there not a danger that the emphasis will move away from the intended beneficiaries of the development?

Brown (1997), for example, describes a development project, the Belize Chamber of Commerce and Industry (BCCI), set up in 1920 as the representative body of large commercial enterprises in Belize City. Between 1989 and 1993 the BCCI grew into a national development agency involved in various activities, such as training, publishing, provision of guidance and assistance for exporters, and the organization of missions to international trade fairs. In order to fund these activities, BCCI received a grant from USAID to cover the 1986 to 1993 period, but came under pressure to demonstrate its 'potential sustainability', based purely on criteria of financial self-sufficiency. In response, BCCI devised a three-pronged strategy to achieve this:

(1) expand and retain its membership;
(2) become the local agent for Western Union;
(3) establish a national lottery.

The third point in particular was intended to generate enough revenue to replace the USAID funds and to demonstrate its sustainability. However, the lottery quickly took on a life of its own and gradually came to dominate the organization to such an extent that development activities were severely neglected. The moral of this story for Brown (1997) is not that institutional sustainability is necessarily bad, but that donors need to recognize that an organization charged with development may have limited means to generate its own revenue and to become self-sufficient.

Nevertheless, given its appeal it is doubtful whether the drive for institutional sustainability and self-reliance, particularly with FS, will relent in the short to medium term. The concept is simply too well ingrained, and many NGOs will be reluctant to admit that what they are doing is unsustainable. It is likely that they will continue to pay lip service to the concept as a means of placating the donors. Some have even suggested that organizations that argue against sustainability may be doing so as a means of diverting 'attention away from their own highly cumbersome and inefficient operations' (Berenbach and Guzman, 1994). Even worse may be the danger of being described as following a 'paternalistic approach to helping the poor' (Microcredit Summit Document). Clearly, given such views, NGOs who dare argue against an overriding domination of financial sustainability could find themselves in a rather vulnerable position, and one is entitled to question whether this is healthy for development.

Institutional sustainability has one further point in common with the sustainable city programmes mentioned earlier: SI development and use has shown great progress. The SIs for each context are being applied as tools to help achieve concrete goals and not as academic curiosities or even as lip service. One can certainly question the goals, as in institutional sustainability, but the use of SIs remains a reality. There are a number of reasons for this, some of which have already been spelt out, including the fact that institutions and cities are well-defined entities. One also has to consider the limitations of what the SIs set out to achieve in each case. In the Norwich programme, the SIs act as a tool to encourage enablement, while in institutional sustainability the SIs are essentially measures of financial self-reliance. As for motive, the Norwich programme may have been sparked by the Rio Conference and nurtured by the city council officers, but the momentum has come very much from the people of the city. A cynic may suggest that this is only true in an indirect sense since sustainability is a word that tends to resonate very well with an electorate, and consequently with politicians and their officers; however, this does not diminish the fundamental ethos of what is being achieved. In institutional sustainability the motive is also very clear, and like the Norwich programme, one tends to hear an emphasis on empowerment – although, can it be denied that there is also a desire on the part of those funding development to achieve value for their aid money?

PROJECTS, APPRAISAL AND SUSTAINABILITY

In the final section of this chapter we will continue to focus on the institutions charged with delivering development in the field, but will also broaden the discussion to look at the development being 'delivered'. Development often takes place within the context of a defined project linked to an institution or set of institutions. A project may have a clear spatial dimension that typically relates to a political or administrative boundary (such as an urban centre, local government area or state). It will also typically have a clear life span, or at least the funding that it receives will be on a renewable (subject to performance or some other factor) basis. However, in many cases the aim of the development initiative may not just be to achieve a goal over a discrete area in a set time, and then simply evaporate, but to introduce an improvement that is intended to last after the money has been spent. For example, the project may be intended to improve the effectiveness of an existing government agency, and this improvement is supposed to be long lasting. Similarly, aid money may be intended to help establish a development project that will ultimately become self-sufficient in terms of finance – no longer requiring funds from the donor agency or others to fulfil its function.

Consideration of sustainability within development projects, whether institutional sustainability or sustainability of the development, may be thought by the reader to represent a rather narrow perspective, as indeed it does! However, it should be noted that the 'blueprint project' approach is extremely common in development, and its popularity, in part, rests upon the fact that goals can be clearly set at the outset and performance matched against those goals. One has to remember that aid agencies, usually located in developed countries, are often constrained by the availability of financial resources; not surprisingly, these donors are anxious to ensure that they get the best value for money. Money is provided for finite periods of time and to achieve definable goals that can be monitored. This is nothing new, and in order to check whether the goals have been attained, the art and science of project evaluation and appraisal has been developed. Indeed, as narrow as it may at first appear, we believe that the major impact of the sustainability paradigm in development will be in the setting of project goals, plans and appraisal. It is also in this realm that the need for practical SIs will be greatest. As a result, the remaining chapters of this book will focus on the use of SIs within development projects.

Problems with incorporating sustainability in the setting of project goals are essentially the same as those discussed in Chapters 1 and 2 – including definition and identification of spatial and temporal dimensions. One also has to be aware of what trade-offs there are between the need for sustainability and other desirable goals of the project (van Pelt et al, 1990). These are commonalities that also apply to the sustainable city concept and indeed to any situation where sustainability is a goal.

In terms of gauging whether a project has achieved its goals, we have already looked in depth at one such approach – financial self-sufficiency as the goal and two simple SIs as the means of gauging whether that goal has been reached. However, this is but one rather specific example, and in order to address the diversity of goals that projects have been charged with achieving (in education, health, transport, agriculture, etc), a whole host of techniques and methods of project appraisal have been developed and applied. However, despite the diversity, these methods can be divided into two broad groups:

- Cost-benefit analysis (CBA): the cost of the project relative to the benefits gained by that expenditure. CBA requires that the benefits can be expressed in financial terms.
- Multi-criteria analysis (MCA): a generic term covering a host of different approaches that may well include an element of CBA. Some of these may generate quantitative results, as does CBA, while others may be based on systems of scoring more qualitative effects.

CBA may be understood in terms of an investment process. Money invested by a factory owner in a new machine will help to generate more output that is eventually sold, thereby providing a return on investment. The CBA may be the cost of the investment (allowing factors such as interest on any borrowing or additional maintenance that may be required) and the product of the quantity (number of units) and unit price of goods sold. This is a straightforward use of CBA since it is based on economic prices (economic cost-benefit analysis, or ECBA). One can extend the idea further and include social prices in a CBA (social cost-benefit analysis, SCBA). The aim here may be to look at distribution of effects in monetary terms in order to check equity across social groups. For example, are the costs and benefits equally spread between men and women?

As an approach, CBA may be attractive because it is fundamentally a quantitative technique, and as already discussed in Chapters 1 and 2 quantification is popular with scientists, technocrats, administrators and policy-makers. In addition, the quantification is monetary, and the appeal for those concerned with managing money and looking for best value is not difficult to imagine. However, there is substantial variation on the basic CBA theme. For example, Turner (1991) suggests that there are four main approaches to the use of CBA in project appraisal:

(1) conventional CBA;
(2) modified 'extended' CBA;
(3) radically modified CBA;
(4) abandonment of CBA.

These four approaches essentially represent a spectrum from narrow CBA at one extreme (the first approach), where all components are taken to have a use for humans, to the other extreme (the fourth approach), where components can have no practical use for humans but instead have an intrinsic value of their own. This latter situation prevails in what is termed the 'deep ecology world view' (roughly equivalent to the strong or ecological sustainability mentioned in Chapter 1); the basic premise of CBA breaks down for philosophical rather than practical reasons. This is a point that will be returned to in Chapter 4. Modified CBA represents a relaxation of conventional CBA to accommodate intergenerational equity (sustainability). It allows for higher costs than gains if this means that natural assets are maintained. Even so, both the conventional and modified CBA can be thought of as occupying the weak sustainability (= economic sustainability) ground. However, it has to be said that in keeping with the diverse set of views of sustainability, all we can do with these different approaches to CBA is to treat them as peaks in a very complex landscape.

Nevertheless, even if we accept the premise that valuation is philosophically acceptable, what if the outputs of an investment cannot be readily converted into monetary terms? This is where the limitations of CBA as a basis for assessing environmental impact and sustainability begin to appear. If one just considers environmental impact within sustainability, as in the AMOEBA approach discussed in Chapter 2, valuation of effects is difficult because of the following:

- How does one translate biological indicators (such as species diversity, presence/absence of key indicator species) into a financial impact? Does one assign a monetary value to each of the 'arms' in the AMOEBA, with distance from sustainability representing a financial gap (positive or negative)? Pearce (1995) illustrates some of the issues involved in the valuation of species and biodiversity.
- One should remember that changes in the ecosystem can occur because of factors outside of the control of humans (for instance, the El Niño effect described in Chapter 2). How does one cost such factors, or should they be discounted?

One practical approach may be to estimate what it would cost to return the system to the sustainable condition. For example, with the AMOEBA, how much would it cost to return the individual arms of the AMOEBA to the reference condition, provided of course that the reference condition can be reasonably defined? One could perhaps think in terms of the cost of other projects required to achieve this compensation (Barbier et al, 1990; Pearce, 1993). If one could do this, one could literally assign a monetary value to sustainability. Therefore, once the arms of the AMOEBA have been defined, as illustrated in Chapter 2, one is costing the actions that would return them to sustainability rather than incorporating any value of the species themselves. Once the system has been returned to a sustainable medium, one could cost the actions designed to keep the system there. In a development project context the aim may be to design the project so that its outputs have little or no environmental impact so that the cost of compensation is either zero or as little as possible.

Nevertheless, the CBA approach to sustainability is problematic, and the problems involved can be illustrated using the River Cynon example already alluded to in Chapters 1 and 2. If one wishes to make the river system sustainable, then presumably the level of pollution noted in the 1971 publication is unacceptable. The costs are relatively easy to define and involve removing the pollution and returning the river to a natural state (perhaps defined in terms of the fish and other fauna found in a neighbouring river that is unpolluted), along with an ongoing cost to keep it that way. The system is clearly defined (the river and its tributaries), and as human influence is a major factor in determining the fauna of the river, then spending money on appropriate treatment plants and personnel would go a long way to returning the river to its natural state.

However, there are a number of complicating factors with this simple model. To begin with, how is futurity costed? Costs of treatment and personnel are likely to change dramatically in the future for a whole host of reasons, including the fact that industries may close and new ones may arise. Defining this in the early 1970s for 30 years to the turn of the century would be difficult, to say the least. In addition, the 'benefit' side of the equation is also not very easy to determine. Clearly a cleaner river closer to its natural state would have an intrinsic appeal to residents and visitors, but how does one cost that? One could try to value recreational activities (fishing and boating) on the basis of a nominal charge or some other rationale (Pearce et al, 1989), but how realistic would these figures be? Again, one needs to consider futurity and include estimations of future benefits. The central conundrum we are faced with is that sustainability is, by definition, a property defined by time; but accurate extrapolations into the future can be extremely difficult.

It has to be admitted that the River Cynon example, although illustrative of the complexities of CBA as the basis for measuring sustainability, is a rather extreme one in that it deals with a resource that is difficult to value financially. Agriculture, forestry and fisheries are much easier because the harvested product can be valued, and one can include adjustments for inflation. However, even here one has to remember that these activities can have undesirable environmental impacts, and essentially one is back in the same position as outlined above.

The alternative appraisal approach of MCA is intrinsically far more flexible than CBA, and this very diversity makes it more attractive to some as a means of approaching sustainability. However, although a diverse and unlimited number of criteria can be included in MCA, there is a fundamental requirement for standardization. Which criteria are included, and how does one 'weigh' the value of each of the criteria in relation to sustainability? Clearly, the choice of criteria to include and how they are to be weighted relative to each other are key decisions and will have a major effect on the final result (van Pelt et al, 1990). Indeed, replace 'criteria' with 'SI' and this language is already very familiar from the earlier chapters. Therefore, MCA can be thought of as an appraisal approach that could incorporate SIs alongside other criteria that are deemed important.

As can be seen from the above discussion, gauging sustainability as part of project appraisal has received much attention. Indeed, so well established are many of the appraisal techniques that three problems could arise:

- The temptation may be to take some of these 'off the shelf' and adapt them to gauge sustainability rather than to develop new, innovative techniques specifically for sustainability.
- Project appraisal may not be carried out by staff trained in the broad issues that surround sustainability.
- Appraisal may have to take place in a relatively short time scale (perhaps just a few days), although monitoring of the goals by the project may be continuous.

In the remaining chapters of this book we would like to revisit sustainability in a development project context and suggest alternative approaches, drawing upon the experience of others such as those involved in the sustainable city programmes. Many of the issues and problems raised in Chapters 1 to 3 will reappear in the later chapters, and we will provide what we think are reasonable answers. Some key questions discussed are:

- Is sustainability important in the project context, and if so, then whose visions of sustainability count and what are those visions?
- Can SIs help to address the problem?
- What SIs do we need?
- How are the SIs to be gauged?
- How are the SIs to be interpreted and used?

The glue that binds all five questions together is people and participation – who makes the decisions and how? Recognizing that sustainability means different things to different people is at the heart of the matter, and for this reason much of the discussion in Chapters 4 to 6 revolves around participation and stakeholders.

Part II

The Application of Realistic Systemisism?

Chapter 4
Paradigms and Professionals

INTRODUCTION AND OBJECTIVES

So far in this book we have developed our discussion as follows:

*   In Chapter 1 we reviewed the concept of sustainability, the problem and need for measurement and sustainability indicators (SIs).
*   In Chapter 2 the issue of indicators was explored – individual technical indicators such as MSY and the combination of indicators seen in AMOEBA.
*   In Chapter 3 we expanded this vision of indicators to the concept of sustainable cities, development institutions and projects.

So far, ranges of problems have been identified in the development of SIs. At this stage we will step back from the SI discussion and move on to discuss problems relating to mindsets, and particularly mindsets relating closely to reductionist and mechanistic worldviews – the worldviews which we argue are dominant in the work described in the first three chapters. This chapter focuses on an alternative 'systemic' mindset. We will start the chapter by setting out the thoughts of two authors – Chambers and Hobart – who provide some seeds of thought for us to develop.

Drawing from Plato's *Republic*, Chambers powerfully sets out problems with mindsets:

> *Unwitting prisoners, professionals sit chained to their central places and mistake the flat shows of figures, tables, reports, professional papers and printouts for the rounded, dynamic, multidimensional substance of the world of those others at the peripheries. But there is a twist in the analogy. Platonism is stood on its head. Plato's reality, of which the prisoners received only the shadows, was of essences, each simple, unitary, abstract and unchanging. The reality, of which core professionals perceive only the simplified shadows, is in contrast a diversity: of people, of farming systems and livelihoods, each a complex whole, concrete and changing. But professionals reconstruct that reality to make it manageable in their own alien analytic terms, seeking and*

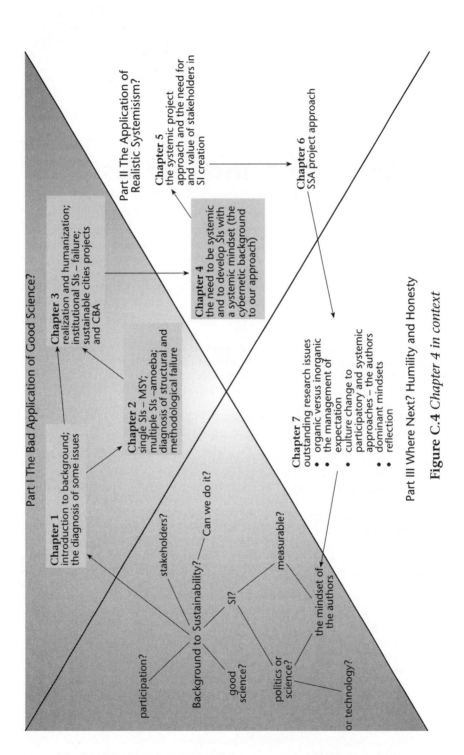

Figure C.4 *Chapter 4 in context*

selecting the universal in the diverse, the part in the whole, the simple in the complex, the controllable in the uncontrollable, the measurable in the unmeasurable ... For the convenience and control of normal professionals, it is not the local, complex, diverse, dynamic and unpredictable reality of those who are poor, weak and peripheral that counts, but the flat shadows of that reality that they, prisoners of their professionalism, fashion for themselves.

Chambers (1997, p 55)

On a similar, illustrative theme Hobart argues:

Local knowledge often constitutes people as potential agents. For instance, in healing, the patient is widely expected to participate actively in the diagnosis and cure. By contrast, scientific knowledge as observed in development practice generally represents the superior knowing expert as an agent and the people being developed as ignorant, passive recipients or objects of his knowledge.

Hobart (1993, p 5)

In the first three chapters of this book we have reviewed the production of SIs generally without reference to local peoples and their knowledge. In the chapters which follow an alternative approach is developed and described. In this chapter we discuss the value of different approaches to thinking about SIs, and we question if SIs are 'scientifically' derived in all cases. The process of their development, for instance, may be scientific, but may just as plausibly be developed by a technocratic belief process or pseudo science.

In this chapter we will look at a number of new topics:

- changes in thinking;
- the demise of narrow scientism;
- a systemic approach to problem solving;
- introducing a range of systems approaches;
- new definitions and new thinking – holism, eclecticism, systemisism;
- emerging premises for SI development.

Building upon the layered examples of sustainability indicators set out in the previous chapters (single SI, AMOEBA, sustainable cities combining SIs, institutional sustainability), and taking forward the scientific or technocratic approaches to sustainability analysis which we described there, the aim of this chapter is to introduce and discuss an alternative, systemic approach to thinking and problem solving. We will compare this with what we might call the traditional, scientific and technocratic approach. In this process we draw out the implicit problem of using SIs – by definition a reductionist technique and tool, to describe sustainability – by definition a vision of wholeness. In this chapter we justify why we are using a systems approach to developing a different way of gauging sustainability which we describe in Chapter 6. In our view, our approach builds off and develops from a practitioner perspective the work begun by Clayton and Radcliffe (1996).

CHANGES IN THINKING – FROM SCIENCE TO SYSTEMS

The value of different perceptions and the necessity for individuals involved in problem situations to learn from one another in a participatory fashion are two of the themes of this book. Changes in perception can involve changes in thinking, and this can be thought of as a 'paradigm shift'. A definition might be helpful here.

> *Paradigm = example, pattern ... an outstandingly clear or typical example or archetype ... a philosophical and theoretical framework of a scientific school or discipline within which theories, laws and generalizations and the experiments performed in support of them are formulated.*
>
> Webster (1995)

We might say that there is a Western scientific tradition which is a paradigm of thinking. We might argue that this paradigm is dominant but that there are alternatives to it. One alternative might be described as a systemic approach. This is an alternative paradigm of thinking, but one which we feel does not deny the value of science; instead, it complements it and is sympathetic to its contribution while recognizing that there are other contributions which can also be made by other forms of thinking from other individuals and groups.

Alternative views or even multiple views of reality are encouraged in a truly systems approach. The unpacking of ideas relating to participation, learning and thinking in different ways requires an understanding that local people often have clear ideas of their own about what is sustainable (from their own perspective and in their own terms) without an expert's view. From one perspective the development of SIs, as set out in the papers described in Chapter 2 (see Verbruggen and Kuik, 1991; Pettit and Sarwal, 1993) exemplify the hegemony of the technocrat. We have already reported in other aspects of the review that this hegemony is challenged by individuals within the scientific community (see Richards, 1979; Biggs, 1990; Biggs and Farrington, 1990; Richards, undated).

There has been a dramatic change in thinking in many related areas among sections of the scientific community (for example, the focus on participatory approaches is exemplified by the work of Robert Chambers: Chambers, 1981; Chambers, 1992; Chambers, 1997; Chambers, undated). The changes we are discussing here do not represent movement from a wrong way to a right way of thinking, rather it is a movement from one paradigm (and thus a set of assumptions about the world) to another. In an earlier work Bell (Bell, 1996) described this movement of mindset in terms of a continuum (see Figure 4.1).

The horizontal line, the spectrum or continuum, provides one perspective of the range of thinking which can be undertaken in any problem-solving exercise. The range extends from the most *reductionist* to the most *holistic*. Koestler describes these two as referring to individuality and wholeness respectively, but again does not see either approach as being opposed to the other:

> *...partness' and 'wholeness' recommend themselves as a serviceable pair of complimentary concepts because they are derived from the ubiquitously hierarchic organization of all living matter.*
>
> Koestler (1964, p 290)

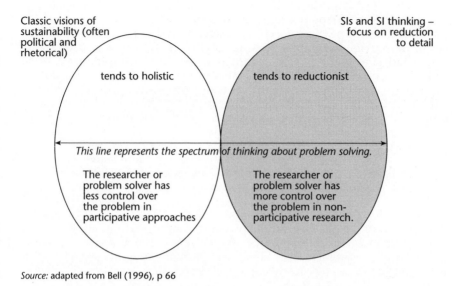

Classic visions of sustainability (often political and rhetorical)

SIs and SI thinking – focus on reduction to detail

tends to holistic

tends to reductionist

This line represents the spectrum of thinking about problem solving.

The researcher or problem solver has less control over the problem in participative approaches

The researcher or problem solver has more control over the problem in non-participative research.

Source: adapted from Bell (1996), p 66

Figure 4.1 *A continuum of research approaches*

Whether we argue with the 'hierarchic organization of all living matter' or not (a subject for another discussion), the idea of complementary concepts is one which we support. However, it is possible to see them as being opposed; therefore, before going on, we need to define these terms and understand more clearly what they include and exclude. In our work we intend to show that holism, in reality, always includes scientific and reductionistic modes of thinking. If holism were to be seen as exclusive or extreme, then it would not be holistic (by definition). To clarify the meaning of the terms, we will set them out against the background of current trends in the discussion within the academic community. An overall and rather dramatic phrase which we use to describe this stage of our description is: 'the demise of narrow scientism'.

THE DEMISE OF NARROW SCIENTISM

Another new term has been inadvertently introduced, so before we look at what reductionism and holism mean, let's get a clear idea about scientism.

> *scientism n (1877) (1) methods and attitudes typical of or attributed to the natural scientist (2) an exaggerated trust in the efficacy of the methods of natural science applied to all areas of investigation (as in philosophy, the social sciences, and the humanities).*
>
> Webster (1995)

The key phrase to keep in mind here is the term 'exaggerated'. In Chapters 1 and 2 we discussed a range of approaches to sustainability which worked on the premise that sustainability was a quantity which could be more or less defined in an absolute sense: 'the measure of sustainability for wheat production, as a weighted figure, is 42'. This form of approach (if expressed a little facetiously here) might also be defined as an 'exaggerated trust in the efficacy of the methods of natural science applied to all areas of investigation'. For examples of this type of approach, the reader should recall that in Chapters 1 and 2 we provided examples of sustainability analysis which made use of mathematical formulae to gain quantitative measure. Such formulae give the analysis a degree of respectability, but the formulae themselves colosally simplify the true complexity of the context. Unfortunately, the definition of scientism used here also raises another phrase which we need to define for clarity's sake –scientific method. What is *the* scientific method?

> *scientific method (1854): principles and procedures for the systematic pursuit of knowledge involving the recognition and formulation of a problem, the collection of data through observation and experiment, and the formulation and testing of hypotheses.*
>
> Webster (1995)

The method of science seems to involve observing the world in a systematic way, seeing problems (or opportunities), collecting data and testing theories about why the problems are there and rejecting hypotheses which are perceived to be 'wrong'. In this approach issues such as: whose problems? whose perception of problems? whose justification for action? whose idea about what data is legitimate? who are legitimate stakeholders in the problem context? what are their views? are not relevant questions. On a similar tack Dawkins has put the essence of this issue as follows:

> *If I ask an engineer how a steam engine works ... I should definitely not be impressed if the engineer said it was propelled by 'force locomotif'. And if he started boring on about the whole being greater than the sum of its parts, I would interrupt him: 'Never mind about that, tell me how it works.' What I would want to hear is something about how the parts of an engine interact with each other to produce the behaviour of the whole engine.*
>
> Dawkins (1986, p 11)

Dawkins' statement is indicative of the mindset of many scientists and also expresses the notion that within the scientific community there is an assumption that science is its own justification, that parts explain the whole and that objectivity is an accepted given truth of a well-undertaken scientific method. We will return to these issues. To get back to our definitions of reductionism and holism, it can be argued that this idea of scientific method finds its logical extreme in reductionism.

> *reductionism n (1943) (1) the attempt to explain all biological processes by the same explanations (as by physical laws) that chemists and physicists use to interpret inanimate matter; also: the theory that complete reductionism is possible (2) a procedure or theory that reduces complex data or phenomena to simple terms.*
>
> Webster (1995)

Reductionism reduces wholeness to individual parts and bits. Its scientific approach to understanding is to stand back, take an objective (scientific?) worldview and seek the truth. As Bell puts it:

> *A reductionist approach rejects ideas about the reality and importance of unscientific aspects of life (hunches, guess-work, instincts for rightness and even in certain circumstances illogical activity, ie activity which is not consistent with narrow definitions of efficiency). The universe is seen through empiricism as fixed, knowable, measurable and, therefore, predictable.*
>
> Bell (1996, p 63)

Developing an understanding of what we mean by reductionism, Dawkins argues that there are two forms: 'reductionist' and 'hierarchical reductionist'. The first type, which we might refer to as the classical reductionist, is in Dawkins' words set up by 'trendy intellectual magazines' as a kind of straw man:

> *To call oneself a reductionist will sound, in some circles, a bit like admitting to eating babies. But, just as nobody actually eats babies, so nobody is really a reductionist in any sense worth being against. The non-existent reductionist tries to explain complicated things directly in terms of the smallest part.*
>
> Dawkins (1986, p 13)

Alternatively, the second type of hierarchical reductionist, of which he counts himself:

> *...believes that carburettors are explained in terms of smaller units ... which are explained in terms of smaller units ... which are ultimately explained in terms of the smallest of fundamental particles. Reductionism, in this sense, is just another name for an honest desire to understand how things work.*
>
> Dawkins (1986, p 13)

A problem is that this form of analysis does not stop at carburettors but is used in all forms of social, environmental and ecological analysis as well. In these contexts, the limitations of the approach are already evident. Reductionism as a paradigm adopted by scientific professionals, whether the baby-eating or hierarchical form, is from one extreme of the continuum or spectrum which we set out in Figure 4.1. It is expressive of one way of thinking about the world and how we understand it. It is arguably the approach or method of understanding the world which has been the basis for much of Western science and it has been responsible for amazing and revolutionary advances in all branches of human thought and discovery. However, on the negative side, the process of dividing up the world in order to identify small parts is questionable in many areas of understanding and has led to partial analyses and the development of answers to problems which themselves cause still greater problems (a difficulty with all approaches which extrapolate from the part to the whole). There is another problem with reductionist approaches. Dividing an entity means that the concept of wholeness is often rendered dead by the process of examination! Studying 'dead' parts can be informative but can often do little to help us understand the living whole. Furthermore, the paradigm of a reductionist can be very limiting. If one considers the world as disconnected parts rather than as an inclusive whole, the resulting worldview can be restricted in terms of understanding the relationships and processes which combine to make the whole. However, we are developing the argument for our approach before providing the definitions. So far we have looked at what we mean by reductionist approaches and have argued that such approaches deal with parts. Set against this is holism, but what is holism?

> *holism n (1926) (1) a theory that the universe and esp. living nature is correctly seen in terms of interacting wholes (as of living organisms) that are more than the mere sum of elementary particles.*
>
> Webster (1995)

Another definition takes us even further into our understanding of this approach:

> *...the theory that the fundamental principle of the universe is the creation of wholes, ie complete and self-contained systems from the atom and the cell by evolution to the most complex forms of life and mind.*
>
> Macdonald (1979)

Holism deals with wholes and in this paradigm we see the universe comprised of 'self-contained systems'. This kind of approach can be said to find a logical end-point in the notion of the world as a living system, as expressed in the work of James Lovelock and the establishment of the theory of Gaia (Lovelock, 1979; Lovelock, 1991). Systems approached as wholes are fundamental and need to be understood in their entirety. To break them down into elements is to lose the point of the wholeness. Lovelock has dscussed wholeness and reductionism in terms of Gaia:

> *Consider Gaia as an alternative to the conventional wisdom that sees the Earth as a dead planet made of inanimate rocks, ocean and atmosphere, and merely inhabited by life. Consider it as a real system, comprising all of life and all of its environment tightly coupled so as to form a self-regulating entity.*
>
> Lovelock (1991, p 12).

To adopt an approach which deals with wholes has many implications. Possibly the first point is to recognize that the premise of the traditional, reductionist scientist – which is that the knowing process works by 'a procedure or theory that reduces complex data or phenomena to simple terms' – is no longer valid for us (nor would we agree that simplicity depends on reductionism). This does not mean that the traditional scientific approaches are invalid in all cases and in all contexts; however, if we are to understand complex wholes, we will need to adopt a different paradigm or extend the old. Later in this chapter we will describe a process within the systems thinking movement, from first-order to second-order cybernetics, which attempts to explain this adoption of a different paradigm. The process can be thought of as a movement of mindset from an observer divorced from context (first order) to an observer deeply involved in the context (second order). For now it is worth noting the comment of Buddrus upon this process: there is a parallel between first- and second-order cybernetics (which we discuss in more detail shortly) and with the movement from reductionist to holistic paradigms:

> *What is needed is a transformation of awareness from cybernetics of the first order to cybernetics of the second order...This seemingly simple transformation has fundamental impacts when applied to self-aware-*

ness and belief systems. It can cause considerable mental problems in
orientation: the transition of oneself from an observer of a reality which
is considered to be outside oneself, to a participant in the same reality,
and then towards being a co-creator of that reality, requires fundamen-
tal cognitive and emotional reorientation.

Buddrus (1996, p 1)

In understanding sustainability we argue that we need to recognize and work
with unities, of which we, as observers, are also part. This is not to suggest that
complex unities cannot be better understood by identifying key components,
interactions and processes (for example, the River Cynon described in Chapters
1 and 2), but that scientific approaches need to be seen in terms of the greater
whole of which the observer is a part; the observer therefore brings ideas and
actions into the context.

The traditional scientific paradigm has its value and its place in our understanding, but as one view among many – and we would argue that it should
not be the meta-theory which dominates all others. The benefit of the holistic
approach is that we can deal with complex wholes without losing their
complexity or 'killing the whole' (as also recognized in Hardi and Zdan, 1997),
and we can ask wider questions than those which relate to individual parts. The
downside for our analysis is that analysis itself becomes terribly difficult and
can lose all sense of focus and organization if the practitioner is not careful. We
will develop this idea and discuss potential means to achieve holistic analysis
in Chapter 6. To make holism work we need to grasp the principles of systems
thinking which lie at its heart.

The 'seed' idea which we want the reader to take away is the value of a
more holistic approach within the analysis and measurement of sustainability.

SYSTEMS APPROACHES TO PROBLEM SOLVING

In this book the word 'system' probably arises more often than any other. As
we described in the foreword, often the word is not used in a strict and exact
fashion. In terms of daily usage, the word is almost redundant, occasionally
meaning little more than 'thing' or a set of related things (for instance, a dish
washing system, a driving system, an office system). We now want to develop
what we mean by system – but we should say at the outset that there is considerable discussion within the systems community about this definition and
there are many interpretations of what a system is. There is also a vigorous and
developing discussion on systems and sustainability; (see the discussion in
Stowell, Ison et al, 1997). Here we make use of widely accepted definitions. One
view of the systems approach is, as the American systems thinker Peter Senge
puts it, the primacy of the whole:

The primacy of the whole suggests that relationships are, in a genuine
sense, more fundamental than things, and that wholes are primordial
to parts. We do not have to create interrelatedness. The world is already
interrelated.

Senge et al. (1994, p 25)

From this perspective, the idea of systems is a perfect foil for Senge's thinking:

> *A system is a perceived whole whose elements 'hang together' because they continually affect each other over time and operate toward a common purpose. The word descends from the Greek verb sunistánai, which originally meant: 'to cause to stand together'. As this origin suggests,* **the structure of a system includes the quality of perception with which you, the observer, cause it to stand together.**
>
> Senge et al. (1994, p 90), emphasis added

This view of systems has echoes of the work of Checkland (Checkland, 1981; Checkland and Scholes, 1990; Checkland and Holwell, 1998) in the UK, where there is great emphasis placed upon systems existing within our minds as perceptions which we throw out into the world as a means of describing and understanding it.

Systems thinking has a number of strands but is fundamentally based upon a few simple concepts. The lists of components vary with different authors, but there are substantial similarities between them (for alternative, useful definitions, see Checkland, 1981; Bignell and Fortune, 1984; Open University, 1987). For our definition of a system we make use of the one provided by Avgerou and Cornford (1993). These authors present the major features of systems as sixfold, and these are set out in Table 4.1.

Although there are different ideas about the fundamentals of systems, a systems analysis of a problem context can be undertaken. Such an analysis, whether an information system (as we might expect from the example of Avgerou and Cornford cited) or an ecological or a social organization, would be expected to provide an understanding of processes and relationships within a 'wholeness'. Emerging from this set of features and the earlier description taken from Senge, we can say some fundamental things about the basis for a systems approach:

(1) System is a term which can be applied to a vast number of different things, and this application is variable depending upon the individual or shared perception of an onlooker. A system can be a physical entity (such as the carbon cycle), a social entity (a political constitution), or an abstract idea (the idea of sustainability – as we shall demonstrate).

(2) Once defined the system will have a boundary (unless it is an infinite system!), and the boundary is defined by the onlookers – or we might say stakeholders. Ison (1993), quoting Russell (1986), draws actor and boundary together in saying:

> *...the observer is seen as part of the system's construction and not independent of the system. Russell takes this debate further. He emphasizes that 'a system is always a short-hand way of specifying a system environment relationship'.*
>
> Ison (1993, p 94)

(3) The system conceived by the onlooker will take place in a larger environment which is defined by being outside the boundary agreed. The environment will have a relationship with the system but the degree to which it affects the system will largely be dependent upon the system itself.

(4) Systems are changing and can be self-changing. As a purposeful wholeness, the system will be expected to seek its own optimum.

The final point is critical. If a system is purposeful then it might be expected to seek its own continuance and therefore *sustainability.*

Table 4.1 *Defining features of systems*

Systems feature	Description
Identification of a boundary • Interaction with the environment	This defines the system as distinct from its environment. The environment is not the system itself, since it is outside, but it does affect it.
• Being closed or open	Concerns the interrelation of the system with what lies beyond its boundary.
• Goal seeking	A system is capable of changing its behaviour to produce an outcome.
• Being purposeful	Systems select goals.
• Exerting control	A true system retains its identity under changing circumstances.

Source: adapted from Avgerou and Cornford (1993)

Figure 4.2 provides one view of the systems approach so far described. Although it is rather artificial, let's compare this systems view of the world with an equivalent, taking the most reductionist stance possible (Figure 4.3). The difficulties which this approach raises for the study of sustainability can be juxtaposed to the advantages of systems as set out in Table 4.2.

Arising from the discussion so far, the systems approach to understanding complex contexts is of interest for three reasons:

• The system is stated and explicit as a construct in the mind of the onlooker(s) or stakeholder(s); the system is brought forth or created as an artificial construct by those studying it. Therefore, the system can be the

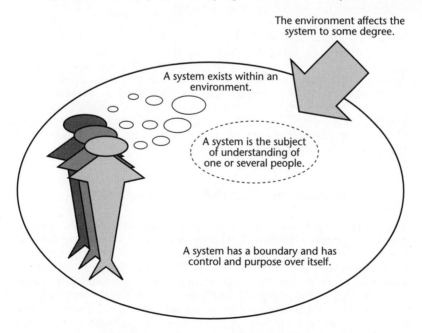

The environment affects the system to some degree.

A system exists within an environment.

A system is the subject of understanding of one or several people.

A system has a boundary and has control and purpose over itself.

Figure 4.2 *A systems view of a particular context*

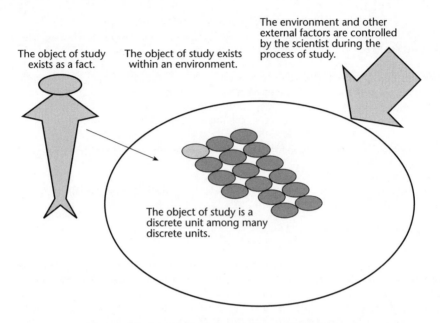

The environment and other external factors are controlled by the scientist during the process of study.

The object of study exists as a fact.

The object of study exists within an environment.

The object of study is a discrete unit among many discrete units.

Figure 4.3 *A reductionist view of a particular context*

result of an eclectic process (eclectic signifies elements drawn from various sources; Webster, 1995).
- The system is a whole and has the potential to change itself.
- The system is involved with its own sustainability; it can change as its environment changes in order to be sustained.

These three seed ideas, developing on the idea of wholeness set out in the previous section, will be fundamental to our thinking in later sections. In Chapters 1, 2 and 3 we reviewed the results of some traditional approaches to SI development. So far we have described the reductionist mindset, which we argue is behind much of the scientific method expressed by advocates and developers of SIs. As yet we have not discussed systemic approaches to problem solving or SI development. This will be dealt with in detail using a specific approach in Chapter 6, but for now we want to briefly describe some forms of the systems approach to problem solving.

A RANGE OF SYSTEMS APPROACHES

As we said in the previous section, there are numerous ways of thinking about and applying a systems approach. This is quite consistent with the systems view that the variable perceptions of different stakeholders in a problem context are legitimate but need to be justified. In this section we will quickly describe four different approaches, some analytic and some more descriptive, which are either explicitly or implicitly systems-based. We argue that they can all be understood in terms of the axis which we set out in Figure 4.4. The approaches which we illustrate here and which we will apply elements of later in Chapter 6 are from the fields of problem solving, problem description, project appraisal and project planning.

Table 4.2 *Comparison of systems and reductionist approaches*

Systems approach	Reductionist approach
The problem is shared by legitimate stakeholders in the problem context.	The problem is in the mind of the scientist.
A wholeness is reviewed.	A part of a complex whole is analysed.
The environment affects the system.	The environment is expected to be controlled.
The boundary of the system is flexible and dependent upon the perception of the stakeholder.	The boundary of the part is defined by the expert.

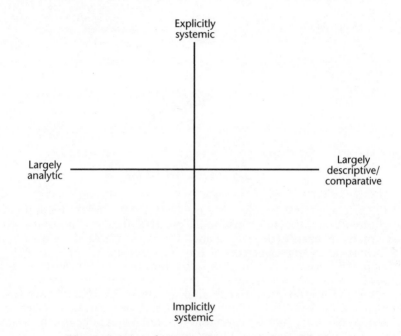

Figure 4.4 *Axis for comparing systems approaches*

The first form of systems approach is set out in Figure 4.5 and is known as the soft systems approach or method (SSM).

A Problem Solving Approach – the Soft Systems Method

To describe the approach, we set out the main elements in Figure 4.5. This provides a view of all the elements of the approach and shows the manner in which they combine.

The SSM was developed, and has since been extended, by Peter Checkland and colleagues at the University of Lancaster in the UK (Checkland, 1981) and has since been developed by him and others (see Avison and Wood–Harper,

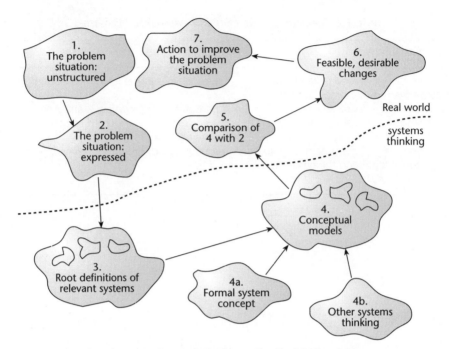

Source: adapted from Open University (1987), building on Checkland (1981, p 163)

Figure 4.5 *The soft systems method*

1990; Checkland and Scholes, 1990; CCTA, 1993). Today the approach is taught by universities and consultancy agencies in many locations and has taken on many nuances depending upon the requirements of the teaching and the specific aims and objectives of the practitioners. The way in which we develop our perception of the approach varies from others but is essentially related to the format set out by the Open University (Open University, 1987). From our perspective, the fundamental insight of Checkland's work is that problems in the world are usually 'soft'. By soft we mean that objectives are unclear, purposes are muddled and solutions are not usually initially available. This contrasts to the traditional 'hard' approach (of, for example, reductionist science, which sees problems as being definable and objectives as self-evident), which has been the hallmark of problem investigation in much of academia. We will not go into detail about the nature of SSM, but features worth bringing out from Figure 4.5 are:

- It is often necessary to spend considerable time in perceiving the problem and exploring the tasks and issues implicit in it (a point also recognized in Hardi and Zdan, 1997). These are set out in elements two and three in Figure 4.5.
- There is not an assumption that the 'problem' is clear. It may have many definitions.
- The next key point is that a definition of a transformation within the problem context needs to be agreed upon (element three). It is not assumed that because, for example, I am a fish biologist looking at the problem, the solution to the problem will be production (as in the MSY

example quoted in Chapter 2). We need to see that other domains may contain the 'solutions' to a given problem. For example, in the Peruvian anchovy example described in Chapter 2 where the fishery collapsed essentially because of overfishing, the emphasis was originally on setting an MSY of production, which itself became invalid because of the El Niño effect. But if the emphasis was on helping the fishing industry, perhaps other perceptions could have been brought in.

- The next point is that identifying a transformation is the basis for an activity plan which is then compared to the problem context as first reviewed (elements four and five). It is often the case that in analysing a given problem we lose sight of the issues which first excited our attention. This loop encourages us to compare our analysis with the problem as first perceived.
- The next point is that stakeholders are brought together to discuss the analysis (element six). Ideally this is not an expert-driven approach and stakeholders are performing the analysis too, but this idea of inclusion prior to action is another strong feature of the SSM approach.
- Finally, the process is cyclical. We do not definitely 'fix' problems. Rather, we achieve ways forward mutually and then work on the next issue which arises (elements seven and one).

The main features of the soft systems approach which we wish to emphasize at this point are that the process of thinking systemically about problems is iterative, participatory and ongoing. The second systems approach arises from the work of Senge et al (1994) and relates to his work on the learning organization (LO).

Problem Description – the Learning Organization Approach

Senge set out five 'disciplines' for encouraging and developing the learning organization which is the focus for his work in making use of systems approaches. The five disciplines are: systems thinking, personal mastery, mental models, shared vision and team learning. As with the work of Checkland et al, the five disciplines have been developed and applied by various agencies and academic institutions in different contexts and have produced a rich range of approaches and adaptations (for a review of these it is useful to take a look at the learning organization email list at <*http://www.learning-org.com*>).The five disciplines as we interpret them are set out in Table 4.3 with a brief definition of each discipline, a note on where they might be applied and some indication of what might be the expected outcome of their application.

As with the work of Peter Checkland, the LO approach does not see problem solving as being easy or objective. Focusing heavily on dialogue and team learning, the list of outcomes shows how closely the LO approach relates to the discussion which we have had so far about the relative merits of scientism and systemisism. In defining sustainability, group consensus and insight are more vital than reductionist objectivity, as could be witnessed in the sustainable cities examples given in Chapter 3 (for example Norwich 21, 1997).

In the LO approach, the systems approach is a core discipline associated with others in order to provide learning and consensus. As with SSM, processes are important and systems analysis relates to cycles of understanding. Senge makes use of what he calls 'archetypes' to be compared against the real world.

Table 4.3 *The five disciplines*

Discipline	Definition	Where applied?	Expected positive outcome?
Systems thinking	This focuses on links and loops – loops which can be reinforcing (small changes become big changes) or balancing (pushing stability, resistance and limits).	Contexts where cause and effect are unclear	Description and insight
Personal mastery	Numerous interpretations, but one threefold explanation of what this means is: • articulating a personal vision; • seeing reality clearly; • making commitment to the results you want.	Contexts where change processes threaten the individuals' ability to cope	Empower-ment
Mental models	We are all making mental models of the world as we experience it. The fifth discipline develops this tendency. Such models are based upon reflection and enquiry.	Any action learning situation	Clear self-analysis
Shared vision	Built around six core ideas: • the organization has a destiny; • a deep purpose is in the founders' aspirations; • not all visions are equal; • there is need for collective purpose; • and to provide forums for people to speak from the heart; • creative tension is useful and can be encouraged.	Contexts of dramatic change	Organization-wide clarity of purpose
Team learning	Learning through conversation, dialogue and skilful discussion – the aim is to achieve 'collective mindfulness' (Senge, et al, 1994 p 359).	Contexts of team development	Group consensus

One such archetypal model is shown in Figure 4.6. In the snowball archetype, a situation of continuous decline or improvement is described – here demonstrated by the River Cynon example described earlier. The snowball is not a virtuous cycle in either contexts of decline or growth – it epitomizes continuous change, feeding on itself. It therefore requires a balancing and adapting action (contained in the balancing archetype described by Senge) to cause stability and equilibrium.

By using a range of archetypes such as these, situations can be considered and the consequences of actions modelled and discussed by stakeholders in the process. The approach appears to be largely descriptive and comparative (there is a similarity here to the 'failures' approach adapted by Bignell and Fortune, 1984), but it allows contexts to be reviewed for change processes, and therefore it appears a useful method to apply to analysing sustainability – particularly where known forces of change are at work and their consequences need to be considered.

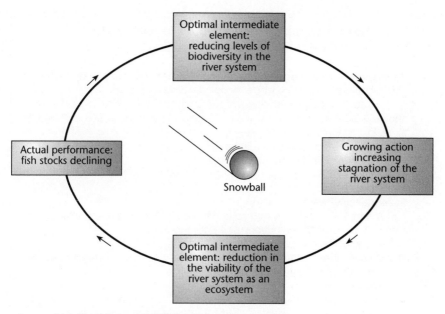

Source: adapted from Senge et al (1994), p 116

Figure 4.6 *The reinforcing loop (snowball)*

Appraisal – the Participatory Rural Appraisal Approach

In Chapter 3 we discussed project appraisal. In that chapter the focus was largely on the inclusion of sustainability issues into cost-benefit analysis (CBA). Developing on from this we now describe the application of participatory rural appraisal (PRA), which we argue is a more systemic approach to the range of issues which arise in project appraisal.

Although PRA does not set itself out to be explicitly a 'systems' approach, it contains much in common with what we described so far as central to a systems ethos in understanding complex situations (see systems concepts as noted in Chambers, 1997, p 138). There is no consensus as to what constitutes PRA techniques as opposed to any other set of methods for analysing populations – as with SSM and LO the approach has been taken up and developed globally, and there is a rich literature on the various ways in which it has been applied and developed.

Working from literature produced from various sources (see Chambers, 1992; Natrajan, 1993; Shah and Hardwaj, 1993; McPherson, 1994; Webber and Ison, 1995; Bell, 1996; Chambers, undated), some of the techniques for PRA are set out in Box 4.1 with a brief description of what they involve.

Chambers (Chambers, 1997), the major author of the approach, indicates three pillars to PRA. These are:

- the behaviour and attitudes of the development professional;
- the need for sharing between different actors;
- the requirement for participatory methods (p 105).

Box 4.1 *Some of the techniques in participatory rural appraisal (PRA)*

- **Participatory mapping and modelling (all participatory diagramming)**
  This technique encourages local people to draw and mark the ground with colours, sticks, cigarette packets and string (and anything that comes to hand, although one should be wary about bringing in pens and paper as these can block local people from expressing their views readily) in order to show variation from a local perspective of 'mapable' phenomena.
- **Transect walks and participatory transect**
  To gain a quick overview of local practices, the team walk a transect through the appraisal area.
- **Seasonal calendars**
  This is a form of modelling or mapping where villagers are asked to show the seasonal or monthly distributions of inputs and outputs.
- **Activity profiles and daily routines**
  This is used when it is important to understand how daily patterns of activity are evolving.
- **Time lines**
  When there is a need to gain a view of local history. The time lines can be collected at community interview (see rapid approaches below).
- **Local histories**
- **Venn (Chapati) diagrams**
  To gain a systemic view of the overlaps between different groups, commodities, inputs and or outputs in a village setting.
- **Wealth rankings**
  To gain an insight into the distribution of wealth over time and space. Small groups can be asked to rank the wealthiest from the poorest in the village. Often piles of stones are used to indicate relative wealth. This can be done as part of the exercise to map the village social context. In this case the community as a whole might rank itself.
- **Matrices**
  Communities are asked to set out a matrix for technologies and to set out attributes in the rows. Another approach might be to map the productive area of the village and then to set out problems and opportunities in the rows.
- **Inventory of local management systems and resources**
  This can be used in focus group or community group interviews (see below). Local people know their management practices best. The interviews focus on how local management is undertaken. Use local classifications wherever possible.
- **Portraits, profiles, case studies and stories**
  These include summaries of family histories, farm coping mechanisms, conflict resolving. Use focus group technique as described below.
- **Folklore, songs and poetry**
  Sitting, listening (usually with an interpreter) and absorbing – principles of direct observation; see below.
- **Team interactions**
  Evening discussion and morning brainstorming sessions with teams which can be mixed and changed but must be carefully monitored by one member of the team. The monitor should record locations of people during the interaction and draw attention to the way the team works:
  - draw a circle around the person who is talking; break the circle when they are interrupted;

- draw an arrow from the talker to the person being talked to with a note of duration;
  - record each contribution in seconds.
- **The night halt**
  When it is important to show that the outsiders are 'with' the village: too often consultants are not in the village when people have time to talk – in mornings and evenings.
- **Survey of villagers attitudes**
- **Intriguing practices and beliefs**
  When we have the time to try to absorb the richness of local life – taking a sideways look at expected project outcomes.
- **Key informant interview**
  Interview a select group of individuals. They are preidentified as having insights and are usually owners or major stakeholders in problem areas. They are usually preidentified as being 'reliable'.
- **Focus group interview**
  A recent addition to semi-formal techniques. The technique is historically based in market the research to gauge reaction of customers to new products. The focus is on reactions to potential changes. Participants discuss among themselves.
- **Community interviews**
  Focus groups are for local people to discuss their own issues and problems; in community interviews the investigator asks questions, raises issues and seek responses. The primary response is to and from interviewer to participant.

These three are set out and developed in Figure 4.7.

SSM has many advocates and LO is now adopted by many practitioners in management science, but PRA has been adopted by the development community almost as an orthodoxy in project practice. This has raised questions about its value and there is considerable debate around the capacity of PRA to work in context. Biggs (1995) indicates three concerns with the approach:

> *Firstly, there is the risk that an exaggerated confidence in certain techniques and management tools associated, in this instance, with 'participatory' approaches, can limit critical awareness of how their application proceeds in practice...Secondly, there is a tendency to assume that simply 'including' certain kinds of people (in a team process) is sufficient to affect the 'participation' of the group which they are taken to represent ... Finally, it cannot be assumed that 'inclusion' guarantees meaningful participation.*

Biggs (1995, pp 4–5)

We will return to this critique later as we develop our participatory model for measuring sustainability. PRA is widely regarded as including populations of stakeholders, and it values the insight of this population. As with both SSM and LO, all three approaches provide the stakeholders in a given context with a say in the process of understanding, a responsibility for the sustainability of the enterprise and a legitimate place in developing analysis. PRA is interested in setting boundaries to appraisal but not in narrowing the boundary to a prespecified topic. The object of appraisal is treated as a system since it is recognized as a whole.

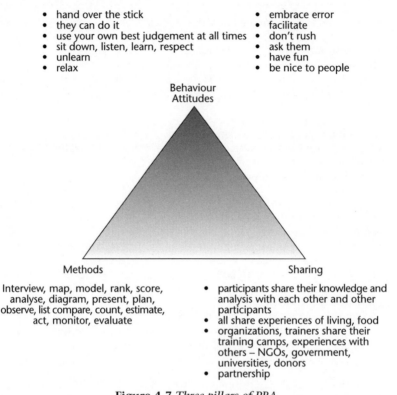

- hand over the stick
- they can do it
- use your own best judgement at all times
- sit down, listen, learn, respect
- unlearn
- relax

- embrace error
- facilitate
- don't rush
- ask them
- have fun
- be nice to people

Behaviour
Attitudes

Methods

Interview, map, model, rank, score,
analyse, diagram, present, plan,
observe, list compare, count, estimate,
act, monitor, evaluate

Sharing

- participants share their knowledge and analysis with each other and other participants
- all share experiences of living, food
- organizations, trainers share their training camps, experiences with others – NGOs, government, universities, donors
- partnership

Figure 4.7 *Three pillars of PRA*

In this section we have been considering the PRA approach as a systemic manner of dealing with project appraisal; however, if systemisism can work in appraisal, can it be applied to project development, planning, monitoring and evaluation? In the next section we examine one approach which can be argued to provide this.

Project Handling – the Logframe Approach

We have already described project appraisal by using CBA in Chapter 3. The value of CBA as described in Pearce (1993) lies in its ability to apply costs to processes and things. The logical framework, as we will discuss, can be a useful vehicle for applying CBA to provide indicators of process, project impact or sustainability. Much has been written about the logical framework or logframe (LF) approach to project planning and management (see Coleman, 1987; Cordingley, 1995; Bell, 1996). Unlike SSM, LO and PRA, LF does not have a single point of reference or champion as provided by Peter Checkland, Peter Senge and Robert Chambers respectively. LF appears as an evolved approach with no single point of original authorship.

This approach is only implicitly systemic in that it encourages its users to think widely about their project and to represent it as a totality, with both hard and soft elements clearly demarcated. The approach can be participatory and requires a great deal of agreement within the project team to work effectively

Table 4.4 *An overview of the logical famework (LF)*

GOAL	VERIFIABLE INDICATORS	MEANS OF VERIFICATION	ASSUMPTIONS
The higher-level objectives towards which the project is expected to contribute (mention target groups)	Measures (direct or indirect) to verify to what extent the goal is fulfilled	The sources of data necessary to verify status of goal-level indicators	Important events, conditions or decisions necessary for sustaining objectives in the long run
PURPOSE The effect which is expected to be achieved as the result of the project	**VERIFIABLE INDICATORS** Measures (direct or indirect) to verify to what extent the purpose is fulfilled	**MEANS OF VERIFICATION** The sources of data necessary to verify status of purpose-level indicators	**ASSUMPTIONS** Important events, conditions or decisions outside the control of the project which must prevail for the goal to be obtained
OUTPUTS The results that the project management should be able to guarantee (mention target groups)	**VERIFIABLE INDICATORS** Measures (direct or indirect) to verify to what extent the outputs are produced	**MEANS OF VERIFICATION** The sources of data necessary to verify status of activity-level indicators	**ASSUMPTIONS** Important events, conditions or decisions outside the control of the project necessary for the achievement of the purpose
ACTIVITIES The activities which have to be undertaken by the project in order to produce the outputs	**VERIFIABLE INDICATORS** Goods and services necessary to undertake activities	**MEANS OF VERIFICATION** The sources of data necessary to verify status of activity-level indicators	**ASSUMPTIONS** Important events, conditions or decisions outside the control of the project necessary for the production of the outputs

(see Thompson and Chudoba, 1994; Team Technologies, 1995; Thompson, 1995; Thompson, undated). (Note that the approach is not *always* participatory; see Chambers, 1997 pp 42–44, for a description of ZOPP – a version of logical frameworks.) The basic LF is a four-by-four matrix and is shown in Table 4.4.

The LF can be both descriptive and analytic. Descriptively, it allows a team or stakeholder group involved in a project to set out the formal aspects of the project (activities leading to outputs, resulting in purposes and, hopefully, achieving the project goal), and also the informal or 'soft' elements of the project at each level – this is shown in the 'assumptions' column on the right. Therefore, the project is described in both soft and hard, formal and informal terms. Furthermore, the middle two columns allow the project to be monitored and analysed, either qualitatively or quantitatively, in terms of the performance of the project. Performance can be measured on activities (the spending of money and the achievement of activities to date), on outputs (giving a notion of the projects impact – has it achieved what it originally set out to do?) and at the level of purpose (evaluation – was the result as expected?).

In all, the approach can be said to be systemic in that it sets a boundary around a complex unity and explicitly treats this unity as a whole. It involves a range of participants in the project process (although this is not always the case

Table 4.5 *Explaining logical fameworks*

Activities of various types	Measured as OVIs[*]	and by MOVs[**]	In the light of certain assumptions, should lead to...
Outputs (deliverables of the project)	measured as OVIs	and by means of MOV	In the light of certain assumptions, should lead to the realization of...
Purpose of the project	measured by OVI	and by means of MOV	In the light of certain assumptions, help in realizing the...
Goal which is beyond the project but is its vision	measured as OVI	and by means of MOV	In the light of certain assumptions

* OVI – Objectively Verifiable Indicator
** MOV – Means of Verification

in practice), and the project as a system is able to change in response to changes in the environment (it has properties of control and self-regulation). But how is the LF approach applied? When employing LF to develop or monitor a project, project activity is set out in the bottom-left cell. The activity described here can be measured and controlled by use of the related verifiable indicators and by means of verification (these can be indicators of project progress as argued in Bell, 1996). On the second row from the bottom, directly above activities, the verifiable indicators relating to outputs can be regarded as indicators of the project's impact. On the third row the indicators of purpose can be used as the main evaluation points for assessing the project's capacity to meet its original objectives. All indicators can, if required, be developed as indicators of sustainability (as we shall discuss further in Chapter 6). The diagram might be better understood as set out in Table 4.5.

The LF approach might be argued to be 'goal driven' and rather positivist (for a discussion of this type of argument, see Checkland and Holwell, 1998). The approach (as with all others) depends on the method of application for its systemic content (is it participatory; is it inclusive?) by the team involved.

Although LF was not used in the Norwich 21 example of sustainable cities set out in Chapter 3, we could apply it retrospectively to the first elements of the first column as shown in Table 4.6.

An Overview of Systemic Approaches

The four systemic approaches are set out below in one frame (Figure 4.8) in terms of whether they are implicitly or explicitly systemic, whether they are

Table 4.6 *A partial LF expression of Norwich 21*

Goal	**Objectively verifiable indicators (OVI)**
This would relate to the achievement of sustainability in cities at a national level.	Similarly, this would relate to the measurement of sustainability in cities at the national level.

Purpose	
• 'Promoting a prosperus and dynamic with policies for sustainable long-term growth and development that take account of the needs of the present generation of people without compromising the ability of future generations to meet their own needs' (Norwich 21, 1997).	• This would relate to the achievement of the impact indicators set out below and the emerging realization of sustainability which they would produce. This is an exercise for the owner of the Norwich 21 action plan.

Outputs	
• clean air	• 0 days poor air quality due to nitrogen oxides measured at Guildhall
• less domestic waste, etc	• waste produced: 0.36 tonnes per head; waste recycled = 0.018 tonnes per head, etc.

Activities	
• Test against UK National air quality strategy standard, etc.	• etc

problem solving, or descriptive or comparative. Before accepting that an approach is systemic or not, the quote from Buddrus given earlier in this chapter should be remembered as a caution:

> ...the transition of oneself from an observer of a reality which is considered to be outside oneself [eg the traditional role of the scientist], to a participant in the same reality, and then towards being a co-creator of that reality, requires fundamental cognitive and emotional reorientation.
>
> Buddrus (1996, p 1)

A point made regularly among groups of managers training in the use of LF is the tendency to simplify the approach to 'box-filling' in isolation, rather than exploring and describing a project context in a participatory manner. It is almost always possible to apply a systemic approach in a reductionist manner and thus lose the value of the undertaking. This is a point we will need to be aware of when we come to developing our own approach in Chapter 6.

In this section we have tried to demonstrate that systems approaches can vary considerably and can do quite different things, but that they hold to some of the seed ideas of what constitutes a systems study. In Chapter 6 we will make use of various elements drawn from some of the four approaches and will discuss practitioner issues. We now go on to look at what implementing the systems perspective can mean to developing a viable assessment of sustainability.

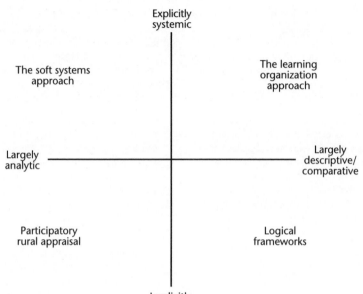

Figure 4.8 *The four approaches*

NEW DEFINITIONS AND NEW THINKING – HOLISM, ECLECTICISM, SYSTEMISISM

We are interested in understanding the issues surrounding the measurement of the 'immeasurable'. It is our contention that the idea of measuring sustainability in absolute, traditional, reductionist terms, as with SIs, is non-viable. It cannot be done *because sustainability itself is not a single thing.* Or better, it can be done but it will be done badly, oversimplifying complexity and reducing a variety of relevant and legitimate views and understandings to the dominant mindset of the scientist. Sustainability is, we believe, a highly complex term open to a wide variety of interpretations and conceptualizations. In short, it is a concept dependent upon the various perceptions of the stakeholders in the problem context. Sustainability is not an absolute quantity to be measured. Sustainability changes as an idea (or as a system) in terms of the perception of the onlookers. According to this approach, the view of sustainability must be developed so that it takes onboard the *legitimacy* of different views of sustainability. When we adopt this mindset we see that the view of a reductionist (even a mythical, 'baby-eating' reductionist) may be legitimate and valuable. However, it is equally true that the view of a local inhabitant may also be legitimate and, although it may vary from the scientist's views, may contain richness and detail which the scientist does not have access to or actually loses in applying the tools of science. Narrow, expert-driven conceptions of sustainability have been problematic (as shown in Chapter 2 with the MSY microcosm); the model for considering sustainability which we develop in this book is therefore developed around three premises. In measuring the immeasurable we are concerned with:

- eclectically derived, *systemic wholeness*; that is, we are concerned with:
- the *perception* of systemic wholeness which derives from legitimate sources;
- the *sustainability* of wholeness which is under observation.

In the following pages we will develop these themes in our approach and we will conduct our analysis using systems tools. It is not the purpose of this text to explore all the thinking and conceptualization behind the systems movement; however, the authors are aware that they are dealing with sets of concepts which require detailed analysis and justification. Such work has been undertaken elsewhere (see Capra, 1996). Behind the discussion of systems approaches and techniques explored in this chapter lies a theoretic discussion specifically expressed in the field of cybernetics; another definition is required:

> *cybernetics ... Gk kybernetes pilot, governor (fr. kybernan to steer, govern)... (1948): the science of communication and control theory that is concerned esp. with the comparative study of automatic control systems (as the nervous system and brain and mechanical-electrical communication systems).*
>
> Webster (1995)

Developing upon this definition, the term was described by Wiener (1948) as the science of 'control and communication in the animal and the machine'. Cybernetics is now organized into first, second and third order categories which can be said to involve in sequence:

- the understanding of feedback loops (Capra, 1996, p 56) and control systems to explain how the world works in a scientific sense (Umpleby, 1994);
- the understanding that individuals construct their own 'reality' (Foerster, 1981) and that this should lead to tolerance of alternative views (Umpleby, 1994);
- reflection on the understanding of multiple realities and the means by which these multiple realities can be contained in a consensus view.

As Umpleby puts it:

> *Whereas the first phase of cybernetics took an empirical approach to the nervous system, the second phase of cybernetics created a philosophy based on the findings of neurophysiological investigations. The third phase, the cybernetics of conceptual systems, looks at the community that creates and sustains ideas and the motivations of the members of that community.*
>
> Umpleby (1994, p 13)

Our discussion in this chapter reflects thinking in the categories of first, second and third order cybernetics.

Perhaps the issue of multiple and inclusive worldviews in the matter of sustainability is expressed most clearly in the work of Maturana and Varela (Macadam et al, 1990; Maturana and Varela, 1992; Maturana, 1997). Their work relates to the nature of biological systems but has implications in many related fields and is, at present, the source of much discussion among systems thinkers (for example, see Mingers, 1995). The core idea we wish to make use of here is that of autopoiesis: the capacity of systems for self-making, self-renewal or self-production. In a revolutionary departure from much of the background of systems thinking, Maturana and Varela postulate that systems are closed but there is an intimate interaction with the environment within this closure. The environment is not 'out there' but, as Morgan puts it:

> *...the theory of autopoiesis accepts that systems can be recognized as having 'environments' but insists that relations with any environment are internally determined.*
>
> Morgan (1997, p 255)

The exciting element for the sustainability debate is in working out what autopoiesis means – again, quoting Morgan: 'Autopoietic systems are closed loops: self-referential systems that strive to shape themselves in their own image' (1997, p 257). Morgan gives some examples of what this means in practice; an example drawn from the fishing industry is illustrative:

> *...the commercial fishing business. This is also in the process of destroying itself because, historically, the key actors involved have seen themselves as being separate from the fish. The firms involved have enacted identities in pursuit of short-term goals, with the result that their actions have, in many parts of the world, already depleted the resource on which their business relies.*
>
> Morgan (1997, p 260)

The lesson seems to be that, for a truly systemic (or second or third order cybernetic) view of complex situations, the autopoietic approach explains why organizations can be progressive and inclusive or narrow and blinkered. Science, therefore, as an autopoietic system can close itself to factors which are not seen as central to the mindset of science itself. In this sense it can be as blinkered as the fishing industry is today. Revelations concerning the sudden explosion in cod stocks in the North Sea (BBC Radio 4, One O'clock News, 18 December 1997) indicates that the scientific analysis of sustainable fishing levels has been proved wrong again – this time resulting in an explosion in stocks. This dramatic increase in stocks occurred against a background of numerous fishing boats being broken up and their crews made unemployed. In Morgan's example of a limited view, quoted above, the culprits are the fishing industry. In this example the problem is the limited understanding and incorrect quantification of stocks as provided by scientists. A fishing industry representative said on BBC Radio 4 that the job for the scientists was now to build trust with the fishermen since they were no longer believed.

In an autopoietic sense, the systems approach to sustainability must mean that we include as much of our environment as possible in our self-referencing. As a result, the views of all involved in contentious projects are included (and their opinions valued) in the decision-making processes. The premises which arise from this section regarding the development of a testable approach or hypothesis are developed in the final section of Chapter 4.

EMERGING PREMISES FOR SI DEVELOPMENT

In the previous four sections we have taken a wide-ranging and provocative view of the role and nature of reductionism, and we have indicated that, although this approach is useful and valid for partial understanding of many areas of analysis, it is not valid as the basis for our understanding of sustainability. We have also described some elements of a systems approach, which is concerned with wholeness and is designed to take onboard the various viewpoints of actors and stakeholders in a problem context. We have described how this approach is related to developments in the field of cybernetics and, most centrally, the autopoiesis of Maturana and Varela.

For our study, these factors were vital in helping us to set the basic premises which we wished to use to develop our hypothesis for systemic sustainability analysis (SSA). As we go through them, the reader should be able to see how they relate back to vital aspects of the discussion so far. The premises for the development of the hypothetical SSA are:

- Sustainability can provide a qualitative measure of the integrality and wholeness of any given system.
- Subjectivity on the part of the stakeholders in any given system (including researchers) is unavoidable.
- Subjectively derived measures of sustainability are useful if the subjectivity is explicitly accepted and declared at the outset and if the method for deriving the measures are available to a range of stakeholders.
- Measures of sustainability can be valuable aids to planning, forecasting and awareness-building (as in Norwich 21).
- Rapid and participatory tools for developing our thinking and modelling concerning measures of sustainability are of value to a wide range of stakeholders within development policy.

These five features will be developed and expanded upon in the next chapter.

Chapter 5

Projects and Sustainability Indicators

INTRODUCTION AND OBJECTIVES

Building on the discussion of systemic approaches to problem solving and project development set out in Chapter 4, this chapter will develop our thinking concerning the specific use of SIs in development projects. We will focus on four major aspects:

- the project scenario: applying systemic methodologies in project contexts to build SIs;
- the stakeholder scenario: how to develop participation and coalition in the use of SIs;
- accommodating multiple views of sustainability within projects;
- introducing the systemic sustainability analysis (SSA) idea.

This chapter builds on the premises set out in Chapter 4 which provided us with our starting points for measuring sustainability. These starting points are:

- Sustainability is a qualitative property of a system.
- Subjectivity on the part of the stakeholders in understanding the sustainability of any given system is unavoidable.
- Subjectively derived measures of sustainability are nonetheless useful aids to planning.

These three elements will be combined in an approach which is both participatory and systemic. The next step is to consider where we want to develop this theory into useful practice. In this chapter we set out our views on where SIs can be developed. In Chapters 1, 2 and 3 we discussed various interpretations of sustainability. We also discussed ways in which sustainability could be considered. It is worth recalling that by sustainability we refer to three domains of practice:

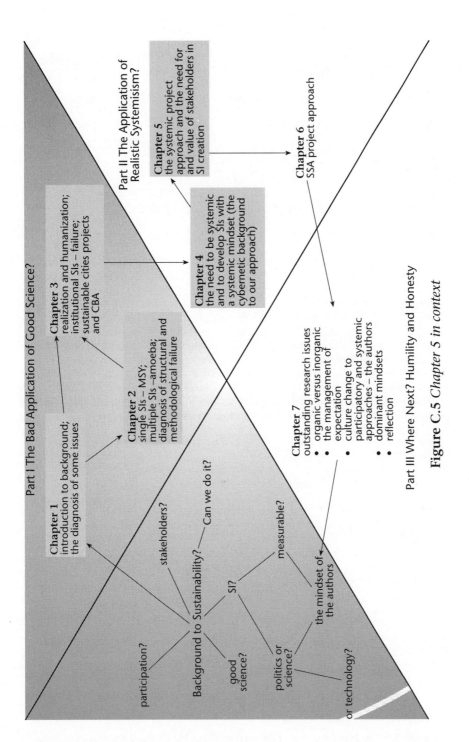

Figure C.5 *Chapter 5 in context*

	State	Process (or driving force or control or pressure)	Response
What is happening right now – pre-project	✔	✔	—
Deliverable (project, implementation)	✔	✔	✔
Deliverer (institution)	✔	✔	✔

Figure 5.1 *The use people make of SIs*

- the domain of 'what is'
- the domain of delivering a project;
- the domain of the deliverer of the project which is instituting sustainability.

These three are set out in Figure 5.1. The project context (the 'what is' prior to the project) can be reviewed for sustainability, and therefore SIs can be produced for it as can the domains of the projects deliverable and the delivering agencies themselves. By keeping the context for the practice of SIs wide, we do not avoid difficult issues relating to where sustainability is of critical importance (the deliverer, the world as it is before the project, etc). This triad or trinity relates closely to what the United Nations has advocated (see the UN internet site <*http://www.un.org/dpcsd/dsd/indi6.htm*>). These are described in Chapter 1 as SIs of state, force and response; they could be loosely linked to our triad as shown in Figure 5.1.

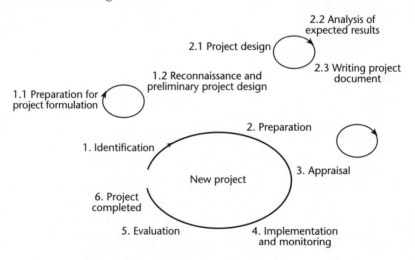

Source: adapted from FAO (1986)

Figure 5.2 *The blueprint project cycle(s); relationship between the phases of project formulation and the traditional project cycle*

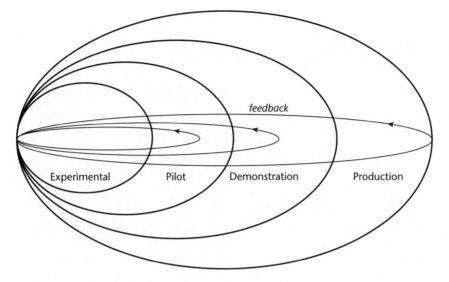

feedback

Experimental   Pilot   Demonstration   Production

Source: adapted from Cusworth and Franks (1993), p 9

Figure 5.3 *The process or adaptive project approach*

We will develop our use of these trinities in developing SIs in Chapter 6. One implication of the different types or forms of SI is that we need to briefly review the nature of the projects in the context in which SIs are implemented. Different types of project format may be more or less sympathetic environments to different types of SI. Following this, we will review the idea of the stakeholder and where and how far this extends within the project. In Chapter 4 we have described the importance of stakeholders participating in systemic practice. The inclusion of stakeholders will, in turn, have an impact upon the nature of the core participatory methods we will use (focus groups, community interviews, key informant interviews, diagramming, team-working, etc).

THE PROJECT SCENARIO FOR SIS

There is a considerable literature on the place and importance of projects in the development context (for a fairly random example of the range of literature on the subject, see Coleman, 1987; Biggs, 1989; Rajakutty, 1991; Cusworth and Franks, 1993; Hulme, 1994; Bell, 1996; Girma et al, 1996). Central to our concern here is the rise in importance of the process project over the traditional blueprint or project cycle approach. Figure 5.2 shows a traditional blueprint project approach; Figure 5.3 shows the main detail of the process project.

The traditional blueprint approach, while being cyclical in presentation, is not iterative or explicitly inclusive of stakeholders' views. It is arguable whether the cycle is really a cycle at all. There is no direct formal linkage between points 6 and 1 in Figure 5.2, nor any reason why the learning from one project should feed into another. Cusworth and Franks argue:

> *The blueprint approach was too rigid and inflexible, that is it placed too much reliance on prior comprehensive data gathering, planning and*

Table 5.1 *Project: blueprint and process*

Traditional, blueprint projects	Process, adaptive projects
Inputs and activities are specified at the outset.	Inputs and activities are only partially specified at the outset, generally only for initial phase of project.
Implementation is according to plans established during formulation process.	Implementation is subject to continual replanning on the basis of formative evaluation.
Stages of project cycle are distinct.	Formulation and evaluation are incorporated into implementation stage of the project cycle.
Focus on efficient conversion of inputs into outputs.	Focus is on realization of project objectives rather than outputs.
Emphasis is on administration rather than management.	Emphasis is on management rather than on administration.

> *control (all of which often appeared as inadequate in developing*
> *countries) and did not give sufficient importance to the acceptability of*
> *the proposed intervention to the intended beneficiaries.*
>
> Cusworth and Franks (1993, p 9)

They suggested an 'adaptive' model. This implies adaptive to the environment and able to change as the environment, in which the project system operates, changes. Building upon the systems view of Maturana expressed in Chapter 4, the environment is seen as being an inclusive part of the project itself. At any stage the project may need to change as it affects and is affected by the environment.

If we draw out the main themes of the two approaches or methodologies to project planning, we will see in how the two vary. Table 5.1 shows the major features of the two approaches.

Each approach has strengths and weaknesses. The blueprint approach is most specifically strong on control and forward planning (a reflection of the thinking in reductionism and first order cybernetics as discussed in Chapter 4). It is probably the best approach in situations where goals are clear and unambiguous and the project's objectives clearly formulated. The process–project approach is more flexible and able to accommodate change and rethinking (second and third order cybernetics?). It would probably be best in situations where the goals of the project can only be semiformulated at the outset, where stakeholders in the project are unclear about the delivery they require and where there may even be a variety of views about the direction of the project and its expected outcome.

As we have said before, we are not arguing that one approach is wrong and the other right. We are indicating that projects come with their own mindsets and assumptions. If we were to think about the two approaches to project formulation in the same terms as we thought about approaches to problem solving as set out in Figure 4.1, it might look like that in Figure 5.4. (For a similar but tabular breakdown on this point, see Chambers, 1997, p 37.)

We have already argued in Chapter 4 that the holistic and systemic approaches to problem solving are more consistent with the approach to sustainability analysis which we develop here. In the same vein, it is apparent

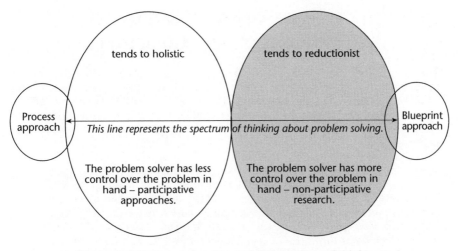

Figure 5.4 *Project approaches and the spectrum of thinking about problem solving*

that the process approach to project planning and management will be more consistent with the SSA approach, which we set out in the next chapter. With reference to the forms of SI which might be produced (what is [state], the deliverer [force] and the deliverable [process]), it would seem that the reflective and learning process which is evident in the process–project approach would be more consistent with SIs reflecting upon processes within and outside the project context; on the other hand, the blueprint project approach is consistent with the necessarily more limited analysis of state. This does not mean that blueprint approaches cannot adopt sustainability measurement, but it does mean that the approach will make the analysis of sustainability relatively static, top down, expert driven and inconsistent with a participatory approach. Long (1992) has summed this difference up as follows:

> *Rather than viewing intervention as the implementation of a plan of action [blueprint], it should be visualized as an ongoing transformational process in which different actor interests and struggles are located.*
>
> Long (1992 p 9, item in parenthesis added)

In this section we have reviewed the underlying assumptions of project approaches. Our concern is to consider and interpret sustainability within development projects. Process projects appear to offer the best chance to achieve this end. Working from this understanding and recognizing the importance of inclusion and participation in process projects, we need to develop our thinking a little further and to consider the nature of participation and stakeholding in projects.

THE STAKEHOLDER SCENARIO FOR SIS – PARTICIPATION AND COALITION

The explicit inclusion of those who have a stake in a project scenario is now a development-project planning orthodoxy. Participation has become something of a holy grail in the development literature. It is often portrayed as the solution to all ills. As we saw in Chapter 4, Biggs (1995) has reservations about the orthodoxy and he has also indicated the range of approaches which are being applied:

> *Participatory process projects are being promoted by many donors, such as the World Bank and ODA, as well as many NGOs [Overseas Development administration (ODA) and Non-Governmental Organizations (NGOs)]. Popular participation is seen as a 'process whereby those with legitimate interests in a project influence decisions which affect them' (Eyben and Ladbury, 1994). Stakeholder Analysis, TeamUp, process documentation and monitoring and DELTA techniques, are some of the methods being advocated.*
>
> Biggs (1995, p 2)

Despite enthusiasm, there are considerable problems in achieving participation (as we saw briefly in Chapter 4). Hirschheim (1989) has noted the problems of participation. In his research on participation in information systems development, he ran across a number of issues which are still relevant in a wide range of project contexts:

> *Participants still required the proactive input of a consultant to keep the design process running. Some participants felt that they did not have enough time to dedicate to the process. The group involved in the design process has to be the right size (an issue which varies between specific projects) otherwise it is non-representative or unwieldy.*
> *Systems boundaries – Hirschheim notes that participants were unclear about the extent of the systems on which they were working and therefore the degree of responsibility they had for design outside their own specific location.*
> *When to begin the participation.*
> *Seniority of participatory staff. In the Hirschheim survey it was found that senior staff have more willingness and greater ability to participate. Junior staff do not have the same confidence to express their ownership of the system.*
> Bell (1996, p 130), adapted from Hirschheim (1989, p 194)

Hirschheim's concerns relate to the procedure of formulating participation. His areas of concern are practical and focus on teams of co-workers. Craig and Porter have other concerns about participation in the development project context, including the element of control which creeps into much project work which explicitly describes itself as participatory (Craig and Porter, 1997). Biggs takes a wider view and questions the mindset of participation itself but also sees development opportunities. Specifically, he makes five 'practical suggestions' for those embarking on participatory project design:

- *Question and unpackage the new participation orthodoxy.*

- *Advocacy and influence: aim to teach these approaches and methods in such a way that, where they appear to have been used effectively, the historical, political, cultural and economic contexts in which this effectiveness was achieved can be fully appreciated.*
- *Claims about efficacy and agency: be cautious as regards two particular kinds of claims which tend to be made by those advocating any set of methods and techniques in development interventions: ... that such techniques and methods possess intrinsic value or efficacy ... the claim that advocates themselves have been the key agents in bringing about this or that development outcome.*
- *Reflective analysis: encourage critical reflective writing by those who have been involved for many years in science technology development.*
- *Coalitions and negotiations: recognize the involvement of contending coalitions in science and technology development.*

Biggs (1995, pp 9–10)

Biggs advocates caution and critical reflection. His concern is that the method becomes the purpose and goal of the project, and that lessons of the past are not learned or that the value of past interventions in development are seen as being heretical. In all, the thrust of the five points is to encourage caution. Key to our argument in this book are the final two points. We advocate reflective analysis elsewhere (see Bell, 1996; Bell and Wood–Harper, 1998), but the notion of coalition requires further development.

ACCOMMODATING MULTIPLE VIEWS OF SUSTAINABILITY

Participation and therefore inclusion in decision-making which will affect your life is a self-evident good; the devil is in the detail. In any development intervention, competing interests will reside in the project constituents. A number of authors have indicated the problems of forming participation in projects (see Hirschheim, 1989; Biggs, 1995; Biggs and Smith, 1995; Mosse, 1995). More recently a crop of papers have indicated problems with the orthodoxy of participatory approaches and have indicated the need for further thought (see Connell, 1997; Jackson, 1997; Khan and Ara Begum, 1997; Reckers, 1997).

The list of those groups which might be seen as participant stakeholders in a process project might appear to be fairly straightforward:

- donors;
- project managers;
- beneficiaries.

Nevertheless, this listing is simplistic and swiftly develops in complexity when we consider the subgroups in Table 5.2. As an example, for a Nigerian project which the authors worked on, the list would appear as shown in Table 5.3. The groups have diversified, but are these discrete groups? The Venn diagram in Figure 5.5 indicates the overlap of membership of the groups from the perspective of the consultants on the project.

There is intense overlap. They are not discrete or permanent. Groups' interests and membership change over time and so do the relationships between them. This ties in well with Biggs's ideas on coalitions:

Table 5.2 *Participant stakeholder groups*

Donors	• International donors: para-statal, eg World Bank, United Nations • International donors: national and binational • International donors, NGOs • Local donors (state), eg government • Local donors (private), eg NGO • Local donors (private), eg national and regional companies
Project managers	• International • National • Regional • Local
Beneficiaries	• Proximate explicitly intended • Proximate implicitly intended • Remote explicitly intended • Remote implicitly intended

Table 5.3 *Participant stakeholder groups in a Nigerian project*

Donors	• International donors: European Union • International donors: ODA • Local donors (state): federal government
Project managers	• International: British Council • National: higher education bodies • Local: universities
Beneficiaries	• Proximate explicitly intended: universities • Proximate implicitly intended: students, lecturers, employers and local and international consultants • Remote explicitly intended: European higher education institutions • Remote implicitly intended: International higher education institutions

> *...while there may be great incentives and pressures to participate in a given coalition, it would not normally be appropriate to regard these as irresistible. Membership of a coalition is not, then, strictly determined by, for example, profession, class or gender, but typically involves some degree of choice.*
>
> Biggs (1995, p 11)

Choice itself may be limited by events, but this does not detract from Biggs's core point:

> *...it corresponds to the view commonly expressed by actors themselves that they have multiple identities and that different situations confront them with varying combinations of both opportunities and constraints.*
>
> Biggs (1995, p 11)

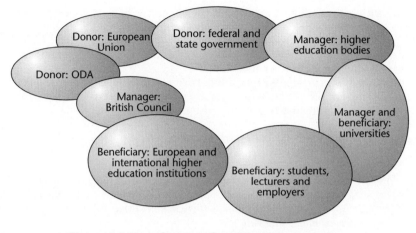

Figure 5.5 *Venn diagram of participant group overlap*

Since there are coalitions of groups in any given context, and since these coalitions will merge and change over time and context, so the need for reflective practice is emphasized and reemphasized; not only do the views of participating stakeholders change over time, their attitudes towards the core project context can also be at variance. On a recent project in China, the authors discovered the following breakdown in views on a project's core purpose between beneficiaries, donors and consultants (see Figure 5.6).

If the views between various participating groups in a project can vary on something as crucial and fundamental as the project goal, there is an even greater potential for differences of emphasis and comprehension on an idea as vague as sustainability. From the foregoing discussion it can be said that any

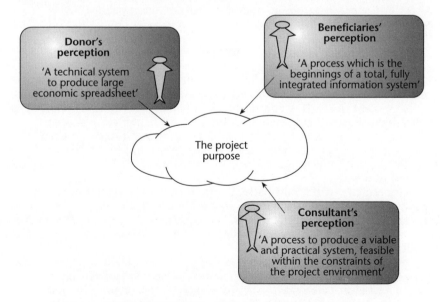

Figure 5.6 *Multiple views on a project's goal*

system which models and interprets the meaning of sustainability across diverse groups needs to keep some key ideas in mind:

- Coalitions of participant stakeholders in the project context merge and vary with changes in the context.
- Individuals and groups within and between coalitions will have differing perceptions of project goals and purposes and may well have significantly different view on what constitutes sustainability.

Guidelines for effectively including stakeholders would be of value. Ison has set out some principles for participation in projects:

> *Projects have the potential for more mutually satisfying outcomes when an invitation is extended to participate, and the resultant communication is based on conversations which acknowledge each person's experience as unique and valid.*
>
> *It is important to understand that experience and knowledge are related to context, and that it is necessary to attempt to appreciate particular contexts.*
>
> *Enthusiasm, which may be triggered , appears to be an emotional state predisposing individuals to action which is meaningful to that individual. Matters individuals are keen to take action on may or may not concur with 'experts' or institutional priorities. Pursuit of these matters in open, collaborative and critically informed ways can lead to locally meaningful and adaptive changes.*
>
> *Knowledge is both individually and socially constructed and because of this, processes are necessary to create learning networks. Pastoralist families and communities already do 'research' and 'extension' (share experience and knowledge – but they place importance on waiting to be asked).*
>
> *Diversity of experience, knowledge, research and 'extension' action is an asset of equal importance to the diversity of the biophysical environment.*
>
> Adapted from Ison (1993, pp 47–48)

These factors indicate again the vital importance of participation, and dialogue between actors. From such dialogue emerges new understandings (McClintock and Ison, 1994, p 6). This approach relates closely to the ideas relating to second and third order cybernetics as discussed in Chapter 4.

If we link together our earlier ideas about systems thinking in Chapter 4 with these ideas of participation, then we need to change our thinking about how development intervention works at a systemic level. Figure 5.7 provides one view of this.

Actors in the world, and participants or stakeholders in a project have separate or linked views of the reality in question. Such a reality can be seen as a system or wholeness of linked parts. Participation in a systemic sense is vital for us to understand and accommodate this range of views. Long exemplifies the idea:

> *...planned intervention cannot be adequately comprehended in terms of a model based upon step-by-step linear or cyclical progression [blueprint or process projects?]. Rather, it must be seen for what it is – an ongoing, socially constructed and negotiated process with unintended conse-*

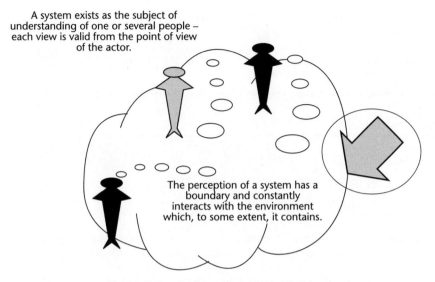

A system exists as the subject of understanding of one or several people – each view is valid from the point of view of the actor.

The perception of a system has a boundary and constantly interacts with the environment which, to some extent, it contains.

Figure 5.7 *A systems view of participation*

quences and side effects. *Applying this insight to the understanding of development projects and the differential responses they provoke requires the deconstruction of orthodox views of policy and planning and their capacity for steering change. We need alternative, more open and less presumptuous ... ways of thinking and acting. This task, we suggest, is best accomplished through the development of theory and methodology that is actor-orientated.*

Long (1992, pp 270–271); item in parenthesis added

In the above discussion we have introduced the context of projects and partici-pation in developing countries. In arguing for participation and the inclusive use of tools such as logical frameworks, we echo the in-country experiences of other groups – most notably, see Hardi and Zdan, 1997, where the development of participatory and reflective analytical mapping (PRAM) is described, includ-ing the use of LF on pages 135–137. Participatory projects are the primary context for our discussion and analysis of sustainability. We have linked project approaches to more and less systemic forms of analysis. We have reviewed a range of problems that arise when thinking about discrete social groups within projects, and have shown that mindsets change among the groups. This is the context in which we are to develop our approach to systemic sustainability analysis. In the following section we briefly introduce the overview of the idea prior to developing one view of its application in Chapter 6.

INTRODUCING THE SYSTEMIC SUSTAINABILITY ANALYSIS (SSA) IDEA

In Chapters 1, 2 and 3 we introduced the idea of the sustainability indicator (SI) and reviewed progress made so far in its development and application, and problems in practice. To get to this point we have spent considerable time

	State	Process (or driving force or control or pressure)	Response
What is happening right now – pre-project	✔	✔	—
Deliverable (project, implementation)	✔	✔	✔
Deliverer (institution)	✔	✔	✔

Figure 5.8 *What SIs we are going to make use of*

introducing the systems approach to thinking about complex issues and problems and also in reflecting on projects. We are not satisfied that narrow approaches to sustainability (such as SIs conceived in reductionistic frameworks) can work without reducing complexity, excluding valid and legitimate worldviews and reducing the area of concern to one which no longer represents the key issue of sustainability. Our belief is that participation, although difficult and problematic in itself, is preferable to projects which are determined top down. Our focus is subjective and systemic, but the tool for measuring SIs needs to be practical and useful. The key terms which we have used in defining the tool conform to principles of contemporary analysis in development studies (see Chambers, 1992; Cook, 1995; Slocum and Thomas–Slayter, 1995). For our purposes it should be a *rapid, participatory, qualitative, descriptive approach with a very clear explicit statement on what it is to be used for.* In developing the SSA, we make use of the SIs (shown in Figure 5.1) which relate most specifically to projects; these we describe in Figure 5.8.

To develop our SSA a number of stages will need to be undertaken. We set out the steps here in general terms and develop the detail in Chapter 6.

Step 1

Identify the stakeholders and the system. The first point in the development of our SSA is the establishment of the system to be measured. This would probably arise from a team of stakeholders. Tools for the development of such a team and the means to achieve cohesion and consensus are described elsewhere (see Thompson and Chudoba, 1994; Thompson, undated). The stakeholder group would identify the system to be reviewed with the SSA, being careful to establish that the system is a system. At this stage the system would probably refer to a task or main issue.

Step 2

Identify the main SIs. SIs are subjective and dependent upon the stakeholder group and the dominant viewpoint of that group. This needs to be affirmed and recognized by the group, but following this, in order to achieve a systems wide view of the item under analysis, SIs need to be drawn from a range of areas reflecting a holistic view. SIs should reflect items that need to be balanced in order for the system to be sustained.

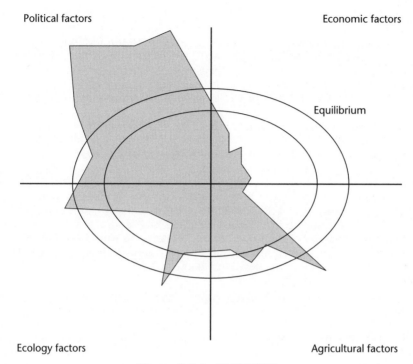

Political factors

Economic factors

Equilibrium

Ecology factors

Agricultural factors

Figure 5.9 *An SI AMOEBA*

Step 3

Identify the band of equilibrium. Measurement of SIs has dogged the literature. The focus of the approach advocated in this book is to provide an SSA which can be appreciated by a wide range of stakeholders without prior access to specialized measurement skills (as exemplified in some of the work undertaken in the Norwich 21 project). In fact, the entire exercise can be undertaken by the stakeholder group, based upon the agreed views and opinions of that group.

Step 4

The development of the AMOEBA. In Chapter 2 we first identified the AMOEBA approach of Ten Brink et al (1991). This was presented as a method to represent multiple SIs in one diagram and has since been developed in a systems manner (see Clayton and Radcliffe, 1996). However, in the Ten Brink et al presentation the AMOEBA was a fairly 'hard' and quantitative tool. Here we develop the AMOEBA, but in the light of the systemic and participative approaches detailed in Chapter 4.

So far the description given here is distinguished from other work only in that it is based on a holistic and systemic approach to the factors which define the sustainability of a project, and upon an explicit recognition of the subjectivity of the analysis and the ownership of stakeholders within the context of the analysis as a tool for reflection. Figure 5.9 shows the development of the original model into the AMOEBA as first described in Chapter 2. The main function of the AMOEBA is to provide a relatively instant presentation of the project's state of health in terms of its sustainability.

Step 5

The extension of the AMOEBA over time. Each time the AMOEBA is drawn from a project review by stakeholders it gives a snapshot indication of the sustainability of a project. Eventually the AMOEBA might move over the surface of the quadrants with each significant movement indicated by the SIs. The resulting 'AMOEBIC' analysis would provide two informing products:

* the overall tendency over time of four major aspects of the project context; and
* a rapid review of what is important now in terms of the stakeholder response to the information provided.

The AMOEBIC analysis set over time indicates continuance (or sustainability or equilibrium) within a given context from the standpoint of a stakeholder group. Of course, other groups might have other ideas and might be candidates for AMOEBIC analysis of their own. In all, the analysis would need to lead to informed discussion and action on items agreed to be in disequilibrium. This approach is described in more detail in Chapter 6.

Chapter 6

A Systemic Approach to Sustainability Analysis

Introduction and Objectives

The knowledge of local people ... has a comparative strength with what is local and observable by eye, changes over time, and matters to people. It has been undervalued and neglected. But recognizing and empowering it should not lead to an opposite neglect of scientific knowledge ... The key is to know whether, where and how the two knowledges can be combined, with modern science as servant not master, and serving not those who are central, rich and powerful, but those who are peripheral, poor and weak, so that all gain.

Chambers (1997, p 205)

Taking a number of cases, we develop the use of the systemic sustainability analysis (SSA) approach. (These cases do relate to real projects but the SIs are suggested.) In Chapters 1, 2 and 3 we discussed the range of approaches to sustainability indicators. In proposing SSA we work off the strengths and 'workable' elements which we have identified in these previous chapters (working with projects, clear boundaries and well-defined terms of reference). Based on this background and using systems approaches, we hope to demonstrate how sustainability indicators (SIs) can be arrived at within project contexts. Whether these are ultimately useful and valuable in project work will be discussed further in the next chapter.

To reiterate from the previous chapter, the five step procedure is:

(1) Identify the stakeholders with multiple views and the system in view.
(2) Identify the main SIs. SIs are subjective and dependent upon the stakeholder group and the dominant viewpoint of that group.
(3) Identify the band of equilibrium – the reference condition.
(4) Develop the AMOEBA. So far the description given here is distinguished from other work only in that it is based on a holistic and systemic approach to the factors which define the sustainability of a project, upon an explicit recognition of the subjectivity of the analysis, and the owner-

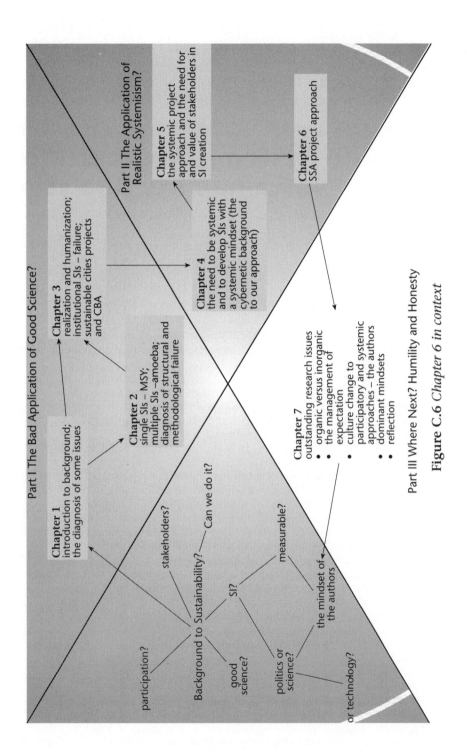

Part I The Bad Application of Good Science?

Chapter 1
introduction to background;
the diagnosis of some issues

Chapter 2
single SIs – MSY;
multiple SIs –amoeba;
diagnosis of structural and
methodological failure

Chapter 3
realization and humanization;
institutional SIs – failure;
sustainable cities projects
and CBA

Part II The Application of
Realistic Systemisism?

Chapter 5
the systemic project
approach and the need for
and value of stakeholders in
SI creation

Chapter 4
the need to be systemic
and to develop SIs with
a systemic mindset (the
cybernetic background
to our approach)

Chapter 6
SSA project approach

Chapter 7
outstanding research issues
• organic versus inorganic
• the management of
  expectation
• culture change to
  participatory and systemic
  approaches – the authors
  dominant mindsets
• reflection

Part III Where Next? Humility and Honesty

participation?

stakeholders? — Can we do it?

SI?

Background to Sustainability?

good
science?

politics or
science?

measurable?

the mindset of
the authors

or technology?

Figure C.6 *Chapter 6 in context*

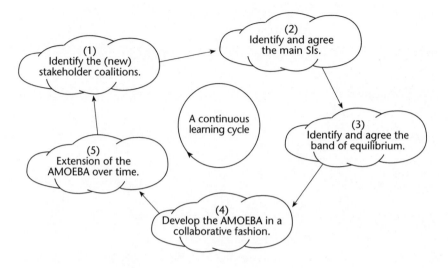

Figure 6.1 *The five steps to producing the SSA*

ship of stakeholders within the context of the analysis as a tool for reflection.
(5) Extend the AMOEBA over time. Each time the AMOEBA is drawn from a
project review by stakeholders it indicates the sustainability of a project.
Over a period of time the AMOEBA might be seen to move over the surface
of the quadrants with each significant movement indicated by the SIs.

These five steps are represented in Figure 6.1.
In this chapter we set out the five steps within a larger cycle of activity,
which is shown in Figure 6.2 and is given as follows:

• Find out how we are – a question of mood.
• Understand the context.
• Identify and invite the stakeholders.
• Be clear on methods.
• Do the five step procedure.
• Unpack the AMOEBA.
• Respond to 'good' AMOEBA.
• Respond to 'bad' AMOEBA.
• A stitch in time… an SI is a valuable thing.

As we develop the SSA we adopt an approach which is most closely related in
style to Western thinking derived from management studies (for instance, the
use of tools such as focus groups and stakeholder analysis). We feel that the
main elements of the approach can be applied in a number of ways (we include
elements dealing with participatory approaches originating in rural development practice). The teams who might make use of SSA may well decide on their
own tools for arriving at the outputs specified. The authors would be interested
to hear about methods used in different sustainability project contexts.
We do not think that the approach should be limited in scope and therefore we expect it to be applicable in a wide range of project contexts (such as
rural development, information systems, organizational learning).

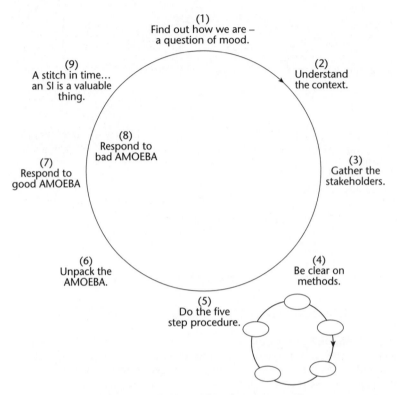

Figure 6.2 *SSA within the greater cycle*

FINDING OUT HOW WE ARE – A
QUESTION OF MOOD

Although the substantive aspect of this chapter which deals with the SSA idea is, we believe, innovative and groundbreaking, the background to SIs is not new. Some of the reasons for focusing on projects within the sustainability context are discussed in Chapter 3. We assume that the tool will be applied by development project planners and others in process or blueprint project contexts. At a later date we may direct our attention to the project context for project intervention, but in this exercise SSA provides project planners with a rounder and more holistic view of the sustainability context.

The first stage of identifying sustainability as an objective for development projects consists of the project team (those entrusted with the development intervention) familiarizing themselves with the mood of the context. Mood is a highly subjective term, but this is a subjective business; it is important to understand if the context is one of historic hope and goodwill or one of despair and anger, or if there is a mixture of both with neither predominating. We want to assess if the mood is positive or negative for future intervention. This is an analysis which can be done quickly in collaboration with local actors. It can be undertaken using some of the participatory rural development and rapid rural appraisal (PRA and RRA) techniques listed in Chapter 4 (for instance, night halt, linked to focus group). For the purpose of clarifying thinking, the resulting

	Positive	Negative
Now	• Strengths: ability to raise finances at a departmental level, ability of faculty to buy time and resources, ability of department to set out true research picture (all income earned).	• Weaknesses: commercialization of the department? current concentration on commercial ventures, problems with faculty operating as consultants, uneven distribution of rewards.
Later	• Opportunities: raise the profile of the department in the university, raise finances to develop projects and opportunities within the department, express the department as a practitioner as well as an academic unit increasing student interest in our courses.	• Threats: commercialism, divisive forces in the department (eg faculty unavailable for routine tasks in favour of more glamorous/interesting work), relative poverty and wealth among colleagues, academic work seen as being the poor relation.

Figure 6.3 *SWOT analysis of mood of a university department concerning a project to develop consultancy within the department*

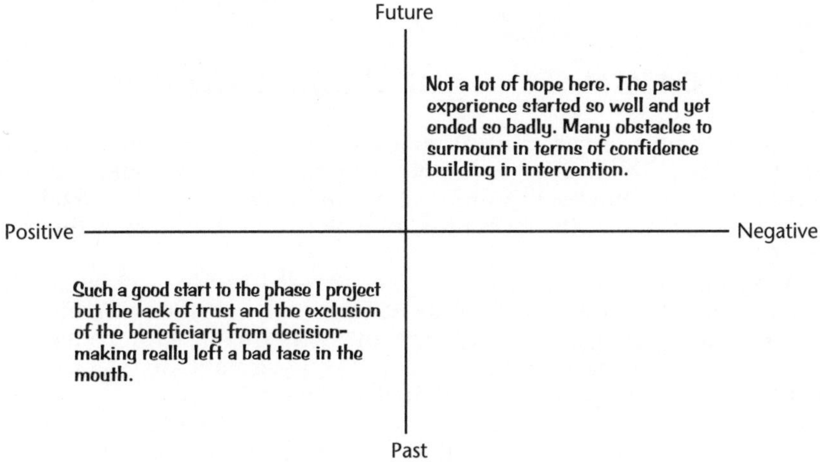

Future

Not a lot of hope here. The past experience started so well and yet ended so badly. Many obstacles to surmount in terms of confidence building in intervention.

Positive ———————————————————————— Negative

Such a good start to the phase I project but the lack of trust and the exclusion of the beneficiary from decision-making really left a bad tase in the mouth.

Past

Figure 6.4 *Quadrants with notes*

insights into the mood can be set out in a strengths, weaknesses, opportunities and threats (SWOT) table (see the example provided in Figure 6.3); more simply, thoughts can be put in a quadrant as the example shown in Figure 6.4.

The intention of the SWOT or the quadrant analysis is to provide insight and to attune the research team to the prevailing mood of the organization acting in the project context. Under normal circumstances the review would remain a personal exploration, and it would not be necessary to circulate the results for wider consultation although the resulting information may well be discussed openly with fellow participants in meetings at a later stage.

It should be born in mind that 'mood' is a very volatile and changing phenomena and variation relates to who is being approached and the 'baggage' of the person asking the questions. Therefore, understanding mood is an iterative process of drawing out major themes and recognizing that few assumptions should be made at this stage.

The outcome of this stage is insight into the potential for the people involved in the project intervention (some of whom may become actors and stakeholders) to deal with the issues and tasks which the context may throw up. It also provides an opportunity for emerging new themes and ideas. Traps and problems of perception will probably also arise. In the example which we described in Norwich 21 participation and local involvement have been central planks of the sustainable cities approach and have been applied and valued from the outset of the project – so much so that the European Sustainable Towns and Cities Campaign invited delegates from Norwich to run a workshop on participation at a recent meeting in Brussels. At the time of writing Norwich has made use of questionnaires, press releases, forums, conferences and round-table discussions to develop understanding and participation in SI development. The experience of the Norwich 21 campaign is that the primary initial requirement for any project in sustainability is 'political will'; following this, participation and sharing ownership of the project idea are vital.

Understanding the mood of those involved in the project context helps the future planning of intervention and the resulting analysis of sustainability: the baseline condition of the context is better understood and therefore the range of possible and feasible interventions can be adjusted accordingly.

UNDERSTANDING THE PROJECT CONTEXT

Understanding the project context builds upon the understanding of mood and, quite often, the two stages can be regarded as integrally linked or even indistinguishable. However, a different approach can be used to track the results of discussions with local people involved in the context – the 'rich picture'.

A word on rich pictures. The rich picture is a fairly unstructured tool for summarizing everything you know about a situation. It is used as a means to develop understanding of context in the soft systems approach set out briefly in Chapter 4. In the Open University course T301 – 'Complexity Management and Change', the rich picture is introduced as follows:

> ... the idea is to get from finding out to action by doing some systems thinking about the situation. To get started on this you need some efficient, economical and illuminating way of summarizing or repre-senting the situation in all its complexity. You do this by building a cartoon-type representation of it.
>
> Open University (1987, Block IV, p 21)

How the practitioner goes about this depends very much on his or her tastes and preferences. Elsewhere (Bell and Wood–Harper, 1998), one way of under-taking the process of rich picture construction is an approach based around four items: hard and soft (these can be thought of as representing formal and informal), structures and processes (things and activities). These four elements need to be identified in terms of core tasks and issues (things to do and problems) which are of concern to the project in question. An element of a complex rich picture is set out in Figure 6.5

The picture can be the personal, subjective portrayal of the researcher or of a group of stakeholders in the project. It is the method used by researchers to express their understanding of the project. As a personal tool, it is a useful, heuristic device. For example, it would be wrong to present the rich picture to a group of project stakeholders as the reality of the project. It is a device to help in a researcher's understanding of that context.

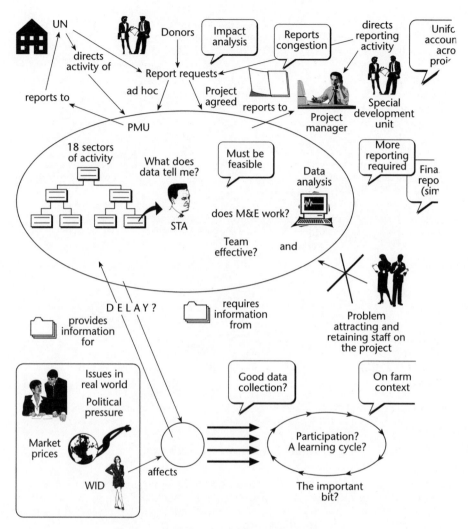

Figure 6.5 *Rich picture of a project context*

The objective is to capture the richness of the context and to be sure that formal and informal elements are represented in future project developments. A rich picture of the Norwich 21 experience as produced by the authors following discussions with the project staff is presented in Figure 6.6. (It should be noted this is the view and perspective of the authors and has had no input from the project staff themselves.)

By the end of the two stages the researcher should have a view (limited and partial, but a starting point) of the prevailing states of mind of those in the context and of the complexities of the project context itself. It should not be forgotten that the knowledge is gained *with* those in the context rather than *about* those in the context. Using the soft systems approach the researcher could (with stakeholders) draw out what might be major tasks and issues and provide a potential root definition or mission statement for the intervention (and transformation), which could be developed with all, or a representative

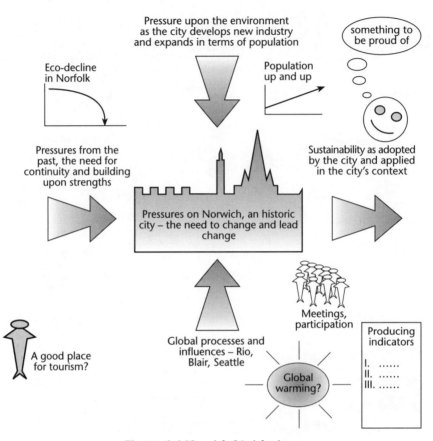

Figure 6.6 *Norwich 21 rich picture*

sample of, actors; from this the researcher could generate a participatory view of an action plan (for more ideas on this, see Checkland, 1984; Davies, 1989; Haynes, 1989). In this book we do not go into such detail, but leave it open for readers to engage with the literature.

Once the researcher feels a degree of comfort and familiarity with the context and the mood of the actors, the analysis can go on to describe the range and type of stakeholders.

IDENTIFYING AND INVOLVING THE STAKEHOLDERS

Participating, learning about and respecting the views of stakeholders is one of the most important aspects of the sustainability indicator approach which we set out in this book. As with the two previous stages, this can be seen in terms of a personal process of subjective learning and recording.

Process

The usual formula for a gathering of stakeholders is a workshop. However, a workshop is a device arising from recent Western management science and is not necessarily in keeping with the needs of a diverse group, which might include:

- donors and their agents;
- project managers;
- agents for relevant ministries;
- international NGOs;
- local NGOs;
- academics;
- representatives of local rural populations (a diverse group which may well include a cross-section of the local hierarchy);
- representatives of local urban populations (ditto);
- representatives from local organizations of other types (such as industrialists).

When considering the diversity of interests and experiences of this group, to suggest that the gathering can produce a workable and consensual plan for action by waving a magic wand called a 'workshop' may be oversimplistic, even naive. We need to consider what a workshop is. Some of the major themes in terms of duration, format and outcome are set out in Box 6.1.

As an alternative to the workshop, an event can be organized. This might be in the format of a meeting conforming to local custom (such as the 'Jirga' of the peoples of North-West Frontier Province in Pakistan). At such a locally recognized event, the topic of the development intervention itself can be set out and discussed in line with local custom.

The event format for developing the stakeholder grouping has a number of advantages over the more managerial workshop.

- The event is the known and expected context in which local people make communal decisions.
- The event is a statement of inclusiveness and should not be as likely to deter some groups and individuals from participating.
- The project outsiders (donors and managers) should be more practised at developmental meetings than local people; therefore, it is appropriate that they, as the representatives of intervention, should meet the potential beneficiaries of intervention on their own ground.

Of course, the event also has some potential negative elements:

- ownership of the event by powerful groups and individuals;
- relegation of minority and disempowered groups (low caste, women) to the position of onlooker;
- capacity for outcomes to be steered towards dominant interests.

Therefore, the design of the event and the individuals involved in that design process are of crucial importance for the integrity of the resulting stages. All formats have strengths and weaknesses, but in the case of the workshop or the event, these approaches include more views than can possibly be contained in the traditional top-down approach to project planning. The main outcome of the process of gathering stakeholders is to ensure that a sufficient and diverse

---

Box 6.1 *Some major elements of a workshop*

(1) Duration
The term workshop can stand for a wide range of gatherings. They can last from one to several days and can sometimes be 'rolling', leading to periodic meetings over several years.

(2) Format
They can include a wide range of devices to promote discussion and under-standing:
- presentations;
- small group work sessions;
- plenary sessions;
- visits;
- video/audio presentations;
- role play;
- discussion groups;
- soap boxing session (opportunities to provide a robust debate).

(3) Outcome
The point of all these devices is to bring the group together on a given topic and to arrive at joint understanding. In small, homogeneous groups (such as a workshop of project contract managers), the chances are that understanding can be rapidly developed. However, in large, heterogeneous groups there may be a need to develop sophisticated tools to gain a workable coalition of inter-ests. In this type of situation it may be necessary to begin with separate, smaller workshops (eg three or four groupings representing donors, managers and local and remote beneficiaries) and then for these workshops to develop their thinking in isolation, concerning major project topics, and to build towards a combined workshop at which nominated representatives for the diverse parties are to be included.

---

range of views is provided for the sustainability analysis process. It cannot be expected that all views will be equally represented, but it must be evident that a representative set of views are provided. The objective is that single views of project sustainability as shown in Figure 6.7 are converted to multiple views as set out in Figure 6.8.

The most challenging aspect of this stage of developing multiple views on sustainability, and therefore the resulting indices, is to regard each stakeholder group's set of views as legitimate and worthy of respect. An anecdote from Liz Edwards, assistant chief executive officer of Norwich City Council and senior activist in the Norwich 21 sustainability campaign, gives an indication of the value of the participatory approach to action:

> *When considering the best way of promoting public awareness of sustainability, we were strongly influenced by the Seattle experience of developing sustainability indicators with the community. We suggested a similar approach to our Norwich 21 steering group, to community representatives and to officers of Norwich City Council, and had no difficulty in promoting the concept of a set of indicators which could be used to measure progress over time. The message which came back to*

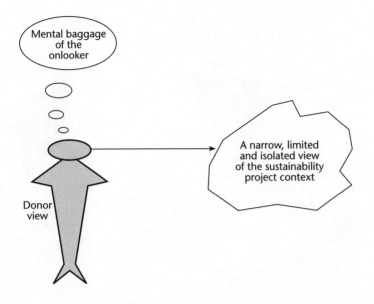

Figure 6.7 *Single view of sustainability*

us repeatedly was : 'keep it simple; keep them short; use plain language and symbols wherever possible'. On this basis we pared down our original long list of indicators to a manageable list of 21 and presented them to a conference in April 1997. The list was warmly received but we were specifically asked to add indicators for art and culture – which we duly did.
Liz Edwards (17 December, 1997), private communication

In the case of Norwich 21 the conference was used as a means to share and develop understanding of the sustainability indicator concept. Further indicators arose from this, including a sense of ownership and responsibility over the resulting activity. We shall return to the theme of simple and short indicators later in this chapter.

Learning, Reflecting and Recording

When the views of all stakeholders have been gathered together, they need to be included in an overall framework for reference, learning and reflection. The method described here is one which is relevant for consultant and management groups who are taking ownership of the overall project flow. The approach can be quite exclusive and 'expert driven', but this does not have to be the case. Stakeholders can (and ideally should) provide their own assessment, although this can be time consuming. The approach set out is based on the work of Team Technologies (1995) and is described in the TeamUp methodology and software. Table 6.1 provides a view of a stakeholder analysis spreadsheet.

Although specific details are not required of this project, it is useful to describe the spreadsheet in outline:

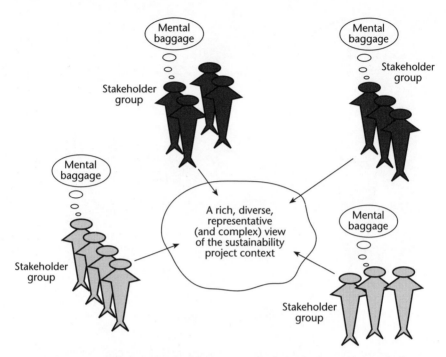

Figure 6.8 *Multiple views of sustainability*

- Stakeholders are given by name in column 1.
- A brief description of the stake which they hold is given in column 2.
- Column 3 contains a plus (+) or minus (-) depending on whether the stake is positive or negative in terms of the success of the project by this organizing group ('n' means neutral).
- Column 4 is the value of the stakeholder. I explain this in the footnotes but 1 would indicate that the stakeholder was non-essential, whereas 5 would mean that the individual or group is critical. It should be noted that these are subjective values applied by the project managing group making use of the spreadsheet. They are not intended to be definitive evaluations but guides for future actions and the assessment of behaviour, and in recognition of variation in the size of stakeholders and stakes.
- Column 5 is the power of the stakeholder and is assessed in much the same way as column 4. A score of 1 would indicate an 'appreciation' of the project, whereas 6 would indicate that the stakeholder has complete control.
- Column 6 provides a view of the overall impact for a stakeholder. This element of the stakeholder analysis approach is the most subjective and potentially misleading: it is produced by multiplying V (column 4) and P (column 5) together. Be wary of what the numbers tell you, but as a general rule of thumb any stakeholder or stakeholder group with a score of over 20 points in terms of impact must be taken seriously. Major stake-holders are set out in italics.
- Column 7 is the activity set related to stakeholders to respond to their potential impact on the project. This is a very important aspect of the table and should not be neglected. As any project develops over time, it

Table 6.1 Stakeholder analysis spreadsheet

Stakeholder	Stake in the project	Overall effect on CFAA system (+, -, ? or n)	Value	Power	Impact*	Activity which is required to assist the stakeholder in the M&E
Donor						
Policy view	Donor to project – need to know impact	++	4	5	20	Include in all discussions. Use LF
Local officer for donor	Local interest in project impacts	+	3	3	9	Include in discussion on preliminary draft
Related donor agency						
Director	Sub-donor – interest in success	+	4	5	20	Include in discussion on preliminary draft
Project manager	Instrumental in project development	+	4	3	12	Include in drafting
Related Chinese agency						
Director	Financial performance indicators	+	4	5	20	Include some financial analysis, MS and National systems?
Sub-Director	Quarterly and monthly reports	+	4	5	20	Review possibilities of monthly more regular reports
Project staff						
Chief	Frustrated by data excess – need systems	+	5	5	25	Include focus, brevity and prioritized system
Staff 1	Will pick up implementation activities	++	5	4	20	System must be feasible
Staff 2	Co-worker in MIS – no training	+	3	3	9	Ditto – as co-worker
Staff 3	Frustrated but vital in participation	+	4	2	8	Valuable person to include in M&E set-up
Related agencies to CFAA						
Agency 1	Need proformas for collection + funds	++	3	3	9	Assist with proformas for data collection + assist with participation
Agency 2	Problems with participation	n	2	2	4	Use objective measures?
Beneficiaries of the system						
Beneficiary 1	Is the money being used for beneficiaries?	+?	2	5	10	Show that monitoring is active and project is fair
Beneficiary 2	Monitoring must be participative	+?	2	5	10	Demonstrate participative aspects
Beneficiary 3	Wants to participate in project	+	2	3	6	Include beneficiaries in impact analysis
Consultant						
Simon Bell	Helps to design the system	+	2	4	8	Need to include range of PIs – impact, financial, etc

Notes: * Major stakeholder impact given in italics. Power is judged as follows: Impact = V×P. complete control = 6; significant control = 5; significant influence = 4; moderate influence = 3; low influence = 2; appreciation = 1. Value is judged as follows: critical = 5; Essential = 4; Necessary = 3; Desirable = 2; Non-essential = 1.

will be seen that stakeholders vary in their scores and actions and reactions to them will also vary.

Taken in this way the analysis provides a view of stakeholders (often not shown in the rich picture of subsequent analysis) and provides a means of developing an agenda of action to respond to needs.

BEING CLEAR ON METHODS

By this stage of the process, the facilitator, or team of agents driving on the process, should have a fairly clear perception of the project context, the primary issues and tasks within the context, the range of stakeholders within the context, and their relative weighting (as well as insights into the various agendas). It is important that this information is not held back and used as a resource purely for the facilitator. The information is 'case history' and is valuable for all those involved in the exercise of arriving at sustainability indicators.

It is important within the project process to be sure that all members of the team who are to devise the SSA are clear on the range of methods and likely outcomes (in form, not content) which are expected. In this book we advocate a range of techniques, some of which may be well understood, many of which may be quite novel to the participants in the exercise. It is useful to spend some time in clarifying what is being done, why it is being done and what is the expected outcome of each stage. The participants may well have their own views on the manner in which techniques are applied or may be able to substitute or supplement techniques with ideas of their own. The process for the team is a learning one and depends upon the ability of all members to make contributions and to gain ownership of the overall process. Indicators themselves are often new and unclear and need introducing. SIs are the result of global processes and may appear irrelevant and alien to many stakeholders. The more that can be done to make their appearance relevant and useful at this stage helps avoid rejection or avoidance of the project at a later date. While attempting to establish this process of SI development as a process which gains wide agreement, it should not be forgotten that the driving force behind the global SI phenomena is the outcome of global political forces; this in turn is remote from most people's lives. Since the background is now complete, the project can move onto the SSA process itself.

THE FIVE STEP PROCEDURE

Identify the Stakeholders with Multiple Views and the System in View.

So far, the process we have been describing has developed our background understanding. The first step in developing the SSA itself is to identify and bring together the stakeholders in the project and to gain a clear vision of the sustainability system which is expected to emerge from the project process.

Processes for developing shared vision and learning teams are described elsewhere (this is dealt with in considerable depth by Senge et al, 1994, whose approach we described in Chapter 4). For the purposes of the approach which we set out here, the main factors to keep in mind are the following:

- In order to represent the diverse interests which are within any project scenario, stakeholders should ideally represent dominant and non-dominant mindsets within donor, manager, recipient and beneficiary groups (and the coalitions of these groups).
- Stakeholders agree and 'vote into' the participatory group.
- There is an explicit recognition by all stakeholders that the outcome of the project process is a sustainable system (no need for detail at this time, but plenty of need for a hands-on facilitation process in agreeing, firstly, on the group's understanding of what a sustainable system is and then agreeing to it in principle).

The gathered stakeholder group is the basis for all future decisions at this time (the group may change in future iterations of the process). The sustainable system, agreed to in principle, now needs to be developed as a root definition of the project process (see Checkland, 1981; Checkland and Scholes, 1990).

The term root definition has a specific meaning in systems terms and is derived from the soft systems approach described in Chapter 4. As we apply it here, the root definition is the 'vision' of the system which we wish to create (which, as described in some of the sustainability literature, can be thought of as the reference condition or target, but also contains the notion of transformation). Normally the root definition is contained in a paragraph which should have the following elements:

- The *customer* of the system: this can be multilayered. The customer may be the person for whom the system will provide benefit – the beneficiary – the customer can also be the person who is paying for the transformation; this can be the donor who provides the capital and the beneficiary who provides the labour and will sustain disruption and change during the lifetime of the project. The team needs to be sure who is the customer and what the customer's expectations are.
- The *actors* who will engage in the work of the project: these may include people who are also customers. For example, the actors may be the project managers but may also be members of the beneficiary group who will enact the change procedures which the sustainability project is focused upon.
- The third element of the root definition, the most critical for the purpose of the project, is the project's *transformation*. This will be the process or processes of change which are to arise and which we wish to understand and (to some extent) measure. Later we will describe what we mean by impact and process SIs.
- The fourth element is the *worldview* or set of assumptions behind the root definition. These are the underlying and working assumptions which are shared by the team. Assumptions might relate to the project's expected delivery, fears about the impact of certain aspects of the project, concerns over the boundary of the project, and its expected impact beyond the immediate project area.
- The *owner* of the transformation is the fifth element. Owners, customers and actors can all be linked, depending upon the nature of the project. They are all stakeholders.
- The last element of the root definition is to set out the *environmental constraints* under which the project must work. These may also be the first indication of the sustainability factors which the project team needs to address and agree upon.

These six factors, customer, actor, transformation, worldview, owner and environmental constraints combine to form the acronym CATWOE. The CATWOE criteria should all be in the root definition statement, for example:

*This project is owned by **owner** who deals with the **transformation**. The core agents involved in the project will be **actor** and the underlying thinking behind the project is **worldview**. The customer for the project is **customer** and the project will operate under the following sustainability issues and **environmental constraints**.*

By the end of this stage the team is gathered and the basic vision or reference condition of the project is agreed upon. The next task is to identify the main SIs which will measure the project's impact.

Identify the Main SIs

SIs are subjective and dependent upon the stakeholder group and the dominant viewpoint of that group, but by including representatives across the project the intention is that the SIs conform to a holistic worldview. In Chapter 1 we discussed a range of quantitative approaches to SIs. These usually relate to the precise measurement of the project's features which can be measured and which provide a view of long-term (anything from five to 20 years) sustainability. The IISD describe sustainability as:

> *Sustainable development is not a 'fixed state of harmony'. Rather, it is an ongoing process of evolution in which people take actions leading to development that meets their current needs without compromising the ability of future generations to meet their own needs.*
>
> Hardi and Zdan (1997, p 9)

At this point it is important to describe what we expect an SI to indicate. In Chapters 2 and 5 we described 'state' and 'process' SIs and explored the current interest in the development of process SIs, in particular, as a means to explain sustainable or unsustainable activities and outcomes. Here we argue that state SIs should largely describe project impacts whereas process SIs are more exploratory and analytical. We suggest that state SIs of impact, being largely descriptive, are relatively less difficult to agree upon and initiate. They provide the 'snapshot' of sustainable development. However, process SIs, linked to state SIs of impact, while being more complex and difficult to initiate, provide projects with more information about the factors affecting the achievement or non-achievement of sustainable development. Figure 6.9 demonstrates the use of state SIs over time. Figure 6.10 indicates how process SIs relate to state SIs in our approach.

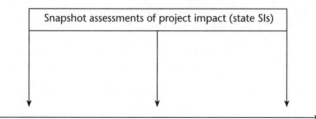

Figure 6.9 *State SIs*

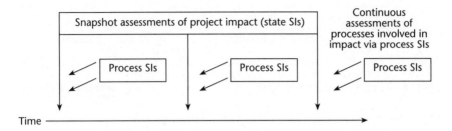

Figure 6.10 *State and process SIs*

We therefore argue that state SIs are the primary measure applied to sustainability projects, but that process SIs may be developed at a later stage by the project team in order to help the team understand what the state SIs are describing – and thus to explain exactly what influences and drives the state SIs.

Beyond state and process SIs, we could differentiate between internal and external process SIs (that is, internal and external to the project boundary). Internal process SIs would necessarily be controlled by the project. External SIs would deal with factors beyond the project's direct control as shown in Figure 6.11.

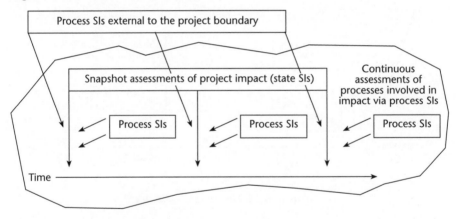

Figure 6.11 *Internal and external process SIs*

The project's ability to control process SIs will vary and in some cases internal process SIs may be less controllable than external process SIs. We might represent the degree of control in terms of thickness of arrow, as shown in Figure 6.12.

This may all seem rather theoretical and abstract; to develop the concept Figure 6.13 shows the way in which state, internal and external process SIs might be considered in terms of the River Cynon example discussed in Chapter 2. Note that in this example we set out SIs for the purpose of explanation only.

In terms of developing SIs, some practical issues need to be explored. As we have already mentioned, state SIs (SSI) of impact are relatively less difficult to develop, whereas external process SIs (PSI) are more difficult. A project team might begin the SI development with SSIs and then develop related PSIs as the team becomes well grounded, trust increases and clear insight in the project process correspondingly improves. Therefore, without being prescriptive, we would expect the range of SIs to develop over time, moving from SIs of impact to

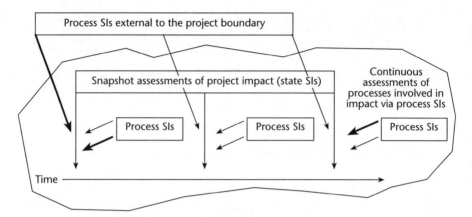

Figure 6.12 *Relative controllability of internal and external process SIs*

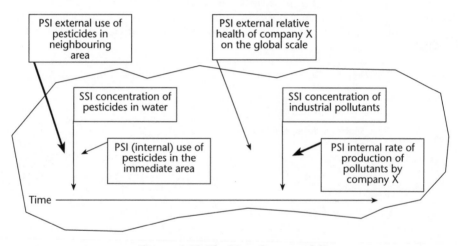

Figure 6.13 *The River Cynon and SIs*

SIs which measure processes. The analysis of the team itself and its sustainability is an issue requiring the ability of the team to reflect and analyse its own behaviour. We shall return to force SIs in Chapter 7. The discussion relating to SIs, and taking the discussion forward from theory to practice, is shown in Figure 6.14.

At the outset the indicators should gauge whether the project is meeting its impact criteria and is achieving the transformation as set out in the root definition, without – at the same time – leaving the resource for the project 'depleted or permanently damaged' (from a definition of sustainability taken from Websters *New International Dictionary*).

To this end we need to clearly define SIs and to be aware that in so far as SIs comprise different types (as described in Chapters 1, 2, 3, 5 and above), so they describe different things and indicate differences in the maturity of the project in question.

In line with the critique made in Chapter 3 of an overemphasis on institutional sustainability, we focus in this chapter on SIs of impact and process relating to the deliverable – the actions and transformations of the project.

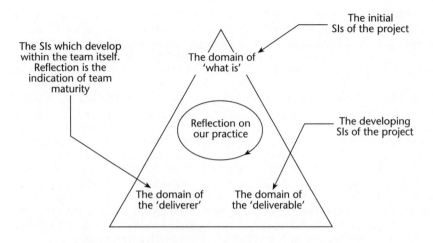

Figure 6.14 *Different types of SIs evolving in the project*

Examples of state and process SIs are provided in Chapter 1. The means to achieving an understanding of the nature of SIs are many and varied and the reader may wish to make use of well-known approaches. In this book we approach the process of identifying SIs by using an explicit 'Kolb' learning cycle. The cycle is shown in Figure 6.15.

The cycle can be set out as follows.

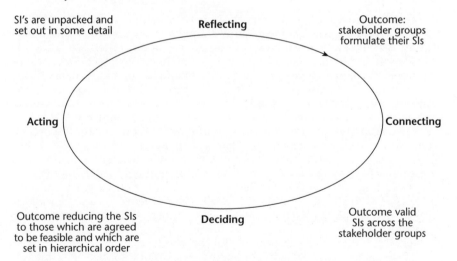

Figure 6.15 *The SI learning cycle*

Reflecting

The team breaks up into groups, reflecting the different and possibly disparate stakeholder groups within the context. Each group reflects upon the initial state SIs needed from their perspective. A group of scientists, social scientists and policy-makers might come up with the type of indictors which we identified within Chapters 1, 2 and 3. Local people may come up with indicators related to conceptions of welfare and social improvement (quality of life) which are not strictly measurable in an absolute sense; see Chapter 1. Donors might come up with indicators of profitability or returns on loans (see Chapter 3). Each group has to keep in mind that despite subjective interest and personal bias, there needs to be a 'meshing' between the transformation and the identification of factors which would indicate permanent damage to resources within the project context. The question to be addressed is: 'What are we going to change and what might this impact upon?' Each group would probably benefit from the assistance of a facilitator who would be responsible for keeping the conversation on track and who would act as a reporter for the next stage. The outcome of this stage is the development of a set of indicators. We are not concerned with their feasibility or contentiousness. The focus is on good indicators which tell us if the project's long-term sustainability is being achieved. The outcome is a set of indicators which are focused but may well be 'outrageous' (in the sense of reaction to them by other stakeholders). For example, in a project in higher education in West Africa, stakeholders suggested indicators which were plainly not feasible. They related to counting students in classrooms in their use of the seating throughout each semester. However, although the method devised by the stakeholders was not feasible (in terms of employing 'counters' and in verifying the results), raising the issue encouraged debate, which in turn resulted in feasible (if less ambitious) indicators being produced by the entire project team at a later date. We will deal with the notion of long-term sustainability shortly.

Connecting

At this stage the team makes connections between disparate aspects arrived at so far. The various groups come together and present the SIs which have arisen. The SIs will represent a vast cross-section of view and counterview. They will include soft and hard methodologies and no methodology at all. There will be a range of thinking processes which cover the range of stakeholders in the project context. The project team has voiced its variations in approach and thinking during the opening stages, but it is at this stage that real differences of approach emerge and potential areas of conflict and outcome arise. This is to be expected, although it also requires skilful facilitation to help the process going and to keep people involved. From a study made in Pakistan (Bell, 1996) it was found that even highly diverse groups of stakeholders could be brought together to form useful focus groups, providing mutually satisfying insights. The variations noted here are the real variations which exist within most projects and which are often not addressed. The connecting stage is a learning opportunity for all involved in the project to understand what development, transformation and sustainability mean to different people with different mindsets and different needs from the project effort.

There are few short ways of developing state SIs of impact. The facilitators need to map out (usually using 'post-it' pads), the core SIs (irrespective of feasibility and cost). The team then needs to agree on the following questions:

- Is the SI real? Does it exist for all the team or is it an idea which some of the team do not recognize? This is often a problem, and so this is the first question. The SIs as quantitative measures produced by technocrats often mean nothing to local peoples and vice versa. An SI which is not perceived as realistic needs describing, discussing and explaining. At the end of this process it may well be real to all or it may need to be changed or dropped.

- Does the SI tell us something about the impact of the project upon the context?
- Does the SI, reviewed over time, tell us something about the sustainability of the context? This is an important point. Sustainability involves the maintenance or continuity of project outcomes over time. An SI can relate to a short-term gain (such as yield increases due to massive fertilizer input), but such an SI will quickly become redundant when the project ceases and fertilizer is no longer available. The focus of this stage in the SSA process is to provide the project with impact SIs which will be collectable, viable and feasible for an indefinite period. If this is not the case, the SI itself is non-sustainable. Selected SIs should show little redundancy (ideally) and be robust in terms of long-term durability. To some extent this means that SIs provide projects with continuity beyond their life time, and this in turn means that the SI encourages sustainability.

As each SI is discussed by the team it is either adopted – in which case it appears on a post-it on the wall – or it is changed so that it can be adopted, or it is dropped. The end of the connecting stage is for the team to learn about the whole project context, to develop wide-ranging state SIs and to agree to the validity (not yet feasibility) of these SIs. Therefore, the outcome is a set of 'valid' SIs. Figure 6.16 shows an example of a post-it collection of 'valid' SIs based on the Norwich Agenda 21 programme.

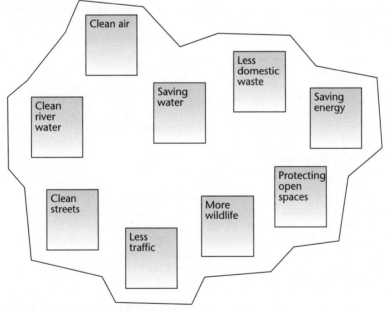

Source: adapted from the Norwich 21 SI list in Table 3.2

Figure 6.16 *A collection of 'valid' SIs*

Deciding

This is the third stage of the learning cycle. During this stage the issues of feasibility and hierarchy are dealt with by the team. It is agreed that the SIs are valid; now each SI is looked at in terms of the following:

- Can we get at or construct the information which we need for the SI? We do not necessarily need to know about data for quantitative SIs. We are not assuming that all SIs are quantitative. Instead, we need to know if we can get at data of a qualitative or quantitative format (eg yield data or conversations with farmers).
- What is the cost of getting at this information? Part of the issue of feasibility is cost. There are numerous ways of measuring a project for impact or sustainability, but they are of little use if the cost involved in getting the information is disproportionate to the value of the information gained.
- How important an SI is this? Does it rate a position in the top ten, 20 or 30? This may seem an arbitrary operation but it is important. Part of the process of gaining clear and valuable SIs is to focus on the key sustainability issues which give the greatest insight into the project. Fifty or 60 SIs would require a considerable effort from a small project. As a rule of thumb, 20 to 30 should be adequate so long as they cross the full (whole) breadth of the project's concerns and stakeholder interests. In this sense we are ranking SIs in terms of importance (see the River Cynon example discussed in Chapter 2 – are trout more important to local people than chiron? – or Ten Brink et al's AMOEBA: are bottle-nosed dolphin more important than sea potato?). Because this analysis is explicitly subjective, we are building in the importance the project team and wider stakeholders put upon the SIs.

At the end of this deciding stage the team should be confident that they have outlined the top 30 or so SIs which the project will use as its measures of sustainability in terms of impact (eventually this will include process).

Acting

This is the fourth element of the learning cycle – which in our approach is concerned with unpacking each of the selected and verified SIs in some detail. To be able to establish equilibrium, which is the main focus of the next stage, each of the agreed SIs needs to be taken back to the small stakeholder groups and worked through in detail. Core elements which should be worked out here are:

- What is the procedure for producing the SI?
- What is the expected band of output from the SI? This is vital. What does the subgroup expect the SI to produce? For example, for a yield-related SI, what would be the maximum and the minimum yields which one might expect? If it were a focus group of farmers discussing the uses of scrub land, what would be the extremes which such a group might produce? If it were a group of managers describing their responses to automation, what might be the extreme which the team would expect?

After the state SIs have been identified, we need to identify the major processes which influence or 'drive' that SI. This is an important element of the unpacking. With the unpacking of the SIs, this stage of the approach is completed. Considerable progress has now been made:

- There is a clear vision of the project and agreement on the basis for SIs.
- A representative stakeholder group has been formed.
- A view of the sustainable project transformation has been arrived at.
- Each set of stakeholders has agreed upon a common store of SIs related to the project transformation.

- The SIs have been explained to the team as a whole, and relevant and feasible SIs have been agreed upon as the basis for the SSA.
- The potential range of responses for each SI have been agreed upon.

The next stage is to consider what measures conform to being sustainable (the target reference position?)

Identify the Band of Equilibrium/the Reference Position

Equilibrium is a contentious phrase with many applied meanings derived from academics and practitioners who work on the theme of sustainability. We take our definition from Webster: 'a: a state of intellectual or emotional balance: poise b: a state of adjustment between opposing or divergent influences or elements' (Webster, 1995).

At the end of the last stage, the small groups of stakeholders were unpacking each of the SIs. During this process the range for each SI was established. For example, consider an SI which covers a local population's response to healthcare. The SI has been provided by local stakeholders from rural communities involved in a project focusing on infrastructure improvements in a developing country. The SI is centred on the perception of local focus groups on the establishment of better health within their families. The continuum for the SI is agreed as taking in a range of related factors and processes, such as child mortality and prevalence of infant disease. The bottom of the continuum would indicate that local healthcare was as bad as ten years ago when the area was subject to prolonged drought. The top of the range for the SI would be to indicate that the factors were of little to no concern. The focus group would be senior women within the community. In this case the band of equilibrium, which would indicate a sustainable state of affairs, was a qualitative assessment (see Figure 6.17) with the focus group.

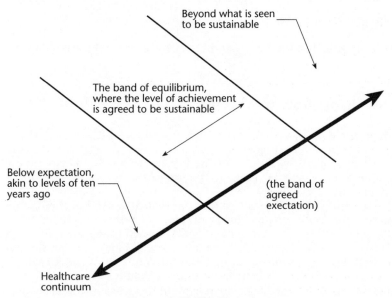

Figure 6.17 *The SI continuum*

As we show in Figure 6.17, equilibrium is integrally related to the management of people's expectations. We deal with this issue more fully in Chapter 7.

The equilibrium band is reasonably well expressed in terms of its definition 'below expectation' range. It is not so easy to define equilibrium in terms of 'beyond the sustainable'. It will be the job of a social organizer working on the project to tease out this response from the focus group. The equilibrium band sets out the target or reference position for the project, but this band should be more realistic and useful than those used by Ten Brink et al and described in Chapter 2: it has been agreed upon and is known to be relevant to local people. It is an intrinsic target for the project and the indicator is thus defensible in encouraging the necessary behaviour for its achievement.

Another SI might relate to sustainable levels of education. This might be more quantitatively arrived at. Because statistics on attendance and achievement are readily available in the project area, the SI provides a quantitative measure of what is less than sustainable equilibrium in education. The process is very much one of expectation management. The figures are worked out with the local community who know what is possible (given the other callings on the children, such as farm labour and other paid employment). A second continuum is produced for this new SI. The team needs to provide such a continuum for each state and process SI, indicating a broad band of responses (qualitative or quantitative) which indicates a sustainable level of progress. The team also needs to produce the outline of responses which are non-sustainable in terms of overachieving or under achieving from the band.

This can be a lengthy process with a great deal of discourse within the team about what is and is not the limit of the equilibrium (and therefore 'sustainability') band. This is to be expected. While researching for and writing this book, the authors have been struck by the difficulty that various academic and practitioner communities have had in coming to any agreement about what constitutes sustainability. This is not because of perverse pride on the side of the communities; rather it is because sustainability is a difficult term to tie down. Nevertheless, time spent at this stage on this problem is time saved for the project as a whole. We suggest that understanding what each SI measures and what each SI means by sustainability will lead to insights into what is realistically achievable within the project context.

The output of this stage of the approach is substantial detail on, and ranking of, the state and process SIs and the establishment of the equilibrium band.

The Development of AMOEBA

The concept of AMOEBA as set out in Chapters 2 and 5 (and as extended and developed under a different label, for example in the work of Clayton and Radcliffe, 1996) is relatively simple. We use it here as a device to map out the series of SIs as a simple graphic guide to the sustainability of outcomes of the project in question.

In the previous section we showed how, for each SI, a band of equilibrium was indicated on a continuum ranging from severely lower than equilibrium to substantially beyond equilibrium. The AMOEBA is used to represent these SIs in their initial state – see Figure 6.18. The three general bands are: not sustainable by deficit, not sustainable by surfeit and the equilibrium band itself. SIs can be placed anywhere in the circle but in our example, which relates to a multisectoral development project, we group SIs in four categories of economic,

Economic SIs

Social SIs

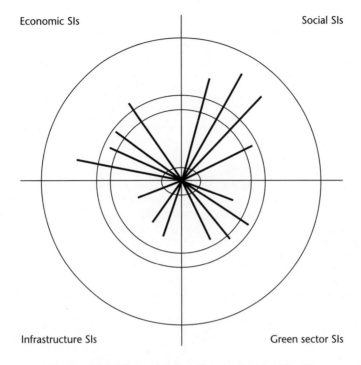

Infrastructure SIs

Green sector SIs

Figure 6.18 *The equilibrium band – drawing the SIs*

social, green sector and infrastructure. The SIs can now be used to produce the AMOEBA; this is represented in Figure 6.19.

In our example we have an immediate visual expression of the project, with a clear view that infrastructure and green sector SIs indicate that the project is not achieving sustainable outcomes. In contrast, the social indicators show that the project is overextending itself and producing SIs which indicate that the outcomes are unsustainable. The economic SIs are more favourable.

AMOEBAE may well not be as neat as this one. Clustering the SIs may be more difficult and the resulting SIs may be much less consistent; for example, see Figure 6.20 relating to an IT project.

The team now has an information product, the means to produce this, agreed SIs, agreed and verified feasible rules for the production of the SIs, and, most importantly, a team which will continue to produce the AMOEBA over time.

Snapshot by Snapshot Extension over Time.

Each time the AMOEBA is drawn from a project review by stakeholders, it gives an indication of the sustainability of a project in a snapshot. Over a period of time the AMOEBA might move over the surface of the quadrants, with each significant movement indicated by the SIs. As the project progresses the AMOEBA can be drawn and redrawn, with attention paid to the indicators which are not in equilibrium. An example of three such AMOEBA is shown in Figure 6.21.

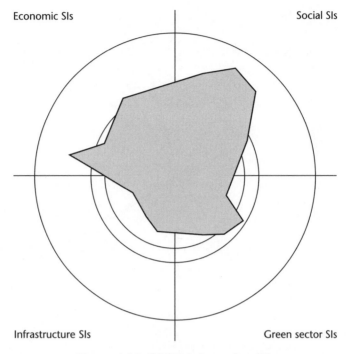

Figure 6.19 *AMOEBA drawn from SIs*

AMOEBA can change shape. Depending upon the project and the decision-making of the team, they can move over the quadrant surface as project focus changes – for example, from green issues to infrastructure and back. In Figure 6.21 the project team has attempted to even out the peaks and troughs and to produce a more even shape. The more the AMOEBA imitates a perfect circle within the equilibrium band, the more the project tends towards sustainability. We would, however, disagree with any tendency (such as that shown by Ten Brink et al with the ecological Dow Jones indicators), to reduce the complexity of the AMOEBA to a single value: such as sustainability = 42, as illustrated in Chapter 2. This loses detail and could mean that vital indicators are ignored; thus their reason for being produced in the first place is negated. The effective use of the AMOEBA as an indicator of moving towards or away from stakeholder understanding of sustainability is the basic theory behind the AMOEBA and the equilibrium band – it should be the informing principle behind the approach.

UNPACKING THE SI ANALYSIS

As with all presentational aids, AMOEBA does not tell the whole story about the project in question. It is a means of displaying how SIs are performing according to a common format. However, we intend the AMOEBA to be an informing device, the results of which will form future action. At a simplistic level, the ideal AMOEBA is a perfect circle within the equilibrium ring; but this is also a problematic point as we shall see. The action arising from analysing AMOEBA can be preventative or corrective depending on whether the SIs show an existing problem or a tendency towards a problem. It is important in all

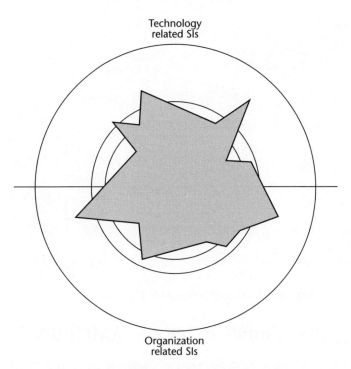

Technology
related SIs

Organization
related SIs

Figure 6.20 *IT project AMOEBA*

project developments to recognise that the AMOEBA is a device for presentation and not a representation of reality. We have tried, through including
stakeholders and developing a wide range of SIs based upon all kinds of
viewpoints, to make the AMOEBA represent a cross-section of sustainability
issues within the project context – but this does not mean that the AMOEBA is
anything more than an artificial gauge which will be more or less correct in
each case. Use the results, but be wary. While Norwich 21 has not made use of
AMOEBA at the time of writing, the experiences of the city are relevant and
another anecdote from Norwich 21 is appropriate for inclusion here.

> *Our task will now be to retain the concept of simplicity in order to meet
> our main goal – that of engaging the general public in the concept of
> sustainability and giving them something concrete to measure it by.
> Already certain interest groups are calling for sophistication with quali-
> tative as well as quantitative data – despite the obvious difficulties. The
> key will be to remember our audience and to listen to what they have to
> say about the purpose and practicalities of developing measurements
> that chart the progress of their community over time.*
> Liz Edwards (17 December, 1997), private communication

The authors would like to express their complete agreement with the sentiment
of Liz Edwards's statement. The idea that local communities should own and
develop their own view of sustainability via SIs is at the root of this book.

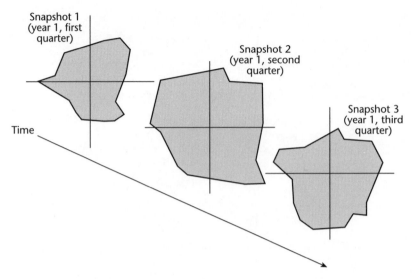

Figure 6.21 *Extending the AMOEBA over time*

RESPONDING TO 'GOOD' AMOEBA

An AMOEBA which shows a strong tendency towards equilibrium in all sectors indicates that the areas which we are monitoring appear to be progressing in a satisfactory way. However, this needs to be considered from at least two further standpoints – time and alternative view.

- In terms of time, an SI or a collection of SIs are a snapshot and nothing more. It is only when there is a selection of AMOEBA to make comparisons that the critical issue of change over time will be apparent.
- Alternative view: when all is well in most sectors, the right questions in the rights areas are not always being asked. It is always sound to review the questions you are asking and the people and events you are focusing upon. A comfortable AMOEBA or a string of AMOEBA indicating that things are going well should prompt the question: 'What else might we look at or what might we look at differently?'

RESPONDING TO 'BAD' AMOEBA

A 'bad' AMOEBA can be seen as a good thing; the system is working and your question-asking process is throwing back problem areas where sustainability is not being achieved. If the measurement over time continues to highlight this there will be a need for remedial action. Various lines of approach can be adopted, but we suggest that we make use again of the soft systems tools for developing an action plan. The checklist of responses to bad SIs can be set out as follows:

- Identify SIs which are 'poor' by deficit of surfeit.
- Identify tasks which the poor SIs indicate. An SI is not just a flag, marking

some problem; it should also point the way to a course of action. A rich picture of the SI context might be useful, setting out the structures and processes which such a result would indicate – for example, an SI in an organization adopting new information technology. The SI measures the adoption of information products by staff. The sustainable level is not being achieved; staff are overwhelming the system with inquiries. The rich picture for such a scenario would include structures such as making use of the system, processes such as use rates, spread of knowledge about the new system, and training procedures in systems use. Identifying major tasks indicates the areas on which the project team need to focus to improve the function of the SI (presuming that we now have confirmed that the SI indicated a real problem and that it was not a case of a poor SI reporting badly).

- Following the identification of the major tasks, the team can produce a new root definition which sets out the *transformation* which should improve the functioning of the project in the light of the poor SI.
- The team can then set out an activity plan or conceptual model which describes the actions which are now required to bring about the transformation. For example, if the result of the root definition work is that the main problem is poor training of staff leading to overuse of the system, then the conceptual model might describe how the transformation of increased systems awareness, skills adoption and practical experience in the use of the information system can be achieved.

If the SI was seen to work well, to flag a real issue and to indicate a real problem for the sustainability of the project then it can be switched on again and, following another cycle (three months, six months, or whatever), the SI can be tested to see if the remedial action has brought about an improvement in the state of affairs.

A STITCH IN TIME...

The AMOEBA is one way of presenting SIs so that they have an initial impact upon the stakeholders in the project process. They are also provocative, since change over time can be used to encourage stakeholders to discuss what is going on in the project context. To this extent Ten Brink et al made an important contribution to the development of SIs. We would invite the reader to compare the AMOEBAs set out here with the lists of SIs which are presented in Chapter 1.

We have deliberately attempted in this section to develop a modest and limited SSA. We have indicated that SIs work well in well-defined projects with clear boundaries and agreed goals. Given this, we have set out how our approach works, basing our thinking on systems and learning models which develop wide-ranging and variable pictures of the project context. Working in a participatory manner and seeking to understand what is important to the stakeholders in the project, we have set out a learning process for SI development and implementation. The result of this is not a perfect SI device. We make use of all types of information and do not have a narrow scientific focus for the work. For this reason the tool becomes more unmanageable as the frame expands and conflicts of interest between stakeholder groups emerge. Nevertheless, although we think that the tool has the virtue of developing SIs to inform the discussion of the project team, we also feel that the very process of setting up SIs will inform the team of the deep sustainability of the project, and therefore may indicate if there are fundamental problems which might otherwise be missed. In this sense the process of developing SIs is part of a virtuous cycle, with the SI itself encouraging sustainable practices and reflecting the result of such practice. In this case the SI becomes the means to the end as well as a simplified description of the project end itself. We argue that this approach is organic and people-focused.

In the next chapter we develop our discussion of SSA and draw some conclusions from the book as a whole.

Part III

Where Next? Humility and Honesty

Chapter 7

Sustainability Indicators – the Rhetoric and the Reality

INTRODUCTION AND OBJECTIVES

Throughout this book we have been chasing a moving shadow called sustainability. This is a term which has achieved Olympian proportions in all brands of ecology, rural development, institutional continuance, city and nation-building. It is one of the words of the latter half of the century. Unfortunately for those charged with the business of making the word mean something fixed, understandable and enforceable, there is no single meaning and there is no agreement on how it is measured and recognized in an objective sense. The situation appears to be that, at the end of the 20th century, a word has been decided upon to conjure up the desirable outcome of social and political endeavours. Scientists and professionals have taken (or been given) the impossible task of achieving definitive measurement of this word. The impossible task was to measure what was never potentially measurable: the immeasurable 'sustainability'.

In Chapters 1, 2 and 3 we looked at some representative samples of this endeavour. From single indicator to multiple indicator to institutional indicators; from reductionist science through to focus groups; from small research organizations to the United Nations we have tried to describe the history of SIs and their understandable failure to achieve an objectively verifiable, scientific measurement of sustainability. Following the review of progress to date, we have explicitly argued for a systemic, participatory and subjective approach to SI development; in Chapters 4 and 5 we described what systemic approaches have to offer and their value vis à vis projects. In Chapter 6 we set out our approach to systemic sustainability analysis (SSA) and described the main steps of the process of developing participatory and holistic analysis. We have not described our approach as definitive or perfect, far from it. Rather, we have argued that it is an approach in need of application and development, but one which we believe will provide useful information to social groupings concerned with their own sustainability (as defined by these social groups). We welcome testing and further discussion.

So far, several items of interest have arisen and we wish to dedicate this last chapter to a review of those which we have found most provocative in our personal journey of discovery. The items we will deal with here are:

- managing expectation;
- organic and empowering approaches compared to inorganic and de-humanizing approaches;
- culture change;
- the essential need for reflective practice;
- future research priorities.

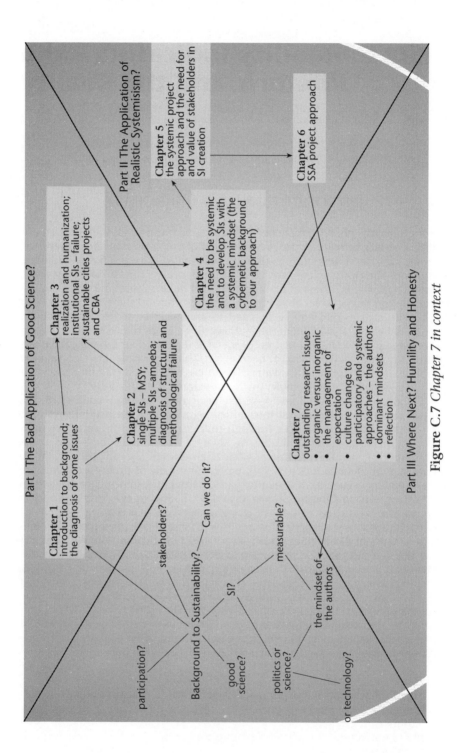

Figure C.7 *Chapter 7 in context*

MANAGING EXPECTATION

In Chapter 6 we described a process for a group of stakeholders to arrive at a 'band of equilibrium'. In this chapter, Figure 6.15 appeared to be a culmination of this and we reproduce it again here with some additions (see Figure 7.1).

One addition to the diagram is the notion of the reasonable limit to expectation. We argue that one strength of our approach is that a stakeholder group has to agree to lower and upper limits to their expectations in terms of what can be delivered (in state and process terms) by a project. Both limits are problematic. Problems for the lower limit are mainly confined to defining an acceptable minimum. This idea is represented today in the UK with the political question of a minimum wage. What is the minimum wage below which UK workers are unable to sustain a reasonable standard of living, but which would not act as a disincentive for capital to invest in the UK economy or for labour to price itself out of work? Arriving at the sustainable figure could be the result of stakeholder discussion, in this case government agencies, employers and employees (as represented by the Confederation of British Industry – CBI – and the Trades Union Congress – TUC). The results of deliberation will hopefully be the 'agreed' figure which will, by necessity, be a compromise. The non-participatory alternative would probably involve the appointment of a panel of experts to devise a figure to which stakeholder groups might or might not agree. In the participatory approach, expectation is explicit and to be bargained with. In the non-participatory approach, expectation is assumed to be known and discounted in deliberation by the expert panel.

Upper limit analysis is even more problematic in the view of the authors. To gain agreement on the upper limit is to gain insight into the preferences of social groupings, but while setting a reasonable limit to this expectation. A good example of an area which might profit from this type of approach is the UK Health Service. When it was originally set up shortly after World War II, expec-

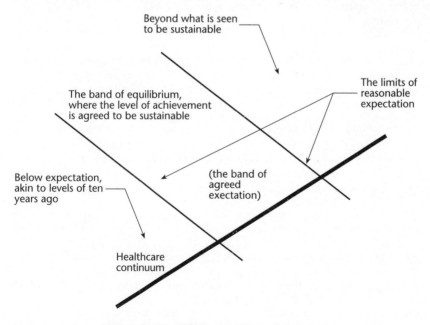

Figure 7.1 *Equilibrium and agreed expectation*

tation was extremely limited in comparison to modern standards of what is possible in health care. The vision of most people was that the health service would patch up the individual in extreme illness but that this would operate from 'cradle to grave'. Today, with mounting costs and expectations which are limitless (triple heart by-pass, AIDS and cancer treatments), there is no agreed upper limit. The argument is not only financial but moral and ethical, with a range of stakeholders from the government of the day, doctor and nurse representatives, patients, and the general public. There needs to be an ongoing negotiation process comparing expectations in order to achieve sustainability. What is the upper limit of expectation? This is a discussion which has proved too sensitive and has not yet been initiated in an open fashion in public forums.

Sustainability indicators, as we have described them in Chapter 6, are intended to relate directly to issues such as these. The purpose of the SI exercise now becomes a discussion around the management of expectation. What is agreed to be sustainable? What effort can the health service sustain? What is the long-term cost of this sustainability? What is a viable system? The approach we set out in Chapter 6 is one way of arriving at this intensely subjective equilibrium band set within these limits. We look forward to working with others in future projects to test out the approach.

ORGANIC AND EMPOWERING APPROACHES COMPARED TO INORGANIC AND DEHUMANIZING APPROACHES

While researching material for this book, it was noticeable how approaches to measuring sustainability often echo the use of indicators in economics, biology and social science. As we have pointed out, this is by no means unexpected given the complexity one is faced with; since sustainability has to be measured to be meaningful, what else can one do but use indicators? The fact that indicators by definition must simplify a complex entity is not ignored, and the question therefore becomes: what indicators will reflect an individual's vision of sustainability? The circularity rather than linearity of this process has already been described, as has its distinction from scientific derivation of indicators in ecology. We have no desire to labour this point any further. However, one interesting facet that emerges from a reading of the literature is how the use and development of SIs is itself an indicator of the very heart of the sustainability debate. Many seem to see sustainability as a property or target that is 'out there' in much the same way as the environment is an entity removed from ourselves. The argument appears to be that no one can define it clearly yet, but given the right SIs, it will enter the domain of being achievable and understandable. It is almost as if sustainability is a mountain to be climbed by those able to generate the 'right' knowledge.

Just what is the right knowledge and who is best suited to get it may well be a matter of serious contention. One only has to read a review in the *New Scientist* magazine written by a scientist (Gribbin, 1998) of a book on research methods in the social sciences (Becker, 1997) to realize the gulf which exists between some members of the disciplines! The rhetoric emphasizing systems, multidisciplinarity and all-embracing vision, sets the height of the mountain and stresses how difficult the climb will be; nevertheless, a flag will ultimately be placed on the summit, and we will know all there is to know about sustainability and how to get it. The fact that most of those going through this live in developed countries is noteworthy in terms of cultural mindsets and what could be called the imposition of 'sustainability imperialism', but not in the context of agreeing upon the need for measurability. After all, knowledge is universal – the mountain is there for everyone to climb.

If our research has taught us nothing else, it is surely that sustainability is the mindset of those who are intimately entwined with its achievement, and not an entity that lies 'outside' of our heads. In other words, sustainability cannot be studied as we can study an ecosystem. Like the term environment but far more so, sustainability is what we want it to be and can change as we change. It is an organic and evolving construct of our minds and not an inorganic and static entity that can be physically probed. Indeed, the very action of trying to implement what one thinks is sustainability may change one's vision of what it is. The best we can achieve is to acknowledge the centrality of people and to put participation at the very heart of implementation. The issue now becomes one of compromise between expectation and what is achievable without causing harm (as we have set out above). This may be vague, but it is the nature of the beast. Indicators can play a very useful role here, but only in terms of empowerment and not as precise measures.

Much of the above may sound very familiar. Other authors have been saying similar things about the environment (Ison, 1994; Blaikie, 1995; Ison, et al 1997) and medical science (Capra, 1982 and 1996). The notion of an act of measurement changing the very thing that we are trying to measure is also very familiar to physicists and, indeed, to social scientists. This is not the most interesting facet of the sustainability debate; rather it is that we feel moved to repeat it here. Why has so much of the debate ignored what to us is a rather obvious conclusion? Why have we been so rooted in a mechanistic and inorganic vision of sustainability? Why have many tried to show that sustainability = 42? In part, the answer lies in a very human desire to understand and make sense of complexity, and this appears to arise with every new human vision of where we want to be. We want to achieve X, so let us first understand it, and to do this we need to measure it.

We sincerely hope that this does not diminish what many people have put much time and effort into trying to understand. While we say that there is no mountain and only a mindset, we do not belittle those who wish to have something tangible rather than abstract. One can think of no greater challenge than trying to address organic visions. Nevertheless we believe we will never achieve a universal and unchanging set of sustainability indicators that provide a handle on sustainability, and the challenge is one of keeping pace with people's dreams and trying to make them real. With sustainability, we (the whole of humankind) really are the creators.

CULTURE CHANGE

Much of the information and discussion which has been set out in this book relates to cross-refereeing between apparently separate cultures or paradigms of understanding. The notion of different worldviews and paradigms is well established in the literature (for a Catholic range of views on the matter, see Koestler, 1964; Checkland, 1981; Wilber, 1996). It appears that part of the problem of SIs is the inability of different agencies and individuals from different cultures, implicitly or explicitly, to espouse different worldviews and assumptions about the way the world works. The result of this is the development of antipathies and incomprehensions between different stakeholder groups and the long-term development of conflict. There is a need to change one's culture to one which is more inclusive and tolerant of other beliefs. This is a challenge long set out in Koestler's work and elsewhere. It is a challenge to science and to all epistemologies (meaning 'the study or a theory of the nature and grounds of knowledge especially with reference to its limits and validity', Webster, 1995). The authors argue that such a change, a merging and toleration of worldviews and the assumptions of these worldviews, would bring about a number of virtuous corollaries:

- an appreciation that 'different' does not mean 'wrong';
- a recognition that variety is the basis for sustainability;
- an understanding that time spent in understanding other people's viewpoints is time saved later when the project starts.

In current and future work the authors intend to develop the vision of culture change and to incorporate new ways of thinking in their analysis. This is a difficult and problematic area – we always tend to view our world from our own perspective, and to see things differently is to see through the lenses of our own prejudices and preconceptions. Nevertheless, recognizing that what has been done in the past with regard to the development of SIs is less than ideal and that multiple perspectives are vital for a rounder understanding, the authors are content to see their view of SI development evolve in practice. Culture change will mean tolerating and inviting different standpoints for a multiperspective analysis of sustainability.

THE ESSENTIAL NEED FOR REFLECTIVE PRACTICE

An essential element for all future SI work must be reflective practice. The authors were surprised when they began this project to find a minimal literature which took into account and reflected upon the existing literature and lessons relating to SIs. The apparent absence of explicit learning about past problems and mistakes was also surprising. It appears that many authors cite those they wish to agree with and ignore the rest. On a related matter, one frightening element of this SI project was coming to grips with and reflecting upon the extreme wealth of literature in the area and the rapidity with which this literature is evolving and developing – but again, with minimal self-reflection on the part of authors. The avalanche of material was and remains incredible, so much so that there were times when both authors despaired at finding the time and space to 'stop' to write this book. We recognized that at the moment of our own pause, we could be sure in the knowledge that several new and interesting articles would be published somewhere on the world wide web.

As with all issues, but most specifically in areas of fast and growing interest, there is a great need for all researchers and practitioners to reflect upon existing material but also upon the reaction to that literature and research. This self-analysis is a vital element of understanding as the world changes and our reaction to that world also alters. We offer the following key to changing mindsets on the part of researchers and scientists who are involved in the process of SI formulation. Table 7.1 (taken from Bell, 1998) sets out in the left column nine problems with regard to unreflective practice in science.

These are some possible outcomes of the traditional scientific mindset. The last three are particularly important in terms of the scientist in the environmental context. When we read the books of, and listen to the lectures of

Table 7.1 *Problems and prizes of vulnerability*

Problem of unreflective vulnerability	*Prize of self-reflective vulnerability*
Unrealistic quality standards	Realistic expectation
Paranoia	Tolerance
Doubt	Humility
Self-preservation	Self-giving
Incessant self-expression	Listening
Undue self-assertion	Self-containment
Out of my depth	But I can learn
Out of my context	But I can experience
Keep it out!	But I am already part of 'it' and 'it' is part of me

scientists, it may appear that they are splendidly confident creatures, comprehending and understanding the world in terms of their science. Yet those of us who count scientists as our friends and know them personally know that, like the rest of us, they are often riddled with self-doubt and concern and anxiety about their work. There is often a mismatch between society's *expectation* of the scientist and the *reality* of what the scientist actually feels and knows. We believe – from our own experience – that in self-reflection the scientist comes to understand more about the issue of managing expectation vis à vis his or her own work and the nature of his or her own *vulnerability*. We argue that to recognize our vulnerability and to reflect upon our own ignorance provides prizes. However, with non-reflection we hide the reality. Reality is multifaceted but it can often mean that we (as researchers) feel out of our depth and out of the context which we know and understand; we sometimes try to keep out the discrepancies (thus always measuring the world according to our long-term prejudices and presuppositions). We would argue that recognizing our vulnerability should develop certain prizes. For example, in accordance with Table 7.1 we could cite three recognitions:

- a recognition (in humility) that we are all learning (the only human being which ceases to learn is a dead human being);
- new contexts can be experienced and from this can follow understanding;
- the object of our study is part of us; if we study and learn about it, we are engaged with it and have become part of it (no matter however slightly).

In this case all systems are linked together in growing and mutual comprehension.

FUTURE RESEARCH PRIORITIES

Upon completion of this book the authors are re-engaging with the literature and with their own research in developing effective SIs from a holistic viewpoint, in collaboration with partners in local government and private enterprise. Figure 7.2 provides a sketch of the research priorities which are derived from the work set out in this book and which we are now developing.

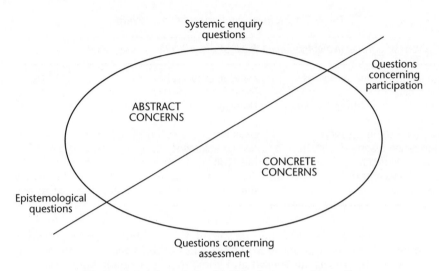

Figure 7.2 *A learning cycle of further research questions*

Epistemological Questions

Our research has taken us into the theory of knowledge and understanding and has left some unanswered questions, such as: how was the original development of SIs conceived? Why did serious minded communities of decision-makers and theorists believe sustainability could be measured? What were the epistemological assumptions which led to this view and are these views still determining policy? Briefly – what was the background thinking which got us into this mess?

The Systemic Approach

The authors continue to develop, through action research practice, a systemic approach to problem solving which can be applied in a systemic manner – expanding on the ideas of second and third order cybernetics (as discussed briefly in Chapter 4). There are numerous systemic approaches to problem solving (SSM in Chapter 4) and some of these are explicitly participatory (PRA in Chapter 4), but we remain unsure that any given approach is systemic in the sense of recognizing and developing the concept of multiple views of reality. Our objective might be to investigate and develop an approach which adapts to individual and social culture in a wide range of contexts.

Participatory SIs in Social Development Projects

Related to the overtly systemic practice advocated above, we are also developing the participatory approach to SI. In collaboration with others already engaged in SI monitoring, we intend to develop the participatory approach advocated in Chapter 6. Questions we engage in relate to empowerment and democratization of decision-making in the formulation of SIs with local people; we also address how SIs can contribute to empowerment.

Assessment of SIs

We have been concerned throughout this book with the means and processes for SI assessment. We have seen in Chapters 1 to 3 that an overtly quantitative approach to SI assessment is often exclusive of the stakeholders involved in the sustainability project context. The AMOEBA set out in Chapter 6 is a fairly user-friendly means but this can, we feel, be further developed and extended. How do we develop SI assessment in a holistic fashion?

In describing the history of information systems thinking, Peter Checkland and Sue Holwell describe the area as 'the anatomy of a confusion' (Checkland and Holwell, 1998, p 31); the review of SIs set out in this book might also be thought of as an anatomy of confusion. However, while in the case of information systems, the confusion lies essentially with blending technocratic and organizational mindsets, with SIs we see a frightening mix of mindsets where the technocratic element dominates. If this book has succeeded in nothing other than alerting the reader to the need for humility and understanding when dealing with different stakeholders with different mindsets, we will consider the exercise to have been a success.

References

Adams, D W (1984) 'Are the arguments for cheap agricultural credit sound?' in Adams, D W, Graham, D H and von Pischke, J D (eds) *Undermining rural development with cheap credit*, pp 65–77, Westview Press, Boulder and London

Adams, D W and von Pischke, J D (1992) 'Microenterprise credit programs: Deja Vu', *World Development*, vol 20 (10), pp 1463–1470

Aikman, P (1997) 'Is deepwater a dead-end?' Greenpeace. Accessed on the internet (13/11/97) at site
<*http://www.greenpeace.org.uk/atlantic/library/biodiverstiy/c_deep.html*>

Ainsworth, E (1989) 'LISA men have called you', *Farm Journal*, vol 113 (February), p 1

Allen, P, Van Dusen, D, Lundy, L and Gliessman, S (1991) 'Integrating social, environmental and economic issues in sustainable agriculture', *American Journal of Alternative Agriculture*, vol 6, pp 34–39

Allen, T F H and Hoekstra, T W (1992) *Towards a Unified Ecology*, Columbia University Press, New York

Avgerou, C and Cornford, T (1993) *Developing Information Systems: Concepts, Issues and Practice*, Macmillan Information Systems Series, London

Avison, D E and Wood–Harper, A T (1990) *Multiview: An Exploration in Information Systems Development*, McGraw-Hill, Maindenhead

Avery, D T (1995) *Saving the Planet with Pesticides and Plastic*, Hudson Institute, Indianapolis

Baldock, D, Bishop, K, Mitchell, K and Phillips, A (1996) *Growing Greener: Sustainable Agriculture in the UK*, WWF–UK and CPRE, Godalming and London

Barbier, E B, Markandya, A and Pearce, D W (1990) 'Sustainable agricultural development and project appraisal', *European Review of Agricultural Economics*, vol 17, pp 181–196

Bawden, R (1997) 'Learning to persist. A systemic view of development' in Stowell, F A, Ison, R L, Armson, R, Holloway, J, Jackson, S and McRobb, S (eds) *Systems for Sustainability: People, Organizations and Environments*, pp 1–5, Plenum Press, New York and London

Becker, H S (1997) *Tricks of the Trade: how to think about your research while you are doing it*, The University of Chicago Press, Chicago

Beets, W C (1990) *Raising and Sustaining Productivity of Smallholder Farming Systems in the Tropics: a handbook of sustainable agricultural development*, AgBe, Alkmaar, Holland

Begon, M (1990) *Ecological Food Production: a food production policy for Britain*, Institute for Public Policy Research, London

Bell, S (1996) 'Approaches to participatory monitoring and evaluation in Dir District, North West Frontier Province, Pakistan', *Systems Practice*, vol 9 (2), pp 129–150

Bell, S (1996) *Learning with Information Systems: learning cycles in information systems development*, Routledge, London

Bell, S (1998) 'Self-reflection and vulnerability in action research: bringing forth new worlds in our learning', *Systemic Practice and Action Research*, vol 11(2) pp 179–192

Bell, S and Wood–Harper, A T (1998) *Rapid Information Systems Development: systems analysis and systems design in an imperfect world*, second edition, McGraw Hill, London

Bennett, L and Cuevas, C E (1996) 'Sustainable banking with the poor', *Journal of International Development*, vol 8 (2), pp 145–152

Berenbach, S and Guzman, D (1994) 'The Solidarity Group Experience Worldwide' in Otero, M and Rhyne, E (eds) *The New World of Microenterprise Finance*, pp 119–139, Intermediate Technology, London

Biggs, S D (1989) *Interdisciplinary Analysis on Rural Poverty in Agricultural Research: an indicative project plan*, University of East Anglia, Norwich

Biggs, S D (1990) 'A multiple source of innovation model of agricultural research and technology promotion', *World Development*, vol 18 (11), pp 1481–1499

Biggs, S D (1995) *Contending Coalitions in Participatory Technology Development: challenges to the new orthodoxy. The Limits of Participation*, Intermediate Technology, London

Biggs, S D and Farrington, J (1990) *Assessing the effects of farming systems research: time for the reintroduction of a political and institutional perspective*. Paper prepared for the Asian Farming Systems Research and Extension Symposium, Bangkok

Biggs, S and Smith, G (1995) *Contending Coalitions in Agricultural Research and Development: challenges for planning and management. Evaluation for a New Century*, Canadian Evaluation Association and the American Evaluation Association, Vancouver

Bignell, V and Fortune, J (1984) *Understanding Systems Failures*, Manchester University Press, Manchester

Blaikie, P (1995) 'Understanding environmental issues' in Morse, S and Stocking, M A (eds) *People and Environment*, pp 1–30, UCL Press, London

Boerema, L K and Gulland, J A (1973) 'Stock Assessment of the Peruvian Anchovy (*Engraulis ringens*) and Management of the Fishery', *Journal Fisheries Research Board of Canada*, vol 30, pp 2226–2235

Bouman, F J A (1984) 'Informal Saving and Credit Arrangements in Developing Countries: observations from Sri-Lanka' in Adams, D W, Graham, D H and von Pischke, J D (eds) *Undermining Rural Development with Cheap Credit*, pp 232–247, Westview Press, Boulder and London

Brinkerhoff, D W and Goldsmith, A A (1992) 'Promoting the Sustainability of Development Institutions: a framework for strategy', *World Development* vol 20 (3), pp 369–383

Brown, D R (1997) 'Sustainability Is Not about Money!: The Case of the Belize Chamber of Commerce and Industry', *Development in Practice* vol 7 (2), pp 185–189

Buddrus, V (1996) *East–West European Centre for Integrative Humanistic Education and Psychology: theoretical background and belief system*, East–West European Centre for Integrative Humanistic Education and Psychology, Morschen

Cairns, J, McCormick, P V and Niederlehner, B R (1993) 'A proposed framework for developing indicators of ecosystem health', *Hydrobiologia*, vol 263, pp 1–44

Callicott, J B and Mumford, K (1997) 'Ecological sustainability as a conservation concept', *Conservation Biology*, vol 11 (1), pp 32–40

Capra, F (1982) *The Turning Point: science, society and the rising culture*, Flamingo, London

Capra, F (1996) *The Web of Life: a synthesis of mind and matter*, Harper Collins, London

Carson, R (1962) *Silent Spring*, Penguin, London

CCTA (1993) *Applying Soft Systems Methodology to an SSADM Feasibility Study*, HMSO, London

Chambers, R (1981) 'Rapid rural appraisal: rationale and repertoire', *Public Administration and Development*, vol 1, pp 95–106

Chambers, R (1991) *Rural Development: Putting the Last First*, John Wiley and Sons, New York

Chambers, R (1992) *Rural Appraisal: Rapid, Relaxed and Participatory*, Institute of Development Studies, Brighton, UK

Chambers, R (1997) *Whose Reality Counts? Putting the First Last*, Intermediate Technology, London

Chambers, R, Pacey, A and Thrupp, L A (eds) (1989) *Farmer First: Farmer Innovation and Agricultural Research*, Intermediate Technology, London

Chambers, R (undated) 'Paradigm shifts and the practice of participatory research and development' in Nelson, N and Wright, S (eds) *Power and Participatory Development*, Intermediate Technology Publications, London

Checkland, P B (1981) *Systems Thinking, Systems Practise*, Wiley, Chichester, UK

Checkland, P B (1984) 'Systems thinking in management: The development of soft systems methodology and its implications for social science' in Ulrich H and Probst G J (eds) *Self-Organisation and Management of Social Systems*, Springer–Verlag, Berlin

Checkland, P and Holwell, S (1998) *Information, Systems and Information Systems: making sense of the field*, Wiley, Chichester

Checkland, P B and Scholes, J (1990) *Soft Systems Methodology in Action*, Wiley, Chichester, UK

Clayton, A and Radcliffe, N (1996) *Sustainability: a systems approach*, Earthscan, London

Coleman, G (1987a) 'Logical framework approach to the monitoring and evaluation of agricultural and rural development projects', *Project Appraisal*, vol 2 (4), pp 251–259

Coleman, G (1987b) *M&E and the Project Cycle*, Overseas Development Group, University of East Anglia, Norwich, UK

Common, M and Perrings, C (1992) 'Towards an ecological economics of sustainability', *Ecological Economics*, vol 6, pp 7–34

Connell, D (1997) 'Participatory development: An approach sensitive to class and gender', *Development in Practice*, vol 7(3), pp 248–259

Cook, J (1995) 'Empowering people for sustainable development' in Fitzgerald, P, McLennan, A and Munslow, B (eds) *Managing Sustainable Development in South Africa*, Oxford University Press, Cape Town

Cordingley, D (1995) 'Integrating the logical framework into the management of technical cooperation projects', *Project Appraisal*, vol 10(2), pp 103–112

Corten, A (1996) 'The widening gap between fisheries biology and fisheries management in the European Union', *Fisheries Research*, vol 27 (1–3), pp 1–15.

Costanza, R and Patten, B C (1995) 'Defining and predicting sustainability', *Ecological Economics*, vol 15, pp 193–196

Cox, P G, MacLeod, N D and Shulman, A D (1997) 'Putting sustainability into practice in agricultural research for development' in Stowell, F A, Ison, R L, Armson, R, Holloway, J, Jackson, S and McRobb, S (eds) *Systems for Sustainability: People, Organizations and Environments*, pp 33–38, Plenum Press, New York and London

Craig, D and Porter, D (1997) 'Framing participation: development projects, professionals, and organizations', *Development in Practice*, vol 7(3), pp 229–236

Cushing, D H (1981) *Fisheries Biology: A Study in Population Dynamics*, The University of Wisconsin Press, Madison

Cusworth, J and Franks, T (1993) *Managing Projects in Developing Countries*, Longman Scientific and Technical, Harlow

Cutter, S L (1985) *Rating Places: a geographer's view on quality of life*, Association of American Geographical Research Publishers

Daly, H E (1990) 'Toward some operational principles of sustainable development', *Ecological Economics*, vol 2, pp 1–6

Davies, L J (1989) *Cultural Aspects of Intervention with Soft Systems Methodology*, University of Lancaster, Lancaster, UK

Dawkins, R (1986) *The Blind Watchmaker*, Longman Scientific and Technical, Bath

Dempster, J P (1975) *Animal Population Ecology*, Academic Press, London

Dichter, T (1996) 'Questioning the future of NGOs in microfinance', *Journal of International Development*, vol 8 (2), pp 259–269

Dominski, A, Clark, J and Fox, J (1992) *Building the Sustainable City*, Community Environmental Council, Santa Barbara, US

Dunlap, R E, Beus, C E, Howell, R E and Waud, J (1992) 'What is sustainable agriculture? An empirical examination of faculty and farmer definitions', *Journal of Sustainable Agriculture*, vol 3 (1), pp 5- 39

Ehui, S K and Spencer, D S C (1993) 'Measuring the sustainability and economic viability of tropical farming systems: a model from sub-Saharan Africa', *Agricultural Economics*, vol 9, pp 279–296

FAO (Food and Agriculture Organization) (1986) *Guide to Training in the Formulation of Agricultural and Rural Investment Projects*, Food and Agriculture Organization of the United Nations, Rome

Fielding, A (1991) 'Chaotic biology', *Biologist*, vol 38 (5), pp 185–188

Flora, C B (1992) 'Building sustainable agriculture: a new application of farming systems research and extension', *Journal of Sustainable Agriculture*, vol 2 (3), pp 37–49

Foerster, Van H and Varela, F J (1984) 'On constructing a reality', *Observing Systems* (2nd ed), Inter-systems Publications Seaside California

Fortune, J and Hughes, J (1997) 'Modern academic myths' in Stowell, F A, Ison, R L, Armson, R, Holloway, J, Jackson, S and McRobb, S (eds) *Systems for Sustainability: People, Organizations and Environments*, pp 125–130, Plenum Press, New York and London

Frans, R (1993) 'Sustainability of high-input cropping systems: the role of IPM', *FAO Plant Protection Bulletin*, vol 41 (3–4), pp 161–170

Fresco, L O and Kroonenberg, S B (1992) 'Time and spatial scales in ecological sustainability', *Land Use Policy*, vol 9, pp 155–168

Garcia, S, Sparre, P and Csirke, J (1989) 'Estimating surplus production and maximum sustainable yield from biomass data when catch and effort time series are not available', *Fisheries Research*, vol 8 (1), pp 13–23

Gause, G F (1934) *The Struggle for Existence*, Hafner, New York

Gibbon, D, Lake, A and Stocking, M (1995) 'Sustainable development: a challenge for agriculture' in Morse, S and Stocking, M A (eds) *People and Environment*, pp 31–68, UCL Press, London

Gilbert, A (1996) 'Criteria for sustainability in the development of indicators for sustainable development', *Chemosphere*, vol 33 (9), pp 1739–1748

Gilot, J and Kumar, M (1995) *Science and the Retreat from Reason*, The Merlin Press, London

Girma, M, Sartorius, R et al (1996) *The Project Cycle Management Resource Guide: a logical framework approach*, Team Technologies Inc, Chantilly

Goldsmith, E, Allen, R, Allaby, M, Davoll, J and Lawrence, S (1972) 'A blueprint for survival', *The Ecologist*, vol 2 (1), pp 1–43

Gribbin, J (1998) 'How not to do it', *New Scientist*, vol 157 (2116), p 41

Gustafson, D J (1994) 'Developing sustainable institutions: lessons from cross-case analysis of 24 agricultural extension programmes', *Public Administration and Development*, vol 14, pp 121–134

Haas, P M, Levy, M A and Parson, E A (1992) 'Appraising the Earth Summit: how should we judge UNCED's success?', *Environment*, vol 34 (8), pp 6–11, 25–33

Hansen, J W (1996) 'Is agricultural sustainability a useful concept?', *Agricultural Systems*, vol 50, pp 117–143

Hardi, P and Zdan, T (eds) (1997) *Assessing Sustainable Development: Principles in Practice*, International Institute for Sustainable Development, Winnipeg

Harger, J R E and Meyer, F, M (1996) 'Definition of indicators for environmentally sustainable development', *Chemosphere*, vol 33 (9), pp 1749–1775

Harrington, L (1992a) 'Measuring sustainability: issues and alternatives' in Hiemstra, W, Reijntjes, C and van der Werf, E (eds) *Let Farmers Judge: Experiences in Assessing the Sustainability of Agriculture*, pp 3–16, Intermediate Technology, London

Harrington, L W (1992b) 'Measuring sustainability: Issues and Alternatives', *Journal for Farming Systems Research–Extension*, vol 3 (1), pp 1–20

Hawkins, S J, Proud, S V, Spence, S K and Southward, A J (1994) 'From the individual to the community and beyond: water quality, stress indicators and key species in coastal systems' in Sutcliffe, D W (ed) *Water Quality and Stress Indicators in Marine and Freshwater Ecosystems: linking levels of organization (individuals, populations, communities)*, pp 35–62, Freshwater Biological Association, Ambleside, UK

Haynes, M (1989) *A Participative Application of Soft Systems Methodology: an action research project concerned with formulating an outline design for a learning centre in ICI chemicals and polymers*, University of Lancaster, Lancaster, UK

Heinen, J T (1994) 'Emerging, diverging and converging paradigms on sustainable development', *International Journal of Sustainable Development and World Ecology*, vol 1, pp 22–33

Hellawell, J M (1986) *Biological Indicators of Freshwater Pollution and Environmental Management*, Elsevier, London and New York

Hirschheim, R A (1989) 'User participation in practice: experience with participative systems design' in Knight, K (ed) *Participation in Systems Development*, Kogan Page, London

Hodge, R A and Hardi, P (1997) 'The need for guidelines: the rationale underlying the Bellagio principles for assessment' in Hardi, P and Zdan, T (eds) *Assessing Sustainable Development: Principles in Practice*, pp 7–20, The International Institute for Sustainable Development, Winnipeg

Hoenig, J M, Warren, W G and Stocker, M (1994) 'Bayesian and related approaches to fitting surplus production models', *Canadian Journal of Fisheries and Aquatic Sciences*, vol 51 (8), pp 1823–1831

Holt, S L (1994) 'The village bank methodology: performance and prospects' in Otero, M and Rhyne, E (eds) *The New World of Microenterprise Finance*, pp 156–184, IT Publications, London

Holt, S J and Talbot, L M (1978) 'New principles for the conservation of wild living resources', *Wildlife Monographs*, no 59, pp 6–33

Hulme, D and Mosley, P (1996a) *Finance Against Poverty*, vol 1, Routledge, London and New York

Hulme, D and Mosley, P (1996b) *Finance Against Poverty*, vol 2, Routledge, London and New York

Hobart, M (1993) 'Introduction: the Growth of Ignorance?' in Hobart, M (ed) *An Anthropological Critique of Development: the growth of ignorance*, Routledge, London

Hulme, D (1994) 'Projects, politics and professionals: alternative approaches for project identification and project planning', *Agricultural Systems*, vol 47, pp 211–233

Idyll, C P (1973) 'The anchovy crisis', *Scientific American*, vol 228 (6), pp 22–29

IITA (International Institute of Tropical Agriculture) (1993) *Sustainable Food Production in Sub-Saharan Africa 2. Constraints and Opportunities*, IITA, Ibadan, Nigeria

Ison, R (1993) *Participative Ecodesign: a new paradigm for professional practice*, Proceedings: Epidemiology Chapter, Australian Vetinerary Association Annual Conference, Gold Coast, Australian College of Veterinary Scientists, Cobar, Australia, pp 41–50.

Ison, R (1993) 'Soft systems: A non-computer view of decision support' in Stuth, J and Lyons, B (eds) *Decision Support Systems for the Management of Grazing Lands*, pp 83–121, UNESCO, Paris

Ison, R (1994) *Designing learning systems: How can systems approaches be applied in the training of research workers and development actors?*, International Symposium – Systems Orientated Research in Agriculture and Rural Development, Montpellier

Ison, R, Maiteny, P et al (1997) 'Systems methodologies for sustainable natural resources research and development', *Agricultural Systems*, vol 55(2), pp 257–272

IUCN (International Union for the Conservation of Nature), UNEP (United Nations Environment Programme) and WWF (World Wild Life Fund) (1991) *Caring for the Earth: A Strategy for Sustainable Living*, IUCN, Gland, Switzerland

Izac, A–M, N and Swift, M J (1994) 'On agricultural sustainability and its measurement in small-scale farming in sub-Saharan Africa', *Ecological Economics*, vol 11, pp 105–125

Jackelen, H R and Rhyne, E (1991) 'Towards a more market-orientated approach to credit and savings for the poor', *Small Enterprise Development*, vol 2 (4), pp 4–20

Jackson, C (1997) 'Sustainable development at the sharp end: field-worker agency in a participatory project', *Development in Practice*, vol 7(3), pp 237–247

Jansen, D M, Stoorvogel, J J and Schipper, R A (1995) 'Using sustainability indicators in agricultural land use analysis: an example from Costa Rica', *Netherlands Journal of Agricultural Science*, vol 43, pp 61–82

Jeffrey, P (1996) 'Evolutionary analogues and sustainability: putting a human face on survival', *Futures*, vol 28 (2), pp 173–187

Jensen, A L (1973) 'Relation between simple dynamic pool and surplus production models for yield from a fishery', *Journal Fisheries Research Board of Canada*, vol 30 (7), pp 998–1002

Johnson, S and Rogaly, B (1997) *Microfinance and Poverty Reduction*, Oxfam, Oxford

Kelling, K A and Klemme, R M (1989) 'Defining "sustainable"', *Agrichemical Age* (May), p 32

Khan, N and Ara Begum, S (1997) 'Participation in social forestry reexamined: a case-study from Bangladesh', *Development in Practice*, vol 7(3), pp 260–266

Kidd, C V (1992) 'The evolution of sustainability', *Journal of Agricultural and Environmental Ethics*, vol 5 (1), pp 1–26

Knox, P L (1974) 'Level of living, a conceptual framework for monitoring regional variation in wellbeing', *Regional Studies*, vol 8, pp 11–19.

Koestler, A (1964) *The Act of Creation*, Penguin, London

Kuik, O and Verbruggen, H (1991) *In Search of Indicators of Sustainable Development*, Kluwer Academic Publishers, Dordrecht, The Netherlands

Larkin, P A (1977) 'An epitaph for the concept of maximum sustainable yield', *Transactions of the American Fisheries Society*, vol 106 (1), pp 1–11

Lawrence, G (1997) 'Indicators for sustainable development' in Dodds, F (ed) *The Way Forward: Beyond Agenda 21*, pp 179–189, Earthscan, London

Laws, E A (1997) *El Niño and the Peruvian Anchovy Fishery*, University Science Books, Sausalito, California

Learner, M A, Williams, R, Harcup, M and Hughes, B D (1971) 'A survey of the macro-fauna of the River Cynon, a polluted tributary of the River Taff (South Wales)', *Freshwater Biology*, vol 1, pp 339–367

Lehman, H, Clark, E A and Weise, S F (1993) 'Clarifying the definition of sustainable agriculture', *Journal of Agricultural and Environmental Ethics*, vol 6 (2), pp 127–143

Lele, S M (1991) 'Sustainable development: a critical review', *World Development*, vol 19 (6), pp 607–621

Levitsky, J (ed) (1989) *Microenterprises in Developing Countries*, Intermediate Technology Publications, London

Liverman, D M, Hanson, M E, Brown, B J and Merideth, R W Jr (1988) 'Global sustainability: toward measurement', *Environmental Management*, vol 12 (2), pp 133–143

Long, N (1992) 'Research endeavours and actor struggles' in Long, N and Long, A (eds) *Battlefields of Knowledge: the interlocking of theory and practice in social research and development*, Routledge, London

Long, N (1992) 'Research practice and the social construction of knowledge' in Long, N and Long A (eds) *Battlefields of Knowledge: the interlocking of theory and practice in social research and development*, Routledge, London

Lovelock, J (1979) *Gaia*, Oxford University Press, Oxford

Lovelock, J (1991) *Healing Gaia*, Harmony Books, New York

Lynam, J K and Herdt, R W (1989) 'Sense and sustainability: sustainability as an objective in international agricultural research', *Agricultural Economics*, vol 3, pp 381–398

Macadam, R, Britton, I et al (1990) 'The use of soft systems methodology to improve the adoption by Australian cotton growers of the Siratac computer-based crop management system', *Agricultural Systems*, vol 34, pp 1–14

Macdonald, A M, (ed) (1979) *Chambers Twentieth Century Dictionary*, W & R Chambers Ltd, Edinburgh

MacGillivray, A (1996) 'How a salmon can save the world', *Green Futures*, no 2 (December), pp 44–45

MacRae, R J, Hill, S B, Henning, J and Mehuys, G R (1989) 'Agricultural science and sustainable agriculture: a review of the existing scientific barriers to sustainable food production and potential solutions', *Biological Agriculture and Horticulture*, vol 6, pp 173–219

Maturana, H (1997) *Scientific and Philosophic Theories*, Open University, Milton Keynes, UK

Maturana, H R and Varela, F J (1992) *The Tree of Knowledge: the biological roots of human understanding*, Shambhala, Boston

May, R (1989) 'The chaotic rhythms of life' in Hall, N (ed) *The New Scientist Guide to Chaos*, Penguin, London

McClintock, D and Ison, R (1994) *Revealing and concealing metaphors for a systemic agriculture*, International Symposium on Systems-Orientated Research in Agriculture and Rural Development, Montpellier

McNamara, N and Morse, S (1996) *Developing On-Farm Research: the broad picture*, On-Stream, Cork, Ireland

McNamara, N and Morse, S (1998) *Developing Financial Services: a case against sustainability*, On-Stream, Cork, Ireland

McPherson, S (1994) *Participatory Monitoring and Evaluation Abstracts*, Institute of Development Studies, London

Meadows, D M, Meadows, D L, Randers, J and Behrens, W (1972) *The Limits to Growth*, Universe Books, New York

Miller, F P and Wali, M K (1995) 'Soils, land use and sustainable agriculture: a review', *Canadian Journal of Soil Science*, vol 75, pp 413–422

Mingers, J (1995) *Self-Producing Systems*, Plenum, New York

Mitcham, C (1995) 'The concept of sustainable development: its origins and ambivalence', *Technology in Society*, vol 17 (3), pp 311–326

Mitchell, G, May, A and McDonald, A (1995) 'PICABUE: a methodological framework for the development of indicators of sustainable development', *International Journal of Sustainable Development and World Ecology*, vol 2, pp 104–123

Moffatt, I (1992) 'The evolution of the sustainable development concept: a perspective form Australia', *Australian Geographical Studies*, vol 30, pp 27–42

Moffatt, I (1994) 'On measuring sustainable development indicators', *International Journal of Sustainable Development and World Ecology*, vol 1, pp 97–109

Mohn, R K (1980) 'Bias and error propagation in logistic production models', *Canadian Journal of Fisheries and Aquatic Sciences*, vol 37 (8), pp 1276–1283

Monteith, J L (1990) 'Can sustainability be quantified?', *Indian Journal of Dryland Agricultural Research and Development*, vol 5 (1/2), pp 1–15

Morgan, G (1997) *Images of Organization*, new edition, Sage, London

Mosse, D (1995) *Process Documentation and Participatory Rural Development: the potential for process monitoring in project management and organizational change*, ODI, London

Munn, R E (1992) 'Towards sustainable development', *Atmospheric Environment*, vol 26A (15), pp 2715–2731

Mutua, A K (1994) 'The Juhudi Credit Scheme: from a traditional integrated method to a financial systems approach' in Otero, M and Rhyne, E (eds) *The New World of Microenterprise Finance*, pp 268–276, IT Publications, London

Natrajan, L E A (1993) *Comparative study of sample survey and participatory rural appraisal methodologies with special reference to evaluation of National Programme on Improved Chulah*, National Council of Applied Economic Research, New Delhi

Neher, D (1992) 'Ecological sustainability in agricultural systems: definition and measurement', *Journal of Sustainable Agriculture*, vol 2 (3), pp 51–61

NEF (New Economics Foundation) (1995) *New Directions for Structural Funds: Indicators for Sustainable Development in Europe*, NEF, London

Niu, W–Y, Lu, J J and Khan, A A (1993) 'Spatial systems approach to sustainable development: a conceptual framework', *Environmental Management*, vol 17 (2), pp 179–186

OECD (1989) *Sustainability in Development Programmes: a compendium of evaluation experience*, OECD, Paris

Norwich 21 (1997) *Norwich 21: Vision and Action Plan*, Norwich City Council, Norwich

Open University (1987) *T301 – Complexity Management and Change: a systems approach*, Open University, Milton Keynes, UK

Otero, M and Rhyne, E (eds) (1994) *The New World of Microenterprise Finance*, IT Publications, London

Otzen, U (1993) 'Reflections on the principles of sustainable agricultural development', *Environmental Conservation*, vol 20 (4), pp 310–316

Patterson, K R, Zuzunaga, J and Cardenas, G (1992) 'Size of the South American sardine (*Sardinops sagax*) population in the northern part of the Peru upwelling ecosystem after collapse of anchoveta (*Engraulis ringens*) stocks', *Canadian Journal of Fisheries and Aquatic Sciences*, vol 49 (9), pp 1762–1769

Pearce, D, Markandya, A and Barbier, E (1989) *Blueprint for a Green Economy*, Earthscan, London

Pearce, D (1993) *Blueprint 3. Measuring Sustainable Development*, Earthscan, London

Pearce, D (1995) *Blueprint 4. Capturing Global Environmental Value*, Earthscan, London

van Pelt, M J F, Kuyvenhoven, A and Nijkamp, P (1990) 'Project appraisal and sustainability: methodological challenges', *Project Appraisal*, vol 5 (3), pp 139–158

van Pelt, M J F, Kuyvenhoven, A and Nijkamp, P (1995) 'Environmental sustainability: issues of definition and measurement', *International Journal of Environment and Pollution*, vol 5 (2/3), pp 204–223

Penfold, C M, Miyan, M S, Reeves, T G and Grierson, I T (1995) 'Biological farming for sustainable agricultural production', *Australian Journal of Experimental Agriculture*, vol 35, pp 849–856

Pepper, D (1984) The Roots of Modern Environmentalism, Routledge, London and New York

Pettit, B and Sarwal , T (1993) *Identifying Indicators of Sustainability: a methodology*, School of Development Studies, UEA, Norwich, UK

Pitcher, T J and Hart, P J B (1982) *Fisheries Biology*, Chapman and Hall, London

Polacheck, T, Hilborn, R and Punt, A E (1993) 'Fitting surplus production models: comparing methods and measuring uncertainty', *Canadian Journal of Fisheries and Aquatic Sciences*, vol 50 (12), pp 2597–2607

Prager, M H (1994) 'A suite of extensions to a non-equilibrium surplus-production model', *Fishery Bulletin*, vol 92 (2), pp 374–389

Prager, M H, Goodyear, C P and Scott, G P (1996) 'Application of a surplus production model to a swordfish-like simulated stock with time-changing gear selectivity', *Transactions of the American Fisheries Society*, vol 125, pp 729–740

Pretty, J N, Thompson, J and Hinchcliffe, F (1996) *Sustainable Agriculture: impacts on food production and challenges for food security*, IIED, London

Rajakutty, S (1991) 'Peoples' participation in monitoring and evaluation of rural development programs: concepts and approaches', *Journal of Rural Development (India)*, vol 10(1), pp 35–53

Reckers, U (1997) 'Participatory project evaluation: letting local people have their say', *Development in Practice*, vol 7(3), pp 298–300

Reid, D (1995) *Sustainable Development: An Introductory Guide*, Earthscan, London

Rennings, K and Wiggering, H (1997) 'Steps towards indicators of sustainable development: linking economic and ecological concepts', *Ecological Economics*, vol 20, pp 25–36

Rhyne, E and Otero, M (1994) 'Financial services for microenterprises: principles and institutions' in Otero, M and Rhyne, E (eds) *The New World of Microenterprise Finance*, pp 11–26, IT Publications, London

Richards, H (undated) *The Evaluation of Cultural Action*, Macmillan, London

Richards, P (1979) 'Community environmental knowledge in African rural development. Whose knowledge counts?', *IDS Bulletin*, vol 10 (2), pp 28–35

Russell, D (1986) *How We See the World Determines What We Do in the World: preparing the ground for action research*, University of Western Sydney, Hawkesbury

Sameoto, D (1982) 'Verical distribution and abundance of the Peruvian anchovy, *Engraulis ringens*, and sardine, *Sardinops sagax*, larvae during November 1977', *Journal of Fish Biology*, vol 21 (2), pp 171–185

Schaefer, M B (1954) 'Some aspects of the dynamics of populations important to the management of commercial marine fisheries', *Bulletin of the Inter-American Tropical Tuna Commission*, vol 1, pp 27–56

Schaefer, M B (1957) 'A study of the dynamics of the fishery for yellowfin tuna in the eastern tropical Pacific Ocean', *Bulletin of the Inter-American Tropical Tuna Commission*, vol 2, pp 245–285

Schaller, N (1989) 'Low input sustainable agriculture' in Smith, D T (ed) *1989 Yearbook of Agriculture: farm management*, pp 216–219, US Department of Agriculture, Washington, DC

Schaller, N (1993) 'The concept of agricultural sustainability', *Agriculture, Ecosystems and Environment*, vol 46, pp 89–97

Schley, S and Laur, J (1996) 'The sustainability challenge: Ecological and economic development', *The Systems Thinker*, vol 7 (7), pp 1–6

Schmidt, R H and Zeitinger, C–P (1996) 'Prospects, problems and potential of credit-granting NGOs', *Journal of International Development*, vol 8 (2), pp 241–258

Schumacher, E F (1973) *Small is Beautiful: A Study of Economics As if People Mattered*, Abacus, London

Scoones, I and Thompson, J (eds) (1994) *Beyond Farmer First. Rural People's Knowledge Agricultural Research and Extension Practice*, Intermediate Technology, London

Senge, P, Ross, R, Roberts, C, Smith, B and Kleiner, A (1994) *The Fifth Discipline Fieldbook: strategies and tools for building a learning organization*, Nicholas Brealey, London

Shah, P and Hardwaj, G E A (1993) 'Gujerat, India: participatory monitoring', *The Rural Extension Bulletin*, vol 1, pp 34–37

Slavin, T (1996) 'Fears grow over microcredit boom', *Green Futures*, no 2, p 13

Slobodkin, L B (1994) 'The connection between single species and ecosystems' in Sutcliffe, D W (ed) *Water Quality and Stress Indicators in Marine and Freshwater Ecosystems: linking levels of organization (individuals, populations, communities)*, pp 75–87, Freshwater Biological Association, Ambleside, UK

Slocum, R and Thomas–Slayter, B (1995) 'Participation, empowerment and sustainable development' in Slocum, R, Wichhart, L, Rocheleau, D and Thomas-Slayter, B (eds) *Power, Process and Participation: tools for change*, Intermediate Technology, London

Southwood, T R E (1978) *Ecological Methods*, Chapman and Hall, Cambridge

Soyibo, A (1996) *Financial Linkage and Development in Sub-Saharan Africa: the role of formal financial institutions in Nigeria*, Overseas Development Institute, London

Spencer, D S C and Swift, M J (1992) 'Sustainable agriculture: definition and measurement' in Mulongoy, K, Gueye, M and Spencer, D S C (eds) *Biological Nitrogen Fixation and Sustainability of Tropical Agriculture*, pp 15–24, John Wiley & Sons, Chichester, UK

Stowell, F, Ison, R, Armson, R, Holloway, J, Jackson, S, McRobb, S (eds) (1997) *Systems for Sustainability: people, organizations and environments*, Plenum, New York

Swift, M J and Woomer, P (1993) 'Organic matter and the sustainability of agricultural systems: definition and measurement' in Mulongoy, K and Merckx, R (eds) *Soil Organic Matter Dynamics and Sustainability of Tropical Agriculture*, pp 3–17, John Willey and Sons, Chichester, UK

Syers, J K, Hamblin, A and Pushparajah, E (1995) 'Indicators and thresholds for the evaluation of sustainable land management', *Canadian Journal of Soil Science*, vol 75, pp 423–428

Team Technologies (1995) *TeamUp 2.0*, Team Technologies Inc, Chantilly

Ten Brink, B (1991) 'The AMOEBA approach as a useful tool for establishing sustainable development?' in Kuik, O and Verbruggen, H (eds) *In Search of Indicators of Sustainable Development*, pp 71–87, Kluwer Academic Publishers, Dordrecht, The Netherlands

Ten Brink, B J E, Hosper, S H and Colijn, F (1991) 'A quantitative method for description & assessment of ecosystems: the AMOEBA approach', *Marine Pollution Bulletin*, vol 23, pp 265–270

Tendler, J (1989) 'Whatever happened to poverty alleviation?' in Levitsky, J (ed) *Microenterprises in Developing Countries*, pp 26–56, Intermediate Technology Publications, London

Thomas, J J (1992) *The Informal Financial Sector: how does it operate and who are the customers?*, Overseas Development Institute, London

Tisdell, C (1988) 'Sustainable development: differing perspectives of ecologists and economists, and relevance to LDCs', *World Development*, vol 16 (3), pp 373–384

Tisdell, C (1996) 'Economic indicators to assess the sustainability of conservation farming projects: an evaluation', *Agriculture, Ecosystems and Environment*, vol 57, pp 117–131.

Thompson, J (1995) *User Involvement in Mental Health Services: the limits of consumerism, the risks of marginalization and the need for a critical approach*, Centre for Systems Studies, University of Hull, Hull, UK

Thompson, M (1993) *A TeamUp Case Study: agriculture project design*, Team Technologies Inc, Chantilly

Thompson, M and Chudoba, R (1994) *Case Study Municipal and Regional Planning in Northern Bohemia, Czech Republic: a participatory approach*, World Bank, Washington, DC

Turner, R K (1991) 'Environment, economics and ethics' in Pearce, D (ed) *Blueprint 2. Greening the World Economy*, pp 209–224, Earthscan, London

Umpleby, S (1994) *The Cybernetics of Conceptual Systems*, Department of Management Science, George Washington University, Washington, DC

Verbruggen, H and Kuik, O (1991) 'Indicators of sustainable development: an overview' in Kuik, O and Verbruggen, H (eds) *In Search of Indicators of Sustainable Development*, pp 1–6, Kluwer Academic Publishers, Dordrecht

Vogt, W (1949) *Road to Survival*, Victor Gollancz, London

Wagner, F H (1969) 'Ecosystem concepts in fish and game management' in van Dyne, G M (ed) *The Ecosystem Concept in Natural Resource Management*, Academic Press, New York

Walsh, J J, Whitledge, T E, Esias, W E, Smith, R L, Huntsman, S A, Santander, H and De Mendiola, B R (1980) 'The spawning habitat of the Peruvian anchovy, *Engraulis ringens*', *Deep Sea Research*, vol 27A, pp 1–27

Watson, R M A and Ollason, J (1982) *Animal Population Dynamics*, Chapman and Hall, London

WCED, World Commission on Environment and Development (1987) *Our Common Future*, Oxford University Press, Oxford

Webber, L and Ison, R (1995) 'Participatory rural appraisal design: conceptual and process issues', *Agricultural Systems*, vol 47, pp 107–131

Webster (1995) *Mirriam Webster's Collegiate Dictionary*, Mirriam Webster, Chicago

Wiener, N (1948) *Cybernetics*, MIT Press, Massachusetts

Wilber, K (1996) *A Brief History of Everything*, Gill and Macmillan, Dublin

WWF (World Wide Fund for Nature) and NEF (New Economics Foundation) (1994) *Indicators for Sustainable Development. Strategies for use of Indicators in National Reports to the Commission on Sustainable Development and in the EC Structural Funds Process*, WWF UK and the NEF, London

Yaron, J (1992) *Successful Rural Finance Institutions*, World Bank Discussion Paper No 150, World Bank, Washington, DC

Zachery, J (1995) *Sustainable Community Indicators: guideposts for local planning*, Community Environmental Council, Santa Barbara, US

Zinck, J A and Farshad, A (1995) 'Issues of sustainability and sustainable land management', *Canadian Journal of Soil Science*, vol 75, pp 407–412

Index

Page numbers in **bold** refer to boxes, tables and figures

UNIVERSITY OF WOLVERHAMPTON
LEARNING RESOURCES

tourism **63**
traffic **63**
transect walks **94**
transport **62**, **63**
travel 16

UN sustainability indicators 24, **25**, 33,
 35, 55, 62, 64
unemployment 16, **63**, 64
United Kingdom 153–4
 see also Scotland; Wales
urban areas *see* cities

Venn diagrams **94**
Vogt, William 7

Wales
 analysing rivers 73–4, 92, **93**
 indicators 135, **136**
 species indicators 18–19, **20**, 21–2,
  51–2, 53
water pollution
 analysing 73–4, 92, **93**
 effluents 18–19, **20**, **25**, 55
 indicators of 18–19, 20–2, 23–5,
  51–2, **53**, 55–8, **63**
 species composition 18–19, **20**, 21–2,
  51–2, **53**, 55–7
WCED 10–11, 26
wealth distribution 16, 23, **63**, **94**, 153
workshops 127, **128**
World Commission on Environment
 and Development *see* WCED